The Best Places To Kiss ™

In and Around New York City

Revised & Updated

Other Books in The Best Places to Kiss . . . Series

The Best Places To Kiss In Northern California $ 9.95
The Best Places To Kiss In Southern California   9.95
The Best Places To Kiss In The Northwest   10.95

To order any or all of these titles, including **The Best Places To Kiss In and Around New York City** ($10.95), please send a check for the total price of each book, plus $1.50 for shipping and handling to:

Beginning Press
5418 South Brandon
Seattle, Washington 98118

The Best Places To Kiss ™ In and Around New York City

Revised & Updated

By Sheree Bykofsky and Paula Begoun

Beginning Press

Managing Editor: Sheree Bykofsky
Copy Editor: Kathryn A. Clark
Art Direction & Typography: *RECAP*: Publications, Inc.
Cover Design: Rob Pawlak
Printing: Bookcrafters

Contributors: Stephanie Bell, Jeanne Muchnick, Maxine Moore, Jack Eichenbaum, Gerry
McTigue, Linda Gruber, Carol Milano, Mark SaFranko, Piri Halasz, Audrey Kurland, Heidi
Atlas, Doug Hoyt, Walter Alexander, Linda Lewin, Adam O'Connor, Karyn Feiden, Susan
Carr, Alison Brown Cerier, Paul Fargis, Sue Katz, Janet Rosen
Kissing Assistant: Stephen D. Solomon

First Edition: September 1989
Second Edition: January 1992
   10 9 8 7 6 5 4 3 2 1

Best Places To Kiss ™
is a registered trademark of Beginning Press
ISBN 1-877988-03-0

This book is distributed to the U.S. book trade by:
Publisher's Group West
4065 Hollis Street
Emeryville, CA 94608
Phone (800) 788-3123

Dedication

Kissing is a fine art. To our husbands, who helped us hone our craft.

Publisher's Note

This book is not an advertising vehicle. As was true in all the *Best Places To Kiss* books, the businesses included here neither were charged fees nor did they pay us. No services were exchanged. This book is a sincere effort to highlight those special places in the area that are filled with romance and splendor. Sometimes those places are created by people, as in restaurants, inns, lounges, lodges, hotels, and bed & breakfasts, and sometimes those places are natural wonders. We've done our best to scour the area to find for you the most special hideaways.

The recommendations in this collection were the final decision of the authors. Please write to Beginning Press if you have any additional comments, suggestions, or recommendations.

"As usual with most lovers in the city –
they were troubled by the lack of that
essential need of love – a meeting place."

Thomas Wolfe

Special Acknowledgments

The most heartfelt thanks to Kathryn A. Clark and Stephanie Bell who assisted us in every possible way: researching, writing, and editing. Thanks to Brian Padol for his compositing skill and great patience, to Constance Bollen for her book-designing ability, and Doris Latino and Janet Rosen for their many suggestions and research assistance in the second edition.

And a special thank you to Avis Begoun, for the original series idea.

Table of Contents

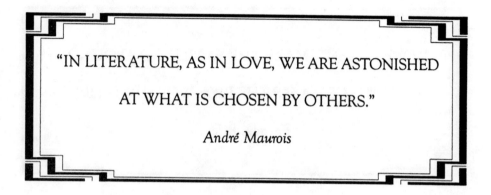

"IN LITERATURE, AS IN LOVE, WE ARE ASTONISHED

AT WHAT IS CHOSEN BY OTHERS."

André Maurois

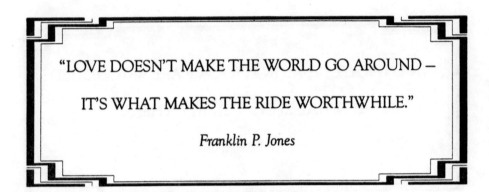

"LOVE DOESN'T MAKE THE WORLD GO AROUND —

IT'S WHAT MAKES THE RIDE WORTHWHILE."

Franklin P. Jones

Kissing in New York City

Why Is It Best To Kiss In and Around New York City?

New York City is one of the most romantic cities in the world — if you know where to look. Always on the fast track but filled with surprisingly tranquil nooks and crannies, New York City's allure is its intensity, diversity, and eclectic eccentricity. There is an incomparable excitement that accompanies everything you do here. You can feel it as you wander (carefully) through the parks, along the avenues, and in and out of the shops and restaurants. When you're in New York, you're at the center of the world. When you're in New York City, nothing else outside of it exists. The world drops off abruptly just west of the Hudson River — but not as far as this book is concerned. Those New Yorkers who know where to find trees and lakes and quiet understand an inner peace that keeps the hectic pace here from getting the better of them, and so we've included our secrets on getting out of the city and into the country in two hours or less.

In Manhattan, one quickly acquires the skills of selecting off-times and thus avoiding crowds when possible, and when not possible, of finding romance in a crowd. When you have each other, plus limitless romantic options at hand and mile after mile of sights and sounds in and around this fascinating carnival we fondly call NYC, what else do you need? Well, maybe blindfolds; you may on occasion need blindfolds to avoid looking too closely at some of the excitement that isn't even vaguely romantic. Okay, okay, and money; you do need some money, but after that, it's all up to you and your own personal kissing preferences.

You Call This Research?

The first edition of this book was the collaborative work of a group of New York writers and was the product of earnest interviews, travel, careful investigation, and observation. The second edition was researched and written almost exclusively by Sheree Bykofsky, but she did welcome the help of three new contributors, three research assistants, an excellent editor, a kissing husband, and her good friend, publisher, and co-author, Paula Begoun.

Although it would have been nice, even preferable, kissing was not used as the major research method for selecting the locations listed in this book. If smooching had been the determining factor, two inescapable problems would have resulted. First, we would still be researching, and this book would be just a good idea, some random notes and nothing more. And second, depending on the researchers' moods of the moment, many kisses would have occurred in a lot of places that do not meet the requirements of this travel guide.

And so, if we all did not kiss at every location during our research, how could any of us be certain if a particular place was good for such an activity? It's simple. We employed our intuitive journalistic instincts to evaluate the magnetic pull of each potential kissing locale. The ultimate criterion, in addition to those listed below, was that if, upon examining a place, the reviewer felt a longing inside for his or her special someone to share what had been discovered, that was considered as reliable a test as kissing. In the final analysis, we feel confident that we have selected for you the crème de la crème of voluptuous places. Once you choose where to go from among the many choices, unless otherwise noted, you are likely to be met with some amount of privacy, a beautiful setting, heart-stirring ambience, and first rate accommodations. When you get there, what you do romantically is up to you.

What Isn't Romantic?

You may be skeptical about the idea of one location being more romantic than another. You may think, "Well, it isn't the setting, it's who you're with that makes a place special." And you'd be right. But aside from the chemistry that exists between the two of you, there are some locations that can add an extra thrill to the moment. For example, holding hands over a hamburger and fries at McDonald's, or sharing a slice of pizza while waiting for your train, might be, for some, a blissful interlude. But the french-fry fight in full swing near your heads, the preoccupied youth who took a year and a day to get your order, or the guy sleeping in front of the entrance can put a damper on heart-throb stuff even for the most adoring types. No, location isn't everything; it's just that when a certain type of place is combined with all the right details, including the right person, you have better odds of making a romantic memory.

With that in mind, the following is a list of things that were never considered even remotely romantic: mildewy, dirty carpet; tourist *traps*; restaurants with no-smoking sections who ignore this policy; over-priced hotels with impressive names and mediocre accommodations; discos; the latest need-to-be-seen-in nightspots (romantic places only count when the most important person there is you and not someone at the table across the room); restaurants with officious, sneering waiters; and last, but not least, a roomful of people discussing the stock market.

Above and beyond these unromantic location details, there is a small variety of unromantic behaviors that can negate the affection potential of even the most majestic surroundings. The following are mood killers every time: any amount of moaning over the weather; creating a scene over the quality of food or service, no matter how justified; worrying about work; getting angry about traffic; incessant backseat driving, no matter how warranted; or complaining in general. Remember the scene on the beach between Deborah Kerr and Burt Lancaster in *From Here to Eternity*, where they're rolling around passionately in the surf? How much kissing would they have gotten to if Burt had started complaining about the water up his nose, the sand down his bathing suit, or the Arctic chill in the air? Get the idea?

So, if the car breaks down, the train stops between stations for what seems like a lifetime, the waiter is rude to you, your reservations get screwed up, or both of you tire out and want to call it a day, try to take comfort in the fact that you have each other. It may only take a new outlook and some tolerant teamwork to turn a dilemma into a delight.

Rating Romance
The three major factors determining whether or not to include a place:

    1. Surrounding splendor

    2. Privacy

    3. Tug-at-your-heartstrings ambience

This one-of-a-kind rating system was used as follows: if a place had all three of those qualities going for it, inclusion was automatic. But if one or two of the criteria were weak or nonexistent, the other feature(s) had to be superior before the location would be included. For example, if a panoramic vista was breathtakingly beautiful in a spot that was inundated with tourists and children on field trips, the place would not be included. Or, if a fabulous bed & breakfast was set in a less-than-desirable location, it would be included only if its interior was so wonderfully inviting and cozy that the outside would no longer mattered.

Of the three determining factors, "surrounding splendor" is fairly self explanatory. "Heart-tugging ambience" could probably use some clarification: wonderful, loving environments are not just four-poster beds covered with down quilts and lace pillows, or tables decorated with white tablecloths and nicely folded linen napkins. Instead there must be more plush or engaging features that encourage you to feel relaxed and carefree rather than rigid and formal. For the most part, ambience was always judged by comfort and gracious appointments as opposed to image and frills. "Privacy" is about how much a particular establishment encourages intimacy. At a restaurant, for example, are the tables squeezed together? At a park, can you find a pretty secluded spot for a private picnic? And so on.

Kiss Ratings

If you've flipped through this book and noticed the miniature lips that follow each entry, you may be curious about their implications. The rating system notwithstanding, **ALL** the listings in this book are wonderful, special places to be, and all of them are heart-pleasing and enticing. The tiny lips only indicate our personal preferences and nothing more. They are a way of indicating just how delightfully romantic a place was and how pleased we were with the experience during our visit. Decor, ambience, service, price, taste of food, and value for the money, were all considerations in assigning lips to restaurants. Therefore, we've aimed to be as descriptive as possible in describing what we've enjoyed. We urge you to read the entries carefully to determine which places best suit your budget, taste, and mood. The number of lips awarded each location corresponds as follows:

Romance Scale

💋 Very Romantic

💋💋 Irresistible

💋💋💋 Magical

💋💋💋💋 Sublime

Cost Ratings

There are also additional ratings to help you determine whether your lips can afford to kiss in a particular restaurant, hotel, or bed & breakfast (almost all of the outdoor places are free or charge nominal fees). The price for overnight accommodations is always based on double occupancy; otherwise there wouldn't be anyone to kiss. Dining establishment prices are based on a full dinner for two, excluding liquor, unless otherwise indicated. Because of the tendency for prices and business hours to change it is always advised that you call and double-check the present status of each place you consider visiting so that your lips do not end up disappointed.

Restaurant Rating

Inexpensive	Under $40
Moderate	$40–$65
Expensive	$65–$100
Very expensive	$100–$150
Very, very expensive and beyond	$150 and up

Hotel/Lodging Rating

Inexpensive	Under $85
Moderate	$85–$135
Expensive	$135–$225
Very expensive	$225–$350
Very, very expensive and beyond	$350 and up

Manhattan Restaurant Strategies

For romance, it's best to have dinner — as opposed to lunch — in most New York restaurants. The most intimate bistro is so often transformed into a boardroom between 12:30 and 2:00. On the other hand, there are many wonderful lunchtime kissing places recommended herein. If you deliberately select an establishment that takes "cash only" or one that sits in a quiet residential neighborhood, you'll be less inclined to find the place filled with businesspeople in suits. Or think about having a picnic at one of the parks. But our best idea for lunching and kissing in New York's fine restaurants is to go at 2:00.

A problem with evening dining is that many of the best and most exotic restaurants are popular beyond their capacity to accommodate the crowds comfortably. Always try to select an off-time. Off-times in New York vary, depending on location, time of year, and flavor of establishment. Some restaurants empty out at 8:00 (near the opera and the theater), whereas others don't start jumping until 10:00. With practice, you'll get to know. Summer Sunday evenings are the best time to get a seat in an otherwise popular dining establishment — because the regulars are sitting in traffic on their way home from the Hamptons. However, many New York restaurants take their own vacations in the summer and on Sundays, and many that serve brunch on Sunday close for dinner. Always call ahead.

If you're selecting a place to celebrate an important occasion such as an anniversary and you have in mind to dress up, look for such buzzwords as elegant, opulent, and ornate. Do not choose one that uses the word casual and then go dressed up in black tie. Also be warned that we've listed a few restaurants that may be considered elegant but which also may be inappropriate for black tie. One such indication is the price. If a restaurant is not said to be Expensive or Very Expensive, generally black tie would be inappropriate. If you're in doubt, call ahead and ask if there are any dress requirements.

One more thing: for a really special occasion, consider going to a not-so-famous restaurant. If you're not a regular or a celebrity at New York's four-star "finest," you may find yourself seated by the bus station — or the restroom! Some restaurants are more notorious for this behavior than others. In a quiet side street bistro that isn't listed in everybody's travel guide, you'll often find they'll treat you like a celebrity when you tell them you're celebrating an occasion. Arm yourself with this knowledge and beware.

New York Notes

In fairness, we must point out that our assessments sometimes were influenced by the chance timing of when we visited a particular locale. It was impossible to go back to every restaurant for breakfast, lunch, brunch, and dinner. Likewise, we saw some parks decked out in fall splendor, some lakes covered with ice, and others filled with splashy bathers. We did make every effort to select the best or most popular time to visit each location, to interview people who had been there at different times, and to determine as best as possible when to go and what to expect. We hope we have accomplished our goal of giving you the whole picture. Still, we ask that you please call ahead, whenever possible, to determine the current hours, availability, weather conditions, or anything else that might put a damper on the romance.

For example, not all sleeping establishments are air-conditioned. If this matters to you, before setting off to a B&B on the hottest day of the summer, call and find out if your room is air-conditioned. Similarly, some inns and opulent large restaurants are so romantic that many couples choose them as the site of their nuptials. You're therefore well advised to inquire of such establishments whether a catered affair is going to be in progress during your visit. If so, be sure to go elsewhere.

Warm Heart, Cold Feet, Empty Wallet

More than in almost any other area in the United States, romance in New York City can cost money and a lot of it, if you're not careful. But with a little effort, a budget, and some strategizing, you'll find scores of romantic destinations in and around this fair city, without breaking the bank. Of course, if you have unlimited resources, you can skip over this section and proceed to the next.

PROBLEM: You want to go out for the evening to someplace intimate and wonderful, but the cost is prohibitive. SOLUTION: Rather than going out for dinner, go to your dream restaurant at an off-time and enjoy an appetizer and a beverage or dessert and tea. Then go home and split a large cheese pizza.

PROBLEM: The theater as an evening out is a great idea but, you can't afford that plus the car fare and after-theater food and drinks. SOLUTION: The myriad of cabarets and jazz clubs that offer great entertainment for under $10 per person, particularly the ones listed in this book, often have romantic environments. Also there are half-price theater tickets to be found at the **TKTS booth, (212) 354-5800**, on **47th and Broadway**, or **2 World Trade Center mezzanine**, the day of the performance, if you're willing to stand in line for an hour or so. There are also Off-Off Broadway shows that are significantly less expensive than Broadway ones. There is a **music and dance half-price**

tickets booth, (212) 382-2323, at **Bryant Park,** on 42nd Street between Fifth and Sixth Avenues.

PROBLEM: You think fancy restaurants are great, but you get hives dressing up. SOLUTION: Afternoon tea at many of the hotels that line Central Park are a wonderful way to spend a dressed down, elegant few hours in a relatively inexpensive manner.

PROBLEM: You want to spend the weekend in Manhattan at someplace really romantic, and that doesn't mean at the apartment, but most of the nice hotels charge as much as you're paying for rent. SOLUTION: Call the bed & breakfast service listed in the Hotel section. They offer incredible getaways for $125 or less a night, including breakfast and, sometimes, amenities such as a Jacuzzi, views or a king-size bed with thick goose-down comforters.

And don't forget, this is a vast region with wonderful nooks and crannies that at any time of year can be safe havens where the two of you can share precious time together, without spending a penny except on transportation. From brisk hikes in the country, long strolls along the avenues, peaceful sunsets in the park, flower markets to browse in, and country roads out on Long Island or in Westchester, a range of magic places hovers close by for you to enjoy. Whether you're married or single, New Yorkers to the core (pun intended), or New Yorkers for the day, your togetherness and this book are sure to enhance the magic.

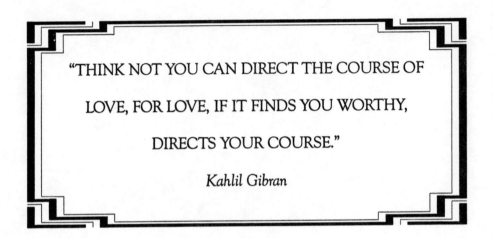

"THINK NOT YOU CAN DIRECT THE COURSE OF

LOVE, FOR LOVE, IF IT FINDS YOU WORTHY,

DIRECTS YOUR COURSE."

Kahlil Gibran

New York City

◆ Hotel Kissing ◆

BED & BREAKFAST NEW YORK CITY STYLE
Urban Ventures
(212) 594-5650
Inexpensive to Moderate

Urban Ventures is a service that is unique to New York City. They list hundreds of locations all over the city that may be loosely defined as bed & breakfast accommodations. It's not that they're not bed & breakfasts; they're just not the sort you may have encountered elsewhere in the world. If you're only familiar with the various assortment of Victorian mansions and private homes in the U.S. that have been renovated to meet the needs of those who have had enough of hotel vacationing, then be warned that Manhattan doesn't have those. A B&B in Manhattan ranges from a basic extra bedroom in someone's house — with or without a private bath — to an extravagant apartment. But for less than $100 a night you probably won't be disappointed, and you might have a real adventure at the same time.

One time the resident handed us the keys to his huge East Side loft. Then he disappeared — never to be seen again. No loss. We found the accommodations to be attractive and convenient. It felt like we were living there: no hotel clerks, no room service charges, and no one to bother us. The kitchen was right there, and so was a nearby Chinese restaurant that delivered. The apartment was very high-tech, equipped as it was with a remarkable stereo system. Another time we stayed with a charming couple in their co-op. Their own bedroom was down the hall, and they personally served us a lavish breakfast. Urban Ventures has over 700 listings and the variations on a theme are endless, but let me make a few recommendations to help make your stay a positive adventure: Be specific about check-in and check-out times; have the space where you will be staying described in detail; ask about size, private bath, smoking, kids, method of entry, location, food served (if any), cancellation policy, type of bed, doorman building, walk-up or elevator, and whether cash or a credit card is acceptable.

I know that sounds more complicated than a hotel, but if you are interested in an alternative, whether it be for business or romance, and especially if your tastes are more than what your budget can afford, then staying in a bed & breakfast, Manhattan style, may be just the thing for you.

THE BOX TREE HOTEL and RESTAURANT ◆◆◆◆
250 East 49th Street *between Second & Third Avenues*
(212) 758-8320
Very Expensive

This is what we call living on love the right way. This is a better place than almost any other in Manhattan to kiss, sleep, relax, eat, soak, read, talk, and do just about any other private legal thing you can think of.

Like a European villa or a miniature Versailles, the fifteen rooms are palatial in style and extravagant beyond compare. From the Chinese suite to the King Boris Bedroom and the Consulate Suite, each is finished with a provocative abundance of gold chandeliers, marble and lapis lazuli baths, marble-mantled working fireplaces, antique screens, and plush furnishings. And the restaurant showcases the same attention to lavish details as the hotel, with the stupendous talents of a kitchen that prepares and serves a prix fixe lunch and dinner fit for royalty.

Note: If you stay in the hotel, you will receive a $100 credit toward your dinner, which will cost more than that.

◆ ***Romantic Warning:*** This, like so many of New York's finest restaurants, is frequented by businesspeople on expense accounts. If there's a loud meeting taking place at the next table and the room is booked, you may be out of luck finding a private table here. It's worth the risk.

THE LOWELL HOTEL
28 East 63rd Street *between Madison & Park Avenues*
(212) 838-1400
Very Expensive and Beyond

Generally you can assume that most of the city's hotels are designed to efficiently handle large groups of people or to encourage businesspeople to take care of business. Every now and then, one chances upon a hotel where slickness is replaced by elegance, and efficiency is embellished with warmth and beauty. The Lowell is just such a place. The furnishings are exquisite and supremely comfortable, with an eye for blending textures and colors. There are wood-burning fireplaces framed by beautifully renovated mantles. The bathrooms are a bit on the small side. We prefer bathtubs large enough to serve dinner in, but the marble surfaces and amenities help obscure the smallness. This is one of our absolute favorite New York hideouts.

◆ *Romantic Suggestion:* Even if the Lowell Hotel weren't so splendid, **The Pembroke Room** would be reason enough to pay a visit here. This room is a radiant composite of a restaurant and tea room. The prodigious dining environment is very English, very civilized, very distinguished, and richly adorned. You'll feel as if you were residing in an English country estate. The cuisine is inspired, with an emphasis on presentation and kid-glove service. We can't think of a more romantic location to partake of breakfast, lunch, or tea. Sunday brunch is equally fabulous and equally expensive.

NEW YORK APARTMENT

East 47th Street *between Second & Third Avenues*
Contact: Alexander Hamilton House
for exact address and reservations
(914) 271-6737
Moderate

Here is all you need to be New Yorkers for a week or weekend: a tiny kitchen with modern appliances, empty refrigerator, a full cupboard and freezer, a small whirlpool bath, a phone with answering machine, color/cable TV, and a comfortable queen-size bed and sofabed. All this is to be found in your own private studio apartment in a pleasant elevator building with a 24-hour doorman. Located in a residential condo, it's very clean and modern while still being cozy and romantic. Step through tall double glass doors into the small rosy-colored apartment, which is tastefully decorated with silk plants and flowers, an antique bureau, recessed lighting, and thick gray wall-to-wall carpeting. For many reasons, not least of which is the price, often we'd rather stay here than at an expensive full service hotel or B&B. We like the fact that, unlike at a B&B, where we have to rise at the announced time and dress for breakfast with strangers, here we can lounge all morning, and eat what we like when we like it. The cupboards and freezer are stocked with the basics: oatmeal, English muffins, cereal, frozen o.j., and coffee. Or really do as the natives do — head out for brunch.

There is hardly a better base from which to explore this funny, crazy island. The apartment is very close to Rockefeller Center to the west and the U.N. to the east, and it's directly across town from Broadway (walkable or easy bus or cab trip). The apartment is a traveler's dream in that it is a quiet refuge in a bustling neighborhood that's home to many nontouristy shops and restaurants.

THE PENINSULA HOTEL
700 Fifth Avenue *at 55th Street*
(212) 247-2200
Very Expensive and Beyond

There are plenty of attractive hotels in New York City, from the Grand Hyatt with its slick greenhouse setting to the Waldorf Astoria's Victorian old-world appeal, but most of the space and beauty of the city's hotels seem to exist only in the lobbies and restaurants. Most rooms are, unfortunately, just hotel rooms, nothing special or extraordinary, with bathrooms that border on small, and nothing is less romantic than a small bathroom.

These drawbacks are far from the case at the Peninsula Hotel. For the same extravagant price as most of the other hotels, the Peninsula offers huge, elegant suites in tones of peach and rose with wonderful king-size beds. And the bathrooms all feature oversized six-foot tubs large enough for a small crowd, but two is enough. Their weekend packages tempt even budgeting couples in the mood for mutual self-indulgence or a special anniversary weekend.

◆ **Romantic Note:** When we get caught in Midtown in the rain, we often make a beeline for the **Gotham Bar** on the hotel's second level. They are happy to let us sit for hours on the large clustered chairs and couches, nursing drinks or hot coffee, and sometimes we splurge on one watercress sandwich that serves two quite nicely. One might expect formality or snobbishness in such an elegant lounge, but we find only welcoming smiles and cordial service. Generally, we prefer the Gotham Bar to the **Pen-top Roof Bar**, despite the latter's view, but take the elevator and decide for yourself.

HOTEL PLAZA ATHENEE & LE REGENCE   ❖ ❖
37 East 64th Street *between Park & Madison Avenues*
(212) 734-9100
Very Expensive and Beyond

After weeks of wandering in and out of the myriad hotels lining the streets and avenues of Manhattan, we were relieved to find the Hotel Athenee. We were beginning to doubt that we would find anything romantic. Most of the rooms we saw were standard. And then we wandered into the Hotel Athenee. Here the rooms, even the simple ones, are charming, and the two on the top floor are exquisite, especially in comparison to most everything else in the area.

The entryways to the suites are large and lined in mirrors. The rooms are spacious with a king-size four-poster bed, soft linens, and a quilt. And then there is the bathroom. A sexy bathroom can take any ordinary room and make it dynamite. A sexy bathroom plus a beautiful room is positively enthralling, and that's what we have here. From the gold-colored marble floors, ceilings and walls to the huge walk-in shower, these are suites designed for two. Plus, if you decide to venture out of your room and don't want to go too far, the hotel's very opulent restaurant **Le Regence** is available for breakfast, lunch, or dinner. It's worth it to forego room service just to have this dining experience. The velvety smooth forest-green bar adjacent to Le Regence warrants making a special toast.

ROGER SMITH HOTEL
501 Lexington Avenue *at 47th Street*
(212) 755-1400
Moderate to Very Expensive

From the lobby to the rooms, the newly renovated Roger Smith Hotel has achieved a true European feel throughout. The location is convenient to touring Manhattan, and the rates are — by Manhattan standards — quite reasonable. In fact the huge suites are some of the best priced in town. This small, plush hotel has spacious rooms and suites with canopy beds, soft lighting, plump carpeting, and cozy loveseats. Although the complimentary Continental breakfast, served in the stylish cafe, wasn't the best when we were there (the coffee was cold and the buffet selection small), it seemed the management was working hard to get its new act together. We recommend the Roger Smith now but predict it will get even better as time goes by.

THE ROYALTON
44 West 44th Street *between Fifth & Sixth Avenues*
(212) 869-4400
Very Expensive to Very, Very Expensive

Of all the entries in this collection, this one has caused the most controversy and frustration, for two reasons. First, the Royalton started off its questionably illustrious beginnings (October '88) with a discrimination suit (the hotel settled out of court), and second, it seems apparent that the staff has been trained not to smile. So why are we including this dubious place? Because it is one of the more uniquely beautiful hotel renovations we've seen.

Directly across the street from the Royalton is the Algonquin Hotel. Whereas the Algonquin is the epitome of charm and nostalgia, the Royalton is the essence of high-tech sophistication and drama. You enter through oversized magenta acrylic doors that bring you to a balconylike hallway that borders the hotel's lounge. Shades of cream and pale lime-green cover the high-backed sofas and chairs; the groupings are well spaced and create an unusual setting for romantic conversation. As you continue past the lounge, a small restaurant is at the end of the short marble promenade. But the rooms are the highlight, after you find them through dimly lit and narrow hallways (like a cruise ship's). Once inside, even the standard rooms carry the slick theme to its conclusion. They have impressive gray and magenta interiors, most with immense bathtubs large enough for bathing *and* dining.

THE STANHOPE
995 Fifth Avenue *at 81st Street*
(212) 288-5800
Very, Very Expensive and Beyond

The Stanhope is something to behold. Overflowing in elegance, it is the stuff of dreams and celebrations. From the moment you cross the threshold you will be taken by the glorious details: the marble floors, Baccarat chandeliers, antique furnishings, stunning four-star dining rooms, and the beautiful flower-quilted king-size beds, most in huge, king-size suites with marble bathrooms. There is even maid service three times a day and an almost overly attentive staff. Even the hotels with impressive reputations can't hold a candle to this.

◆ *Romantic Note:* The Stanhope offers weekend rates; unfortunately, they are as high as the weekly rates at most other New York hotels. But remember The Stanhope for one of those splurges of your lifetime.

THE UNITED NATIONS PLAZA HOTEL
One United Nations Plaza *at 44th Street & First Avenue*
(212) 355-3400
Very, Very Expensive

The guest rooms don't begin until the 28th floor, so regardless of your room number you're guaranteed enviable skyline views of the city and water (an almost priceless commodity in New York hotels). There is a full facility health club on the 27th floor with a full-size pool surrounded by windows, and the rooms are simple but lovely. The area is also one of the quietest in all Manhattan. The weekend rates are among the most reasonable, around $130 per night or $140 for a deluxe room. For weekdays, the rates are pretty much the same as the rest of the major Manhattan hotels. If you want to get up and away, but not that far, this might be an indulgence too good to ignore.

HOTEL WALES
1295 Madison Avenue *between 92nd and 93rd Streets*
(212) 876-6000
Moderate

Inexpensive by Manhattan standards, there is nothing opulent about this very bed & breakfasty feeling hotel. With every inch bespeaking old-world simplicity, it's no wonder this quiet getaway is of particular appeal to Europeans who, on the whole, eschew nouveau riche decor. The rooms are dark with lots of mahogany, and the halls are dormlike. Far from being flowery and lacy, the atmosphere is stark, simple, and comfortable like an old Colonial manor house. On the 8th floor (room #822), there's a large junior suite with a four-poster bed, a separate sitting room and, like the other top-floor rooms, a clear view of the surrounding neighborhood and the Central Park reservoir. Anything comparable in Midtown would be four times the price. The hotel itself was built in 1902 and renovated in 1990 to its original state. Complimentary tea is served everyday at 3:00 in the second floor Pied Piper Room, set up as a private club for guests to enjoy. (Imagine Mycroft Holmes's Diogenes Club, and you'll have an idea of this very stately public room). If you want the newness and amenities of the Hilton, by all means do not choose the Hotel Wales. If you want flowers, wreaths, and lace, stay away. If you want a simple inexpensive romance, here's your choice.

♦ *Romantic Note:* Sometimes less is better. The more expensive penthouse with roof access is less romantic than the less expensive junior suites and cozy, small double rooms.

♦ *Romantic Option:* In addition to the many great restaurants in this revitalized residential neighborhood (**Bistro du Nord, Table d'Hote**), there is a pretty and lively jazz cafe nearby: **Equense, 1291 Madison Avenue, (212) 860-2300.**

"HE GAVE HER A LOOK YOU COULD HAVE

SPREAD ON A WAFFLE."

Ring Lardner

◆ Restaurant Kissing ◆

Given New York's passion for restaurants, and particularly restaurants with invitingly seductive atmospheres, choosing which dining spots to include in this book was a daunting prospect. Keep in mind that the last thing we wanted was for this kissing guide to become strictly a dining guide. On the other hand, we'd be crazy to ignore the obvious: in New York, romantic dining is the primary way couples spend time together.

Our problem of choosing from seemingly endless possibilities created some interesting discussions. We all agreed that a restaurant had to have more than opaque lighting, pretty china, professional service, and yards of linen tablecloths. That "more" part was sometimes difficult to define, but the restaurants listed in *our* guide had to have that elusive "more" quality. Diligently we researched the recommendations of other reviewers, restaurant critics, and the best source of all — New Yorkers. Herein we give you a romantic overview of the best kissing restaurants in New York City for all pocketbooks, palates, temperaments, and a variety of ethnic preferences.

Note: If we missed your favorite romantic restaurant it was probably due more to indigestion than anything else (our hearts were in it, but not our stomachs). The diary section at the back of the book is for your own notes and personal additions to be reviewed at your own pace and when your hearts get hungry.

American Kissing

Europeans say that Americans aren't romantic, that we know very little about matters of the heart (and stomach). They think that there is nothing less endearing than wolfing down a hamburger or hot dog and that "fast food" dining means the death of intimacy. They have a point, but that's not the kind of American dining we're talking about here. Rather, we found many beautiful places that reflected a uniquely American brand of style, food, and romance.

AMERICAN FESTIVAL CAFE at ROCKEFELLER CENTER ◆
20 West 50th Street *between Fifth & Sixth Avenues*
(212) 246-6699
Inexpensive to Moderate

Everything about the American Festival Cafe is so delightfully and casually romantic — somehow even its touristy demeanor. The people you are likely to find here are a rare blend of out-of-towners and locals. During the winter, for breakfast, lunch, or dinner, you can sit inside and watch the fabled ice skaters through large wraparound windows. You might even fulfill your own fantasy and become one of them. In summer, outdoor tables take the place of the slip-and-slide show, and you can enjoy a leisurely meal sans cars, cabs, and street traffic. Coming here is always one of the most romantic things to do in New York.

◆ *Romantic Suggestion:* Depending on your body temperature and ability, the restaurant offers **skate-a-date**, which can prove to be a fabulous evening event for two. Your three-course, prix fixe, well-served meal includes entrance to the rink, skate rental, and hot mulled cider served outside. We can't think of a more congenial, affectionate way to spend time.

◆ *Romantic Option:* **Savories, (212) 246-6457** (Inexpensive), is a stylish cafeteria just around the circle from the Festival Cafe. Good food and the same view are available at much lower prices.

◆ *Second Romantic Option:* Still within the circle that makes up the lower concourse of Rockefeller Center is the **Sea Grill, (212) 246-9201** (Expensive). This is more formal than the casual Festival Cafe, and it fills its niche respectably. Designed for more exclusive dining, the room is stunning, the menu sophisticated and classic, and the view of the rink remains the same. Serving only lunch and dinner, the Sea Grill offers outdoor seating in a romantic garden during the spring and summer.

ANTICS
320 Atlantic Avenue, Brooklyn
(718) 625-0785
Inexpensive to Moderate

Eight minutes from downtown by car; glide over the Brooklyn Bridge and turn left on Atlantic Avenue. Continue for a block and a half and the blue neon lights of the restaurant will be visible on the right. Park on Atlantic.

PROBLEM: It's a comfortable summer day and you feel like dining outdoors in the Hamptons; unfortunately, you've only got a couple of hours. SOLUTION: Come here. Step into the restaurant and the first thing you'll see are the busy chefs hard at work in the kitchen. Keep walking past the open woodburning brick pizza oven, past the small modern dining room, through the large glass doors and onto a secluded garden deck. If you don't live in New York City (and even if you do), you may not know about the "other" New York that exists in tranquil green backyards with gardens, patios, and decks like this. Antics' garden deck is a delight, and so is the good home-style food. Not only will the deck surprise you, but so might the reasonably priced generous portions of delicious food. The pizza made in the open pizza oven is a special treat.

◆ ***Romantic Note:*** If you have a choice, choose to sit under the big green umbrellas on the garden deck, but note that reservations aren't taken for the garden; so come at an off-time, if you can.

AUREOLE
34 East 61st Street *between Park & Madison Avenues*
(212) 319-1660
Expensive a la carte lunch or prix fixe dinner
Jackets Required

Aureole means "halo" in Latin, and you'll certainly feel like you're in heaven here. The first thing you'll notice as you enter are the enchanting white swans on the two-story mural. Perhaps the second thing that will catch your eye is a profusion of colorful flowers against this soft white backdrop. A table by the railing on the small mezzanine looks out over this calming scene and the pretty street, and thus is the best seat in the house for a romantic interlude. Every inch of this delicious restaurant is elegantly simple, every touch purposeful and pleasing. Look up at the subtle ceiling tapestry. We found the comfortable purple chairs perfectly suited for what turned out to be a long evening of fabulous dining and quiet conversation.

◆ *Romantic Note:* There are steps up into an outdoor garden in back. This is one of the few restaurants in New York where we would almost always choose to sit inside rather than out — even on a beautiful day.

THE BLACK SHEEP
344 West 11th Street *at Washington Street*
(212) 242-1010
Moderate to Expensive

Manhattan couldn't go to the country, and so they brought the country to Manhattan. The twinkling white lights call you from two blocks away. Lush green plants droop lazily from the awning over the outdoor tables. The lace half-curtains on the windows intrigue. The cowbells on the door jingle as you enter. Tastefully decorating the restaurant's brick walls are copper kettles, pitchforks, armfuls of dried flowers, wreaths, pinecones, and even hanging chairs. A friendly waiter escorts you to the best available table. The air-conditioner keeps the air cool on warm days, but the whirring fans still spin beneath the high tin ceilings, providing comfort and atmosphere.

The Black Sheep is a perfect choice for a birthday brunch or romantic casual dinner. With real farmhouse flair, the food is thoughtfully prepared and lovingly presented. Dress up or go casual.

COURTYARD CAFE BAR
130 East 39th Street *at Lexington Avenue*
(212) 779-0739
Moderate to Expensive

Whether for breakfast, lunch, brunch, or dinner in good weather, dine in the open air English courtyard garden out back where preside three stone statues of goddesses (my husband is inspired to say "four" and, of course, he means me). No doubt you'll provide your own fourth goddess in the little garden surrounded by white latticework in pretty Murray Hill. In inclement weather, the adjoining greenhouse with a view of the courtyard is casual and pretty (a good spot for brunch), and beside that, the slightly more formal dining room is also a pleasurable, clean, and subtly lit dining spot.

◆ *Romantic Note:* On weekday evenings in summer, the Courtyard hosts a very moderately priced outdoor barbeque feast.

◆ *Romantic Warning:* This is very much a hotel restaurant; the ambience reflects that, and with the exception of the barbeque, the prices do, too. Manhattanites ourselves, we sometimes like to get away in New York to a hotel restaurant. We pretend we're tourists experiencing the wonders of the big city for the first time. It's romantic.

JEZEBEL
630 Ninth Avenue *at 45th Street*
(212) 582-1045
Moderate to Expensive

A lazy, hot, mint julep, summer afternoon is what you will find inside Jezebel's any month of the year or any time of the day. The atmosphere is as intoxicating as the fragrant Southern delicacies that will convince your palate, as well as your other senses, that you are no longer in New York City, but somewhere in the Deep South. Time takes on a new meaning when you visit here: It's a way of dining and courting that could become downright regular.

MARYLOU'S   ◆
21 West 9th Street *between Fifth & Sixth Avenues*
(212) 533-0012
Expensive

Down a few steps on an attractive West Village street, just made for leisurely walking, is Marylou's. Inside, past the elegant but merry bar, alive with the sounds of jazz or classical music, is the more sedate restaurant looking very much like the interior of a country estate and inspiring soft whispers and lingering conversation. Even when crowded, as it often is, the atmosphere is quiet and relaxed. Pink linens and colorful china decorate the tables. Fresh flowers overflow from atop antique hutches placed beneath captivating works of art. The fireplaces in two of the four dining rooms are always put to good use, and the fringed antique lamps are suitably dim. From the wood moldings to the old books, a couple could lose track of time while dining on caviar, the freshest seafood, the tenderest meats, and vintage wine. Add that to the attentive, cordial service and embarrassingly indulgent desserts, and you may forget that there's another couple sitting a bit too close for real kissing privacy. (There are a few tables for two that are all by themselves, and if you're lucky enough to be at Marylou's when it's not crowded, you may request them, but they cannot be reserved.)

◆ *Romantic Option:* Marylou's quiet nightlife is a part of Greenwich Village that is often overshadowed by the frenzied jazz and rock clubs of Bleecker Street. To make it linger a little longer, after dinner, walk over to **One Fifth** at the corner of **Fifth Avenue and 8th Street, (212) 260-3434** (Moderate), and continue the evening and mood. Don't hurry, this is a piano bar worth lingering in.

ONE IF BY LAND, TWO IF BY SEA   ◆ ◆ ◆ ◆
17 Barrow Street *between Seventh Avenue & West 4th Street*
(212) 255-8649
Very, Very Expensive

As we peered in through the windows we knew that the evening was going to be one we would remember forever. The restaurant seemed to be glowing from two well-stoked fireplaces that enhanced the already scintillating atmosphere. The entrees were almost as attractive as the room and they tasted even better than they looked. The waiters were patient and considerate, the surroundings elegant and stately. It was an evening that would make any occasion special. (We wish you a patient cab driver, this is a tricky address to find, although that's an additional kissing advantage.)

RIVER CAFE

One Water Street, Brooklyn Heights
(718) 522-5200
Expensive
Jackets Required after 6:00 P.M.

Take the Manhattan Bridge to Brooklyn. Drive one long block to Tillary Street and turn right. When Tillary ends at Cadman Plaza, turn right again. Follow the road which winds around to the right, towards the East River. At the end of the street, the River Cafe is on your right.

Friends gave us a wedding present of brunch at the River Cafe and, in every way, it was a gift to savor. The food was creatively prepared, very good and caringly served. But the real gift was the thrilling view from the glass-enclosed dining room. Renovated in the mid-'70s, the River Cafe is an immense white barge with an enormous, crystal clear glass wall facing west. A few portholes remain as authentic touches from the past. Towering flower arrangements brighten the dining room and cocktail lounge. Sitting close together, gaze out at the Statue of Liberty, South Street Seaport, the lower Manhattan skyline, and the stonework of the Brooklyn Bridge. Watch the river traffic, as the color of the water changes in sync with the movement of the sun across the sky.

Note: Come for a drink at sunset, for lunch, or dinner, or brunch on weekends. Waterside tables outside are coveted in the summer. This is a popular place, and so make reservations. If you're coming for drinks, keep in mind that the bar gets crowded around sunset.

◆ *Romantic Option:* Just south of the River Cafe on Fulton Ferry Landing is **Bargemusic, (718) 624-4061**, a uniquely romantic concert site. Talented musicians perform "Chamber Music With a Different View" Thursdays at 7:30 and Sundays at 4 p.m. all year round, and at 7:30 on Fridays in the summer. Go topside on this double-decker former coffee barge for preconcert conversation or intermission. Dress is casual, and the prices are very reasonable. (Reservations are needed.)

◆ *Second Romantic Option:* While in Brooklyn Heights, wander along the **Promenade**, three blocks south of historic Fulton Ferry Landing. With its moving views (literally) and many benches, it's a perfect spot for a walk or a sunset. On nice sunny days, it's full of runners, bikers, small children, families, and other couples like yourselves.

RUMPELMAYER'S
50 Central Park South *between Fifth & Sixth Avenues*
(212) 755-5800
Inexpensive

There are going to be more than a few locals who are going to disagree with this entry, but we voted, and this overly pink, Central Park, somewhat out-of-date ice cream parlor won its recognition as a place to enjoy old-fashioned romance, which, when you think about it, is hard to come by these days. There was a time when a sundae wasn't a designer escapade with elite sounding names and price tags. There was a time when a boy would take a girl to the local ice cream shoppe and they would share whatever gooey offering they could handle. Well, indeed, times have changed, but the chance to relive a more innocent way of life is an opportunity not to be overlooked. And, yes, the interior is pink and during the summer or weekends grandma may be taking junior out for a sugar rush, but during off-hours, after a morning hansom cab ride through the park or an afternoon playful romp through F.A.O. Schwarz (see Miscellaneous Kissing), a very serious sundae, with a few discreetly placed kisses in between licks should just about make the day as joyous as they come.

SATURNIA RESTAURANT at the DORAL PARK AVENUE HOTEL
70 Park Avenue *at 38th Street*
(212) 949-5924
Moderate to Expensive

What could be more American than gourmet spa cuisine in a formal and elegant neoclassical garden setting? The menu provides fat and calorie information. Renowned chefs prepare three-course prix fixe meals, including such tasty morsels as "melange of seafood with cucumber, snow peas & rouille crouton" (316 calories; 2.9 fat points) and "sauteed tiger prawns salad with papaya, grapefruit & sesame-ginger dressing" for a meager 261 calories. The main reason people come here is for the food, but the atmosphere is compelling, too. Soft lights show off the muted but colorful murals. Bursts of flowers are everywhere. The tables are set with linens, crystal, and tall candles. This is a good choice for brunch.

◆ **Romantic Warning:** If you plan to eat here, call ahead to be sure the restaurant isn't reserved for a private party.

THE WATER CLUB
The East River *at 30th Street*
(212) 683-3333
Expensive to Very Expensive

We like the quiet, attractive, and elegant dining room at the Water Club, but we prefer to just have drinks here — inside in the cozy piano bar in winter or, even better, outside on the upper deck in summer. If you select the latter, you may be disconcerted at first by the loud noise of the traffic on the FDR Drive as the cars whiz past, but then you remember, this is New York, and the sound is transformed into an exhilarating force, the musical backdrop to the sparkly late evening view. The upper deck presents a ground's eye skyline view of industrial Queens and midtown Manhattan. You'll notice the tops of some prominent skyscrapers and the U.N., but mostly your eyes will rest upon the bejeweled necklace of the 59th Street Bridge. It's easy to feel groovy up here as you sip champagne and watch the Circle Line float past.

◆ **Romantic Option:** Before or after, take a stroll along the promenade past skaters, joggers, and strolling lovers, to **Waterside Plaza**, a little known residential enclave built right up against the East River. Walk up the steps to a private though publicly accessible park, and witness the view from a slightly different vantage point.

British Tea Kissing

AFTERNOON TEA at the PARK LANE HOTEL
36 Central Park South *near Fifth Avenue*
(212) 371-4000
Inexpensive

The Afternoon Tea at the Park Lane Hotel, unlike at other tea rooms, is not generally filled with female shoppers at tea time. It is therefore the perfect place to be together at a time of day when most Americans are too busy to relax.

The large mahogany furnished room, covered in thick, red plush carpeting with a vast window that overlooks Central Park, has a refined British atmosphere that is comfortable without being stuffy. Although this tea room may not be as remarkable as the Helmsley Palace Gold Room, what it lacks in grandeur it makes up for with a stellar view of the park, a fabulous salmon and caviar tray, and the richest pastries anywhere. At very reasonable prices, this is an afternoon affair almost every budget can afford.

GOLD ROOM at the HELMSLEY PALACE
455 Madison Avenue *at 50th Street*
(212) 888-7000
Moderate

The very popular, very opulent Gold Room at the Helmsley Palace is one of the most exquisite rooms in New York. As its name suggests, the room is completely encrusted with gold — shiny, elaborate, metallic gold. Unfortunately, it fits the tea room stereotype of catering largely to female shoppers. Go there anyway. The atmosphere is so seductive you won't notice anything else except, we hope, each other.

LITTLE NELL'S TEA ROOM
343 E. 85th Street *between First & Second Avenues*
(212) 772-2046
Inexpensive to Moderate

We were here on a summer evening right before closing time, and far from being the only couple in the place, we were the only people! May you be so lucky (but may the tea room always thrive). Open for brunch on Saturdays and Sundays and tea every day followed by dinner, both rooms — the pink and the green — are decked out in Victorian Christmas splendor. Charming, delightful, magical, and sweet, this is a place to linger and sip. Tall tapered candles softly light the room. Exposed brick on one side, English wallpaper on the other, tea served in china teapots with home-baked goodies, pictures of Royalty, scores of antique toys and dolls — all bespeak a very proper, very British atmosphere. There are many choice seats for an intimate tea for two. Lift your little pinkies and kiss delicately.

◆ *Romantic Warning:* As with most tea rooms, at tea time it is popular with ladies and sometimes children, but Little Nell's attracts couples as well — particularly during other meals. Try brunch or dinner.

Broadway Kissing

ARTHUR'S LANDING – (See Worth the Trip, New Jersey)

LA PRIMAVERA
234 West 48th Street *near Broadway, of course*
(212) 586-2797
Moderate Italian

With the exception of Restaurant Row, you can look all over the theater district for a place to kiss and not find one. Well, you don't have to wait 'til the lights go out in the theater. At Primavera, you can sit in the back, side by side in a booth, and gaze out past the balcony at the trompe l'oeil mural that will transport you right to the Amalfi coast.

The restaurant is decorated with explosions of flowers, giant faux marble columns, and pink table linens. Curl up some great pastas from the fine china, choose something luscious from the pastry cart, wash it down with a foamy cappuccino, and don't be late for the show!

LE MADELEINE – (See Restaurants, French)

RESTAURANT ROW
46th Street *between Eighth & Ninth Avenues*

Got two hot tickets to a Broadway show? In the mood for some food first? Forget about making reservations. Take a stroll along Restaurant Row and find just what you're in the mood for. Presenting a plethora of pleasurable places to partake of palatable portions, go very early (before 6:00 p.m.) to this thoroughly engaging street and step in and out of some of the most delightful restaurants in Manhattan until you find the one that speaks to your appetite and wallet. Following are a few of our favorites, atmospherically speaking that is.

Barbetta   ◆◆◆◆
321 West 46th Street, Restaurant Row
(212) 246-9171
Expensive Italian Cuisine

The fact that this restaurant is not renowned for its food may be a blessing. If the food were as wondrous as the atmosphere, the prices would be even higher, and you'd never get a reservation. As it is, you can often get in without one. The decor is so astonishing that you're bound to forget you're eating, and you're lips might very well be too busy kissing to eat at all. The food, by the way, isn't bad, and it's often quite good.

Weather permitting, dine in the garden, a magical setting filled with blooming trees and flowers. In its center, like a green jewel, is the crowning glory: a classic Italian fountain where four cherubs shoot sprays of water at one other. This is one of the few gardens in New York where the tables are set with linen, silver, crystal, and china.

Weather not permitting? Never fear. You'll be happy to kiss in any one of the many dining rooms, upstairs and down. Each has its own romantic flavor. One room is lined with old wine bottles in wooden hutches. Another is topped with delicate crystal chandeliers. Still another — the small one with the 350-year old fireplace — can (for a very steep price) be rented for just the two of you. There, as in a fantasy, you'll be wined and dined by a private staff of waiters, and a violinist will appear to serenade you off to never never land. Hello! Snap out of it! Are you there? All of the rooms have working fireplaces and beautiful ornate Italian antiques.

Broadway Pasta
330 West 46th Street, Restaurant Row
(212) 581-1815
Very Inexpensive Italian Cuisine

Feels expensive with its candles and crystal chandeliers, but Broadway Pasta is easy on the wallet as well as the eyes. In fact, you may be so amazed by these non-New York prices you'll forget to kiss!

Carolina
355 West 46th Street, Restaurant Row
(212) 245-0058
Moderately Priced American Cuisine

The woodburning barbeque smells so good, your nose may very well choose this spot for you. Wave to the busy chefs through the glass kitchen window. On your way out, after dining, you'll want to blow them a kiss; go ahead, they won't mind. The downstairs of the restaurant is fine, but it's the upstairs that we recommend. The small quiet room with gentle flute and piano music playing in the background provides just the right atmosphere for cooing and conversation. The only problem is, you may want to stay, and you'll miss the theater.

Danny's Grand Sea Palace

"Restaurant, Piano Bar & Skylight Room Cabaret"
346 West 46th Street, Restaurant Row
(212) 265-8130
Moderately priced Thai and Seafood

You'll be offered two menus here: one is called "Broadway," and it features seafood; the other is called "Bangkok," and it is filled with Thai delicacies. Danny's has great peach lighting, live piano music, and a very special central dining nook for two. Or sit at the raised lamplit table beside the piano. Eat good food or sip a glass of champagne. The service is warm and friendly.

Hourglass Tavern

373 West 46th Street, Restaurant Row
(212) 265-2060
Inexpensive American Cuisine
No reservations; no credit cards

With only eight tables, most of them built for two, and delicious and generous portions of tasty inexpensive food, you don't want to come to this funky American bistro when it's crowded because if you do they just may hold you to their one hour limit (thus the hourglass on the wall and the name of the establishment). If there's no one waiting for your table, there's no time limit. Even so, an hour is a long time here and the service is friendly. Most of the time you won't feel rushed at all. Quite the contrary. Savor the homemade bread, pastas, and other entrees, and be sure to share a big wedge of their famous chocolate cake.

Joe Allen
326 West 46th Street, Restaurant Row
(212) 581-6464
Moderately Priced American Cuisine

Joe Allen's provides romance for two tastes. You can choose between the atmospheric brick-walled front room or the gardenlike sunroom in back. We chose the back, and we weren't sorry. The music played softly in the background, we ate some hearty food, and all was right with the world.

Meson Sevilla
344 West 46th Street, Restaurant Row
(212) 262-5890
Inexpensive to Moderate Spanish Cuisine

Eat some paella, wash it down with a Margarita Conquistador (if you're not driving, of course) and listen to the sounds of Julio Iglesias.

Orso
322 West 46th Street, Restaurant Row
(212) 489-7212
Moderate to Expensive Italian Cuisine
Reservations strongly advised

Orso is believed by many to have by far the best food on Restaurant Row. The quiet ambience when empty can best be described as austere elegance. The effervescent ambience when crowded (which it almost always is) can best be described as star-studded. Your mouth may be too wide open from gaping at celebrities to kiss.

◆ ◆ ◆

Brunch / Breakfast Kissing

We are always searching for the quintessential romantic breakfast, the kind of place where mornings succumb to the heart's longing for time to pass slowly with nothing to do but sip another cafe au lait and prolong morning another hour or two. If you can find your way out of bed before 11 a.m. on Sunday, most of these places will not even have a waiting line. These morning kissing spots are not even vaguely known for the infamous New York power breakfast.

Note: Many of the other restaurants listed elsewhere in this book also offer delicious brunches, and many of the ones listed in this section serve other meals besides brunch. Some restaurants offer brunch on Saturday and Sunday, whereas others just serve brunch on Sunday. Call and ask.

BERRY'S

180 Spring Street *at Thompson Street*
(212) 226-4394
Inexpensive to Moderate

Weekend brunch is only a part of what this lovingly intimate, reasonably priced restaurant does best — particularly on Saturday when the Sunday brunch crowd is out shopping and running errands. Berry's also comes with an emphatic warning: It can get crowded, noisy, very smoky and, because it is so intimate, unpleasant. Until the management institutes a no-smoking policy, go there cautiously or cross the street to the **Manhattan Bistro, 129 Spring Street, (212) 966-3459** (Moderate), where the size and atmosphere and great food can make the morning a beautiful affair.

CAFE DES ARTISTES

1 West 67th Street *at Central Park West*
(212) 877-3500
Moderate Brunch; Expensive Dinner

The outdoors has moved indoors at Cafe des Artistes and it couldn't be more inviting. Well-tended greenery is everywhere and the cheerful room is provocatively lit. The breakfast is Continental food at its best, and the presentation, like the environment, will please your senses. This place is probably too popular to be a truly romantic spot, but we so thoroughly enjoyed our Sunday brunch here that we had to include it. (Very well known and luscious Continental menu for lunch and dinner, too.)

CUPPING ROOM CAFE
359 West Broadway *at Broome Street*
(212) 925-2898
Moderate

Every romance has its first brunch, where sleepy-cats show their true colors before that first cup of joe. Well, morning people, this is the kingpin of brunch places: where stay-at-home East-siders and staunch Upper-West-siders climb into taxis and head downtown for some of the best comfort food and homey surroundings in the city. Sipping the cafe's own blend of coffee or frothy cappuccino wakes up even the grumpiest of non-morning types. (There's usually one in every couple!) The mood is desirably cozy, designed like an old-world European cafe: perfect for long conversations over the strings of Strauss. And the aroma that drifts from the surrounding tables! Muffins the size of two fists, challah French toast, and their specialty — waffle orgies. Waffles with huge dollops of ice cream or yogurt overflowing with dates, nuts, and fruit are just some of the goodies on the menu. Dessert is a must: It all looks so perfect and practically screams for attention. Go ahead. Order one dessert and two forks — sharing makes it that much sweeter.

◆ *Romantic Warning:* Early birds will have no problem getting a table on weekends; but come later than 11:00 a.m. on weekends (Sunday especially) and you should expect a good long wait. There are no lines during the week.

GOOD ENOUGH TO EAT
483 Amsterdam Avenue *between 83rd & 84th Streets*
(212) 496-0163
Moderate

Picture a farmer's cozy kitchen plunked down in the middle of New York's Upper West Side and voilà: Good Enough to Eat is good enough to move into! Its wood tables (antique sewing machines, actually), country baskets, and antique surroundings make for a rustic haven reminiscent of Vermont. This is a place designed for lingering . . . over oversized muffins, homemade granola, or thick fruit-filled pancakes. The cozy interior is perfect for hushed conversations, romantic glances and mimosa kisses. Brunch is a specialty but go on a weekday; weekends are known for their long waits. Dinner is also popular; make reservations if you're dining after 7:30 p.m.

PARIS COMMUNE
411 Bleecker *between 11th & Perry Streets*
(212) 929-0509
Inexpensive

This modest restaurant, with its small array of wood tables, oil paintings, and casual ambience exudes a Parisian Left Bank atmosphere. Weekend brunch is fresh and beautifully served. It's a shame they serve only dinner during the week.

THE PEMBROKE ROOM – (See The Lowell Hotel)

SARABETH'S KITCHEN
423 Amsterdam Avenue *between 80th & 81st Streets*
(212) 496-6280
1295 Madison Avenue *between 92nd & 93rd Streets*
(212) 410-7335
Inexpensive to Moderate

We think it is very considerate of Sarabeth to give us two of the most romantically perfect locations for brunching on the East or the West Sides. Our preference is the East Side Sarabeth's with its tall jade-green French windows, French door entranceway, and a balcony section, which helps separate the two dining areas — a definite yes when it comes to crowded (note: very long lines crowded) Sundays. The restaurants are bright and cheery and practically empty on weekday mornings with a wonderful menu featuring all types of egg dishes, granola, and fresh baked goods. You have to get up early in the morning if you want a pumpkin muffin.

◆ *Romantic Option:* Sarabeth's has recently opened **Sarabeth's at the Whitney** (see Museum Kissing).

SUMMER HOUSE RESTAURANT
50 East 86th Street *between Madison & Park Avenues*
(212) 249-6300
Inexpensive

The omelet was fluffy and it was served with a fresh, sweet strawberry butter with warm melt-in-your mouth biscuits by somewhat distracted (it can be busy), though polite, waitpeople. (Theirs is one interesting brunch menu; they even serve a Huevos Rancheros Pizza). The cafe-style interior is simple and classic, with a warm, casual atmosphere — perhaps a little too crowded to be a quiet spot for two over brunch and Sunday morning conversation, but be patient, once you're at your own table for two, it is possible that you won't notice anyone else except each other.

Cafe Kissing

There comes a time in every romantic involvement when two people look deep into each other's eyes and say: "Let us eat cake and anything else sugary we can get our hands on." At other times, when your beloved is obviously in need of a long talk, the informed romantic will suggest that the mood be supported by a well-brewed espresso or calmed by herbal tea and enriched by something sweetly decadent. Sometimes romance requires the old-world grace and pace that only a cafe can provide. For such times and needs, consult the following tastefully and sincerely compiled compendium. (**Note:** Because the typical fare at most cafes are light, all of them listed here are rated inexpensive.)

ANGLERS & WRITERS
420 Hudson *at St. Luke's Place*
(212) 675-0810

This newcomer quietly appeared and now seems to have always been here. Their business card says it all: three naked cherubs carrying a big fish. Whimsical? You said it. Look closely and you'll see many instances of the offbeat charm that defines the funky candlelit country decor. Punctuating an airy wide open space, each table is different. Some are carved, others are various colors of marble. One table is an antique desk. And the boss's rolltop in the center of it all is open for inspection. You can sit side by side on couches or embroidered chairs. The service is cordial. Expect to smell the coffee brewing. Expect to eat luscious pies, beautifully presented light entrees, and the best soup in town. Expect to hear Billie Holiday music playing in the background. Expect to see books, books, and more books, tackle boxes, nets, a bust in the corner, dried flowers, fresh flowers such as towering rose-colored gladiolas, grapevines hung upside down — oh, and fish.

◆ **Romantic Note:** Although this is a fun kissing spot, it's also a fine place to sit alone with a cup of coffee and a book.

CAFE BORGIA
185 Bleecker Street *at MacDougal Street*
(212) 473-2290

Cafe Borgia is a Village landmark which has been tempting lovers with plates of little delicious cookies for years. On a beautiful spring day, its outdoor table can't be beat.

CAFE DE CORTINA
1450 Second Avenue *between 75th & 76th Streets*
(212) 517-2066

Simply lovely. One of the most affectionate places to partake of everything from Belgian waffles to crepes, desserts, and a perfect cappuccino, which is an emotional experience in and of itself. With the person you love sharing it all, it can be heaven.

CAFE SHA SHA

510 Hudson Street *at Charles Street*
(212) 242-3021

Cafe Sha Sha has two things that make it a good kissing place: It's in the far-west Village and it's very quiet. Technically it's too big for a cafe, but this allows for space between one romance and the next.

CAFE LA FORTUNA
69 West 71st Street *off Columbus Avenue*
(212) 724-5846

A darkly lit dessert cafe with red, black, and brick walls, this has come to be a late night Upper West Side institution. Linger over great cappuccino in big cups and, like a true New Yorker, ignore the frenzy around you. During the warner months, head outside to the garden tables.
◆ ***Romantic Warning:*** The cups are big, but the ice cream tables and chairs are small and close. This is not everyone's idea of romantic. The old-world desserts, on the other hand, are alone worth the price of admission.

CAFE LUCCA

228 Bleecker Street *at Cornelia Street*
(212) 243-8385

Here's a place where you'll want to linger. It has a few tables for alfresco dining which are occupied into the wee hours in the warm months. The cozy interior is a rendezvous spot for a serious — and seriously romantic — cafe crowd. By the way, if you ask them when they open and close, they'll say, "Till late."

CAFFE REGGIO

119 MacDougal Street *at West 3rd Street*
(212) 475-9557

With its jumble of marble tables and imposing coffee urns and samovars, Caffe Reggio is a place where time slows down and moods turn softer. At times it does suffer from the tourist trade, but if you want the look and feel of a real cafe, this is it. Going during off-hours, however, is the best option here, as in most New York hot-spots.

CAFFE VIVALDI
32 Jones Street *at Seventh Avenue South*
(212) 691-7538

Both this street and, as a result, this caffe, are harder to find (for you and everyone else) so you should have more quiet moments here. In winter the fireplace will also keep the two of you warm and glowing. You can also enjoy some of the best and freshest pastries around, in the cafe's peaceful and warm interior.

CLOISTER CAFE (Garden)
238 East 9th Street *between Second & Third Avenues*
(212) 777-9128
No credit cards

When the day or evening is delightfully balmy and you're thinking casual and alfresco, go here. Aptly named, this offbeat European-style find is so well sequestered on this unromantic street that you can walk by it four or five times before you find it, but keep looking and you won't be sorry. Enter the doors into a medieval stained glass sanctuary. During the winter, stay warm sipping big bowls of coffee or tea and munching on fruits, salads, pastas and other Italian cafe fare. The presiding knight in shining armor in the corner may provide kissing inspiration if the tin ceiling, brick walls, flickering candles and centrally located warming wood-stove don't do the trick.

All that said, weather permitting, get thee outside to brunch in the cobblestoned garden enclosed by ivy-covered walls on three sides and a wrought-iron gate on the fourth. In the center a fountain will relax you with its gurgling sounds. Trees, roses, greenery and, in the evening, twinkling white lights will transport the two of you to a far away place of love.

CORNELIA STREET CAFE

29 Cornelia Street *at Bleecker Street*
(212) 989-9318

A little bit of everything a cafe lover could want is waiting at this gem of a coffee house — outdoor seating in summer, a fireplace in winter, poetry and prose on Sundays, and a relaxing, laid-back, easy atmosphere.

DANAL

90 East 10th Street *at Third Avenue*
(212) 982-6930

Ah, the aroma, the setting, the warm service — everything you need except a favorite other to share it with. This may be one of the most enchanting places in the East Village. Danal even has a garden tucked away for outdoor seating in the warmer months.

DE ROBERTIS PASTICCERIA
176 First Avenue *between 10th and 11th Streets*
(212) 674-7137

A handsome, period piece of an Italian cafe, brightly lit with lots of privacy. The pastries can be too sweet — even for the sweet — but two forks and one dessert should fill the bill just right.

EDGAR'S CAFE

255 West 84th Street *between Broadway & West End Avenue*
(212) 496-6126

Someone with a beautiful sense of style created Edgar's. Dropped lights, high ceilings, and trompe l'oeil Pompeiian "ruins" all conspire to create this gem of a cafe. With the fans turning overhead, sit at little marble tables and treat yourselves to light salads, every kind of coffee, and the wickedest desserts in town. As at most cafes, you can sit all day if you like. The best table, if you can get it, is in a little nook under a large painting.

◆ **Romantic Warning:** Expect noisy; you will hardly hear the crashing Beethoven tapes.

HUNGARIAN PASTRY SHOP
1030 Amsterdam Avenue *at 111th Street*
(212) 866-4230

Pleasantly off the beaten track, the Hungarian Pastry Shop is frequented primarily by Columbia University students. Here you can satisfy the sweet tooth in your mouths and the gypsy in your souls. You'd swear through the smoke — the only place in the world where smoke is required for atmosphere — that Jack Kerouac was having a chat with Allen Ginsberg.

LA LANTERNA DI VITTORIO   ◆◆◆◀
129 McDougal Street *between 3rd Street & Washington Square Park*
No phone

Properly dubbed "the fireside caffee," La Lanterna di Vittorio boasts fireplaces upstairs and down, wood-and-brick walls, and a knight in shining armor at every turn. Upstairs the soda fountain recalls a little taste of the old world. Steaming brews and sinful desserts — French, German, and Italian pastries — are served in the most exquisite, antiques-filled Village environment. Be warned that your diets are doomed here.

◆ **Romantic Note:** The slightly more intimate downstairs room opens at 6:00 p.m.

LANCIANI PATISSERIE
275 West 4th Street *at West 11th Street*
(212) 929-0739

A handsome, sparkling room served by a caring staff and patronized by an elegant clientele. An exuberant place at heart, it may be too quick-pulsed for some, but off-hours are more tranquil.

MILLE FLEURS
246 West 4th Street *at Charles Street*
(212) 785-7946

Somehow sunny even at midnight and always comfortably unkempt like home, with the fan always whirring under the tin ceiling and the barely audible sounds of the piano playing softly, you'll feel as if it's Sunday morning in your own French country cottage. There's a menu that includes breakfast at any time of day, but if you prefer, you can just order sumptuous desserts, coffees, cappuccinos, and other typical cafe fare. The atmosphere conspires to woo in its own friendly, relaxed, artistic, and eclectic manner. Amid the watercolors, antique porcelains, magazines, broken chairs, busts, Buddha, and other things strewn about, note the framed print (see the original at the Metropolitan Museum of Art) of Pygmalion and Galatea entranced in a kiss as Cupid looks on. (Pygmalion, the artist, sculpted a woman so beautiful that he fell in love with the statue, and Aphrodite brought her to life). If you encourage her, the fluffy calico (Greta Garbo) or her cohort, Carl Jung, might curl up at your feet. If this isn't relaxed kissing, nothing is.

ODYSSEY ROOM at the DORAL PARK AVENUE HOTEL
70 Park Avenue *at 38th Street*
(212) 949-5924

Tended by the same chefs and nutritionists who have made the spa cuisine of the Saturnia Restaurant famous worldwide, this is a delightful little hotel cafe on elegant Park Avenue. When lines spill out the doors on Columbus Avenue and in the Village, this place is remarkably empty and inexpensive. It hits the spot for lunch, brunch, or whenever the mood demands a salad, sandwich, or dessert and coffee. We love to saunter into this amusing red, black, and white cafe with its little love seats and pretty inlaid wood tables. We argue amiably over whether this small and bright but intimate cafe can be described as Greek deco with Japanese influence or modern Italian with Greek flourishes. By all means, decide for yourself. Whatever else you say, surely you'll agree it's undeniably cute.

RUMBULS PASTRY SHOP
20 Christopher Street *at Sheridan Square*
(212) 924-8900

A quiet cafe whose small, warm wood-paneled rooms take the cake (sorry) for beautiful decoration and heartwarming ambience. Their selection is creamy and temptingly presented.

Chinese Kissing

The best Chinese restaurants are usually crowded with large parties. Perhaps that's because it's so much fun to eat Chinese cuisine in a large group where you get to taste more of the endless variety of meat, fish, and vegetable dishes. But then again, this is New York, a city full of lovers who love Chinese food, and the niche for chopsticks-for-two has been filled quite nicely by a few restaurants that have turned the lights down low, softened the pace, and created just the right blend of ambience and excellent cuisine.

AUNTIE YUAN
1191 First Avenue *at 64th Street*
(212) 744-4040
Expensive

Auntie Yuan borders on too popular because it happens to be one of the best Chinese restaurants on the Upper East Side; it feels romantic anyway. Auntie's (we're on intimate terms) is for when you're in the mood for high style that also radiates coziness and has exotic food to match.

CHEZ VONG

220 East 46th Street *at Third Avenue*
(212) 867-1111
Expensive

From the moment we entered this hallowed, elaborately decorated restaurant we knew that something special waited for us. Everything was set for sumptuous dining from the traditional, dramatic Chinese decor to the extensive (actually, "extensive" is an understatement), well-served menu.

PEARL'S

38 West 48th Street *between Fifth & Sixth Avenues*
(212) 221-6677
Expensive

This striking room is the epitome of elegance, and the gracious staff makes you feel that your meal is something more than special. Even lunch seems more like an event than a mere dining escape. The sleek, sophisticated interior makes an inspired setting for romance.

SHUN LEE

43 West 65th Street *near Columbus Avenue*
(212) 595-8895
Expensive

Shun Lee's is one sexy Chinese restaurant. The setting is a mysterious mixture of blacks with dramatic spotlights poised over each table. The menu, far from mysterious, is blatantly delicious. Any couple will find the experience here worthy of a special occasion.

SHUN LEE PALACE
155 East 55th Street *between Lexington & Third Avenues*
(212) 371-8844
Expensive

Everything about this Shun Lee is designed to be impressive. It is a posh, popular location with a truly excellent menu that makes dining here a treat.

Continental Kissing

There is something very de rigueur about this style of dining. It encompasses the best of many cuisines, with an emphasis on French and Italian dishes. For amorous couples with eclectic appetites there is nothing quite as satisfying as Continental dining — particularly here in New York City, where the chefs are some of the best in the world.

THE AMBASSADOR GRILL
One United Nations Plaza *at 44th Street & First Avenue*
(212) 702-5014
Moderate

Providing an elegant atmosphere, good food, and reasonable prices, the Ambassador Grill is secluded in an out-of-the-mainstream quiet neighborhood. You enter this spacious restaurant through a glass-ceilinged entryway, designed to resemble a contemporary greenhouse, which brings you to a large reception alcove that is separate from the dining room and bar. This entryway prevents you from feeling that you've intruded on someone else's intimate tête-à-tête when you arrive. The dramatic scarlet rug is offset by the skylit atrium of the main room, and the glass-paneled walls make for an airy feeling all around. Inside, the pace is leisurely and the atmosphere soothing. After savoring a delectable four-course meal you can have your espresso in the lounge where the background music stays in the background. This one spot can make for an a complete evening for two, after dark, in New York. The prix fixe lunch is also a good option here.

CAFE DES ARTISTES – (See Restaurants, Brunch/Breakfast)

THE CARLYLE RESTAURANT AND CAFE
35 East 76th Street *at Madison Avenue*
(212) 744-1600
Very, Very Expensive

We are usually skeptical when we hear that a well-known, luxurious hotel dining room is intimate. Most are too stuffy, too business-oriented or they take themselves much too seriously for the tender needs of snuggling and affection. The Carlyle is, in all honesty, a little and, at times, a lot of all those things, and sometimes we wish the staff would just lighten up. But it is also upscale New York at its best, with all the right touches and all the right details to make any time of day seem special. The interior is impeccable. The food is extraordinary. There's a profusion of flowers everywhere, and you can go for breakfast, lunch, dinner, brunch, teatime, or cocktails. At night Bobby Short still plays Cole Porter tunes in the Cafe Carlyle. For a thoroughly suave time of it, come here.

540 PARK
540 Park Avenue *at 61st Street*
(212) 888-7914
Very, Very Expensive and Beyond

If dining in a French country château on a scale only slightly less majestic then Versailles is to your taste, then this location is prime territory for you, with a menu that is simple, classic, and enticing. The only warning this exquisite setting carries is its reputation "power eating," which can create awkward vibes when the mood you want is warm and endearing.

GOTHAM BAR & GRILL   ◆◆◆
12 East 12th Street *between Fifth Avenue & University Place*
(212) 620-4020
Expensive to Very Expensive

The Gotham Bar & Grill is beautiful. Perhaps a bit too much on the formal side for some affectionate tastes, but the sparkling elegance down in the Village has never looked so good. Holding hands over a serious, well-paced dinner here can be an all-night affair; or appetizers alone can serve as a welcome introduction to the four-star menu. From the street the tall windows reveal only a suggestion of the strikingly eccentric interior. Muslin fabrics float like parachutes from the overhead fixtures, diffusing the lighting throughout the restaurant. The dining room itself borders on enormous, which is a kissing advantage; no one feels packed in at this restaurant. Beautiful tones of green and rose are accented by floor-to-ceiling French windows (probably 30 or 40 feet tall), and the tables are softly lit to give a vibrant glow to each setting. You can take this one to heart.

LION'S ROCK   ◆◆◆◀
316 East 77th Street *between First & Second Avenues*
(212) 988-3610
Moderate

This is New York City, isn't it? Manhattan even. But you won't believe it until you see it with your own eyes. The focal point of the restaurant is its grottolike outdoor garden, a many-tiered rapturous affair, set beside a large slab of granite over which trickles a natural waterfall! The water comes from a natural spring that was once Jones' Wood, "legendary location of buried treasure and a Kissing Bridge," a place where lovers met in the 19th century. The theme is the jungle, but we assure you, there's nothing to be scared of here. Huddle together and enter past the lions, past the bar into the restaurant with its exposed brick walls, low lights, and fireplace, and — weather and crowds permitting — march straight out the back into paradise. You'll not only want to kiss here, you'll want to hug, too. Oh, the food? Yeah, it's good, but frankly we'd go there even if it weren't.

PALIO

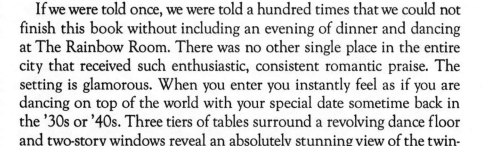

Equitable Center Arcade
151 West 51st Street *between Sixth & Seventh Avenues*
(212) 245-4850
Very Expensive

Palio is a visually impressive restaurant. The circular mural that wraps around the bar on the ground floor fills the room with exciting color. On the second floor, accessible only by elevator, the room is awash in white tablecloths with a decidedly chic, dignified (some would call snobby) air. The patrons are noticably slim and designer perfect (when you mention mousse here, you're not talking about dessert). Regardless of your own personal style, or because of it, there is romance to be found at Palio. The food is remarkable, the service superior, and you're sure to have a thoroughly first class evening.

THE RAINBOW ROOM

30 Rockefeller Center *on the 65th Floor*
(212) 632-5000
Very, Very Expensive

If we were told once, we were told a hundred times that we could not finish this book without including an evening of dinner and dancing at The Rainbow Room. There was no other single place in the entire city that received such enthusiastic, consistent romantic praise. The setting is glamorous. When you enter you instantly feel as if you are dancing on top of the world with your special date sometime back in the '30s or '40s. Three tiers of tables surround a revolving dance floor and two-story windows reveal an absolutely stunning view of the twinkling city beyond. The food is notable, the service graceful and considerate. A twelve-piece orchestra plays music the way it was meant to be played. A two-step into the past couldn't be more beguiling then this . . . unless you consider the price, which is as far removed from the '30s as you can get. On the other hand, because The Rainbow Room charges so much, nearly everyone saves it for the most special romantic occasions, and this charges the air with even more romance.

Note: Dancing and dinner go together, which explains the hefty price tag on this evening out. Although if you dine after 10:30 p.m., the light supper menu is served and the cost can drop to almost half.

◆ *Romantic Option:* If you can't dance or your budget doesn't permit, the **Rainbow Promenade**, adjacent to the Rainbow Room is a wonderful, much less expensive alternative with the same view and the same kitchen preparing very good lighter fare. There isn't a twelve-piece orchestra, but there is a pianist making pretty music in the background.

THE ROSE ROOM at the ALGONQUIN HOTEL   ❤ ❤ ◆ ❤
59 West 44th Street *between Fifth & Sixth Avenues*
(212) 840-6800
Moderate to Expensive

We had heard that the Algonquin was deteriorating. Well, that is just not true. We found the Algonquin to be charm personified. Separate from its history, which alone can send any literature-loving couple into a tizzy, The Rose Room is a quaint and pretty place to have engaging meals (including a late-night dessert buffet) and talk the hours away — as befits the legendary setting. The Algonquin's **Oak Room** (see Cabaret/Lounge section) is one of the handsomest dining rooms in the city, where the best cabaret singers from all over the world perform. No, it is not the slickest place in the city; yes, the rugs in the main room aren't new, and there is a definite feeling of walking back in time to the '40s, but for some that's a preferable atmosphere. This nostalgic location is one of a kind and should not be overlooked when you're seeking an enchanting evening or weekend for two.

SIGN OF THE DOVE

1110 Third Avenue *at 65th Street*
(212) 861-8080
Expensive to Very Expensive

The very beautiful Sign of the Dove is the last word in fine dining. Even though jackets are not required here, the elegant atmosphere inspires dressing up, and you won't feel out of place in the most decked out black tie. On the other hand, you could wander in on a random night and be seated as you are — that is if the large many-roomed restaurant is not filled to the brim as it so often is.

Specific tables may be requested here, but you'll have a hard time choosing. First you'll need to decide which of the four dining rooms suits your taste and mood. Many people think the music room is the most suited to romance with its low coral tones, Tiffany glass, large fringed lampshades, and antique wicker chairs. Here as in all the rooms, the fragrant aroma of fresh flowers permeates. Others may opt for the large main dining room or the gauze-covered sun room (the greenhouse room) with its marble statues and brick walls, looking very much like a bright palatial Italian Court. Our favorite is the very special conservatory room with its four tables for two (among some larger tables). Here the colorful and interesting sun roof dominates, despite the central presence of a captivating marble statue and a ficus tree with branches entwined like two lovers.

◆ *Romantic Note:* Be sure to reserve at least a week ahead for weekends.

THE SUMPTUARY RESTAURANT

400 Third Avenue *between 28th & 29th Streets*
(212) 889-6056
Moderate

"Oh no," I thought as my friends and I stumbled into this enchanting, whimsical, offbeat dining establishment, "not another restaurant for the book." "Oh yes," my own voice countered. I must have stepped out of New York and into Wonderland. Stop the presses, it would be a disservice not to include such a phantasmagorical eating experience as this, with its fine service, quiet flute and violin melodies, pink table linens, the room strewn with little white lights, strangely flickering fireplaces, bird ornaments, paintings, bas reliefs everywhere and little funny touches that would seem out of place anywhere else (is that a tiny green mask that bird on the wall is wearing?). I'm telling you, there's a profound magic at the sumptuous Sumptuary restaurant.

The food is characterized by the same strange charm as the atmosphere (how does Apricot and Plum Duckling grab you, for example?). Our meal was delightful and far less expensive than most comparable meals around town.

TAVERN ON THE GREEN

In Central Park *at Central Park West & 67th Street*
(212) 873-3200
Moderate to Very Expensive

This glass palace set in the heart of Central Park is a staple of the New York dining scene and, although overly well-known places are not usually considered romantic, you'd have to be a true cynic to miss the magic that can be found amidst the twinkling white lights. The abundance of floor-to-ceiling windows allows perfect viewing of a fresh snowfall over the park in winter, the fiery colors of the trees in autumn, the lazy lingering mood in summer, and the fertile rebirth of flowers in spring.

THE TERRACE RESTAURANT

400 West 119th Street *at Morningside Drive*
(212) 666-9490
Very Expensive

It's the little touches that make the Terrace such a special place to visit. Perhaps it's the azaleas blooming in the entry hall where your coats are checked or the live harp music piped throughout the restaurant at just the right decibel level that brings me back to this hidden jewel time and time again. Or maybe the real enticement is the single rose in a crystal vase that sits atop each table or the slim candle that is replaced by the ever-attentive staff before it burns too low. Whatever it is for you, the understated refinement of the Terrace, the dazzling view from its 17th-floor windows, and the nearly perfect cuisine draw a dedicated following night after night. Squirreled away in a Columbia University-owned building, the Terrace is a favorite splurge for a romantic tête-à-tête. Be warned that you won't get away cheaply, although, like us, you may want to eschew the expensive Beluga caviar appetizer in favor of warm goat cheese salad and settle for a lovely bottle of fume blanc over the $500 bottle of 1975 Chateau Petrus. If only all compromises could be this satisfying.

◆ **Romantic Note:** There really is a terrace at the Terrace. Be certain to step outside on it for a moment after you've eaten and admire the extraordinary skyline of an extraordinary city.

THE WATER'S EDGE, Queens – (See Long Island City Waterfront, Outdoor Kissing)

French Kissing

The obvious pun is even too much for us, so please forgive the momentary cheap indulgence – this is not the section for those with athletic tongues – this is the section for true food lovers who feel that their relationship is best reflected in their joint belief that a succulent coq au vin or coquilles St. Jacques is the perfect prelude to amour. For those in search of tantalizing the palate as well as the heart, here are our suggestions for places in which to appreciate the pleasures of a truly smooth complex sauce, a wicked combination of textures and flavors, the ecstasy of art-worthy presentations usually served on the most translucent select china — dedicated to creating rapturous dining pour deux (for two).

ATELIER
436 Hudson Street *at Morton Street*
(212) 989-1363
Moderate to Expensive

Let quiet guitar strings lull you as the candlelight flickers in the small but wide-open space. Giant bouquets emit their fragrance, and dried flowers and wine bottles decorate the walls in this quiet and softly lit West Village charmer. This refined wood-paneled country cafe serves exquisite food in an elegant, relaxed environment. Sit up straight on your spindle-backed chairs at an antique oak table and treat yourselves to a special evening.

AU TROQUET
328 West 12th *between Hudson & Washington Streets*
(212) 924-3413
Expensive

An inviting room, delectable food, and for this high caliber of dining, reasonable prices — those are things that get two hearts beating any night of the week.

BISTRO DU NORD
1312 Madison Avenue *at 93rd Street*
(212) 289-0997
Moderate to Expensive

An unusually small but tall two-leveled bistro, this lovely restaurant specializes in mouth-watering French fare. French lyrical love music and an abundance of tables for two draw many couples. The golden low lighting on the tiny balcony helps to keep them. The restaurant is interestingly decorated in white with white covers over the chairs. In the summer, the tall front of the tiny restaurant is open to the air.

◆ *Romantic Warning:* This has become a popular spot. It is often crowded, and many of the tables are a little too close for true intimacy.

BOULEY ◆◆◆◆
165 Duane Street *between Greenwich & Hudson Streets*
(212) 608-3852
Very Expensive

Gigi, Funny little good for nussin Gigi* Oh, excuse me, we were at Bouley's last night, and we're still singing zee praises. Za flowers. Za lighting. Za waiter. He treated us as he did za celebrities. Za food. Ah, za food. We wanted never to end zis meal.

From the moment you open the big wooden doors until you polish off the complimentary little cookies and chocolate mouse (that's right, mouse not mousse), you'll be swooning with delight. Lovers sit side by side beside other lovers under the vaulted ceiling. Unlike many other four-star New York restaurants, this one is more popular with couples than with businesspeople. With its perfect lighting, food from heaven, a happy and elegant non-intimidating ambience, Bouley is pure pleasure.

◆ *Romantic Warning:* Sometimes large groups do create a noise problem, and this place is, understandably, popular. We highly recommend choosing the quietest times to go, such as early (or late) during an off night in summer when many New Yorkers flee to the Hamptons and points north.

**To be read with a French accent – to put you in just the right spirit.*

THE BOX TREE RESTAURANT – (See The Box Tree Hotel)

CAFE DU PARC
106 East 19th Street *between Park Avenue & Irving Place*
(212) 777-7840
Expensive

Intimate French dining in this extremely pretty location is a must for any discussion that requires good food, truly charming decor and courteous, intelligent service.

CHANTERELLE
2 Harrison Street *at Hudson Street*
(212) 966-6960
Very, Very Expensive

With a handful of tables in a precious setting, Chanterelle serves a gourmet selection of exquisitely prepared creations of French and Continental delights. Given the almost-impossible-to-obtain reservations, careful planning is required for a celebration here.

CHEZ MICHALLET
90 Bedford Street, *corner of Grove Street*
(212) 242-8309
Moderate to Expensive
Dinner Only

You'll feel transported to Old New York the minute you approach this West Village restaurant. Even if you and your partner were pushed and shoved on your subway ride, or had to fight for a cab on a busy Midtown street to get here: It's worth it. The modern-day hustle and bustle of Manhattan seem to melt away from the moment you arrive in the neighborhood. The restaurant is located on one of the prettiest and best preserved streets in New York. Ask for a table by the window and you can look out at a Revolutionary-era house (yes, a real house in Manhattan!), historic brownstones, and a vintage fire station where you half expect to see a Dalmation and hear the clang of a hand-held fire bell.

The quaint, quiet setting outside only complements the soft tones inside. This is a small, intimate restaurant (the best kind for romantic kisses!); there are only about 12 tables, decorated simply with white tablecloths and votive candles. Located in an old brownstone, it has the cozy warmth of a country farmhouse, with its high tin ceiling, Laura Ashley blue-and-white wallpaper, billowing curtains, rustic baskets and discreetly in the corner, a vase of fresh flowers. One side of the restaurant offers the privacy of cushiony banquettes; the other side, the window view. The food is superb — a combination of interesting sauces and French entrees.

The waiters are especially caring and attentive, and know when your glass needs filling or when your hushed tones signal the need for privacy. You'll want to linger here for hours — and you can. No one rushes you, which only adds to its charm. But don't stay too long past your bedtime — we suggest leaving some time to walk hand in hand around the neighborhood, to peer into the many historic homes, their lights blazing, showing off shiny chandeliers and long oak staircases, and to imagine, for a moment, that you've traveled back in time to another era.

CHEZ JOSEPHINE   ◆ ◆ ◆
414 West 42nd Street *between Ninth & Tenth Avenues*
(212) 594-1925
Moderate to Expensive
Amazingly, no music cover

This long thin room with its red drapes and teal-blue tin ceiling gets a little cramped at the height of the dinner hour, but when people leave for the theater, you can really stretch out and relax with some measure of tranquillity. Whenever you come, however, expect an experience. The color and feel of this 1920's Paris-style bistro is as vivid, bright, and bold as the exotic fan dancer and chanteuse Josephine Baker for whom it is named. Sit among the deco palm tree lamps and let your shoulders roll to the timeless jazz piano and blues. Feast on huge portions of enticing and hearty French foods.

◆ *Romantic Note:* Our fun was enhanced by the drill of the teeming rain outside, as seen from our warm and cozy window seat, but we can't guarantee you'll have the same luck.

EZE
254 West 23rd Street *between Seventh & Eighth Avenues*
(212) 691-1140
Expensive

The best part about Eze (rhymes with Pez) is the outdoor garden. There are very few like it in the city, and that makes it a much-sought-after commodity. Tucked in the back of a former townhouse, it has all the elements for kiss-stealing: privacy, a smattering of tables (mostly twosomes), the serene quiet of nature, votive candles casting a hazy light, and lots of greenery. There are real trees here and well-kept plants. The tables fit in with the outdoor decor: crisp green and blue chairs and tables draped with white tablecloths and candles. A small boom box sits unobtrusively by the entrance, playing soft, classical music. You'll feel like you're in the backyard of your best friend's house, that you've been invited over to reap the rewards of a bountiful garden and sample new recipes.

If you come in winter, don't despair — the indoor seating is just as nice, albeit a bit more formal. You'll still feel a bit like you're dining at your friend's — your rich friend's, that is. Because the restaurant is in an old townhouse, the atmosphere is suited to special occasions. The tables are a bit larger here — a lot of fours and sixes — and decorated with tapestry chairs and white tablecloths. Lace curtains hang in the big bay window in the front of the room. If you sit by the back window, you'll get a view of the garden. The marvelous food is French, with a leaning toward Provencal, and most of the main dishes include fish and seafood.

Note: The restaurant is only open Tuesdays through Saturdays. Reservations are a must. You can request the garden.

HULOT'S
1007 Lexington Avenue *at 72nd Street*
(212) 794-9800
Moderate to Expensive

Très French. In fact, you'll often hear couples speaking French at some of the many tables for two. The atmosphere here is casual, pink, and charming. Little peach sconces with fringed shades punctuate the wall. The chefs stand in the very center and cook delicious fresh food in plain sight. This is an ideal spot for lunch on the town.

LA BOHEME
24 Minetta Lane *between Sixth Avenue & Bleecker Street*
(212) 473-6447
Moderate

You won't question why a French restaurant specializes in pizza after you've tasted it! Baked in the flaming centerpiece, an open woodburning pizza oven, it's outstanding. That's not the only thing here that's superb. So, too, is the rest of the menu. And so is the country deco atmosphere where bundles of wood (for the pizza oven) are stacked neatly while long theatrical bulbs are hung haphazardly from the rafters. When the front door is open to let in the spring air, the best seat is right in it. In the winter, opt for the back. Year round, enjoy a slow, leisurely meal on comfortable cane chairs. It's fun to watch the French chefs cook out in the open while you cook up an idea of what to do next in the Village.

LA CARAVELLE
33 West 55th Street *between Fifth & Sixth Avenues*
(212) 586-4252
Very Expensive

Elegant but not stuffy, this is the quintessential French restaurant. With the same artistic ambience, this feels like a smaller and more intimate version of another French favorite, La Cote Basque. The many touches of cherry red, including red banquettes and bright murals of French scenes painted on faux windows, create just the right mood for l'amour. With the drapery pulled aside from the "windows," you can see the colorful carousel making its circles round and round as the people promenade past. You can almost hear the band playing in the kiosque at the Jardin des Tuileries. The handsome couple in the corner, snuggled close on the banquette, does not seem out of place at all.

LA COLOMBE D'OR
134 East 26th Street *between Lexington & Third Avenues*
(212) 689-0666
Expensive

If we tell you about this tiny place, you have to promise not to crowd it up on the nights we want to go there. For a funny, French evening out in a snugly intimate setting, here is one of New York's best secrets. Situated discreetly in a double brownstone, this is a hidden treasure on an unlikely street. Inside it may be filled with people, but you won't notice. For one thing, the maitre d' has an eye for privacy and will not seat people close together unless there is no other option. Moreover, the atmosphere is so charming with its tin ceilings, terra-cotta floors, oak tables, bas reliefs, and exposed brick walls, that you'll be too busy looking around and at each other to notice anyone else. The food, Provencal cuisine, is flavorful, colorful, and well-presented. Enjoy a leisurely meal in either one of the two small rooms. Expect warm and friendly, caring and professional service. You'll feel pampered here.

◆ *Romantic Suggestion:* This restaurant makes a special production over Valentine's Day. On February 14th of each year, the mouth-watering aroma of freshly baked heart-shaped sourdough rolls mixes with that of fragrant roses, one per person to take home.

LA CÔTE BASQUE
5 East 55th Street *at Fifth Avenue*
(212) 688-6525
Très Expensive

La Côte Basque is more pretty than beautiful and more fun than elegant; you wouldn't expect such an enchanting and magical atmosphere from such a New York establishment. Dominated by fanciful sunny seaside murals of la côte basque, the restaurant is elaborately simple. Everything is faux (except the magnificent food!): faux beamed walls, faux awnings, faux blinds, faux shutters opened to reveal faux French scenes. The murals will take you to France: here a port, there the beach, over here an old winding street. And we're suckers for restaurants that encourage you to sit side by side as this one does (although you don't have to). With the friendly atmosphere comes warm and caring, and of course professional, service. In between bites of the most pleasurable French food, a discreet kiss will not seem out of place.

◆ **Romantic Note:** As in most upscale New York restaurants, the lunch crowd is typically composed of businesspeople. Although the expense account crowd comes at night, too, they're easier to ignore from your private lamplit table for two with its small hand painted vase filled with a large bunch of colorful fresh-picked fleurs.

LA GAULOISE
502 Sixth Avenue *near West 13th Street*
(212) 691-1363
Expensive to Very Expensive

This is one of our favorite French restaurants, although sometimes dinner or brunch here can be the agony and the ecstasy. The food is exceptional (our number one choice for brunch), the interior is a stately combination of dark wood paneling, art deco sconces, and well-placed mirrors. You will be impressed from the moment you enter. Our hesitation: Sometimes the service is haughty; sometimes the room can be a bit noisy and crowded; and we always spend more money than we had hoped. Such is the price of love.

LA LUNCHEONETTE
130 Tenth Avenue *at 18th Street*
(212) 675-0342
Moderate to Expensive
Dinner Only

Because this restaurant is a bit remote (there aren't a lot of restaurants on Tenth Avenue), it feels like a stolen moment, away from the kids, the job headaches, the tourist mobs on Fifth Avenue, the honking taxis. As soon as you step inside this former bar/townhouse, you'll experience the excitement of finding your own little private hideaway.

Even more perfect is its funky decor: sort of Left Bank Paris bistro meets Grandma's garage sale. There are fun surprises in almost every nook and corner: postcards behind the bar, an old music stand, an artist's bust, a covered fireplace, an iron door, an old hotel mailbox that now holds wines, and so on. (We don't want to give too many surprises away!)

What makes it great for stolen kisses is its intimacy: There are only about 22 tables in all; half of which are twosomes. Try to get a table in front — this area was originally a bar. Most likely, a very neighborly one. The long bar remains and takes up much of the room; the other half of the room is white-paper-covered tables with mismatched chairs. Tall glasses filled with yellow candles add a romantic touch. The food is French and changes almost daily.

The other half of the room was originally part of a townhouse (you can still see the exposed brick and part of the beam). It's not as filled with old knickknacks but it does have the same old-world charm. Large red curtains drape one side of the room, giving the feeling that Greta Garbo could stroll in, long cigarette in hand, at any moment.

Note: La Luncheonette serves dinner only; the restaurant officially opens at 6 p.m. but they don't serve until 7 p.m.

◆ *Romantic Warning:* Although the out of the way location adds to its funkadelic charm, it is a bit off the beaten track and not a place you want to walk to too late at night. Take a taxi there and back.

LA METAIRIE   ◆◆◆◆
189 West 10th Street *at West 4th Street near Seventh Avenue*
(212) 989-0343
Moderate to Expensive

We don't use the word "charming" lightly when we use it to describe this French bistro. You'll swear by the time you've been wined and dined at La Metairie that the adorable goslings decorating the green awnings are wagging their white feathered tails. These are not the only birds that will steal your heart here. Inside, too, are a pair of snuggling turtledoves perched high above the many country French touches that make La Metairie so appealing: dried flower arrangements in antique planters, a dark pressed-tin ceiling offset by sunny backlit paintings on glass in the spirit of Van Gogh, farm implements mounted on rough hewn boards, Provencal Pierre Deux fabric-covered chairs and stools, decorative firewood flounced with orangy light. With the shutters flung open to let in the soft night air and tall tapered candles dancing light everywhere, it'll all make you feel like you're in a Van Gogh painting altogether. Happily, this is an expensive-feeling restaurant with moderate prices and a full menu until midnight or later. On the other hand, you're welcome just to satisfy your cravings for espresso or Kir Royales (champagne with kir) and something sweet — if that's all you want. But if that's all you have, you'll be missing out on a beautiful bountiful harvest of food: large portions of delicately sauced, succulent entrees arranged like works of art on fine china.

◆ *Romantic Note:* Every evening at 11:00 strolling singers parade about with Latin guitars and a harp. They play classic romantic Latin music. Whenever you come, you're sure to leave with a smile on your face and a song in your heart.

THE LEOPARD
253 East 50th Street *between Second & Third Avenues*
(212) 759-3735
Expensive

In the movie *Green Card*, the character played by Andie McDowell is willing to do anything to rent a particular apartment with an atrium greenhouse. The Leopard restaurant with its well spaced tables surrounding a grand floral centerpiece also has a magnificent atrium that looks just like the one in Andie's dreamhouse, and you'll want to move into it, too. Well, you can't move into it and you can't take it with you; what you can take is a satisfying bellyful of wonderful French cuisine. The creative prix fixe menu changes nightly, and unlimited glasses of house wine (Cuvée Rouge and Blanc de Blanc Sec) are included in the price.

LE MADELEINE (Garden)
403 West 43rd Street *at Ninth Avenue*
(212) 246-2993
Inexpensive to Moderate

You won't believe it! Tucked behind the neon jungle of 42nd Street, an intimate brick-walled French garden. More amazing, this quirky little skylit refuge is climate-controlled and open all year round. Bathed in sunshine and surrounded by vines and trees, clay mask planters, and lattice work, you'll swear you're outside. Ask for the corner table by the French window that looks in. All meals are good here, but this is an especially excellent choice for Sunday brunch.

Note: The service can be slow, but considering how sweet it is to loll about and linger, that is a blessing — unless of course you're cranky from hunger.

LE REGENCE — (See Hotel Plaza Athenee)

LES SANS CULOTTES
1085 Second Avenue *at 57th Street*
(212) 838-6660
Inexpensive to Moderate

If you want to do your French kissing in a non-intimidating setting, this is the place. It's hard not to love this comfortable little well-worn French bistro with its heart-stealing waiters who'll serenade you by cranking pretty tunes out of an 1806 Limonaire music machine. They'll chatter and sing amiably and then applaud themselves as you munch merrily away on a gargantuan basket of sausage and vegetables and look laughingly into each other's eyes. They'll keep you so busy, you may forget to look around at the delightful surroundings.

A painting of the storming of the Bastille would dominate the small downstairs room if not for the many droll touches such as the unusual

French patriot wallpaper, wooden soldiers, barrels, fans and Parisian posters. To say this little bistro — upstairs and down — is cute, fun, and charming would be an understatement. So where's the rub? The food is heavily sauced and, frankly, not that great. For best results, order simply. The menu is prix fixe and the portions are huge (they'll even bring more of something you like), but if you like sausage, salami, bread, semi-fresh raw vegetables, and perhaps a reasonably price bottle of wine, you can make a meal out of that and the great desserts (la crepe maison with ice cream is heavenly), or just come for dessert. Whether you come for lunch, dinner, or after the theater, be prepared to laugh and enjoy the friendly ambience *au français*.

LUTECE   ◆◆◆◆
249 East 50th Street *at Second Avenue*
(212) 752-2225
Very, Very Expensive

All of the restaurant reviewers in the world who have dined at this bastion of culinary excellence rate it as one of the best restaurants in the universe. A gastronomic feat of excellence such as Lutece offers may very well prove to be a richly tantalizing romantic affair.

MAXIM'S — (See L'Omnibus, Cabaret and Lounge Kissing)

NICOLE BRASSERIE DE PARIS
870 Seventh Avenue *at 56th Street*
(212) 765-5108
Moderate to Expensive

This is a lovely French dining experience. It is very simply done, without pretense or frills. A few steps down from street level, this window enclosed dining room offers a soft cafelike atmosphere with an elegant touch that is comfortable and, in a New York sort of way, romantic.

PETROSSIAN RESTAURANT
182 West 58th Street *at Seventh Avenue*
(212) 245-2214
Very Expensive

It is hardly a secret that the Petrossian room is a ritzy place to dine, but I'm not sure its romantic potential has been fully revealed. Caviar, champagne, and thou: the stuff of which dreams are made. From the fluted champagne glasses to the black-and-white patterned Limoges china that sparkles by the glow of an antique crystal chandelier overhead, to the staff that is well versed in gourmet delights, everything is carefully orchestrated to enhance your caviar experience.

◆ *Romantic Alternative:* Although it lacks the finesse and grandness of the Petrossian Restaurant, the **Caviarteria, 29 East 60th Street, (212) 759-7410**, serves up some fine caviar, too. Go shopping here for your own supply and create a caviar atmosphere at home, or take a picnic to the park. Petrossian has its own take-out area, but we assure you, once you're there, you'll want to stay put.

PROVENCE
38 MacDougal *at Prince Street*
(212) 475-7500
Moderate

Everything about this place speaks to the heart — if only it didn't speak to the heart of every couple in town! Albeit large, it would be one of the most delightful environments if it weren't always so darned packed with people. But in the summer months, the garden is still a charm with its ornate stone fountain. If you're thinking intimate, don't go here. If you're thinking, let's see what the fuss is about, try to go for lunch on a weekday.

SONIA ROSE   ❖ ❖ ❖ ❖
132 Lexington Avenue *between 27th & 28th Streets*
New York, NY 10016
(212) 545-1777
Expensive but a value (prix fixe)
Reservations essential

Sonia Rose and Romance are synonymous. A decorative candlelit table for two beckons from the window. Like an invitee at an elegant dinner party, you ring. The door is opened for you, and you're welcomed warmly to this exquisitely intimate restaurant. Like a rose for which the restaurant is named, the room is long and slender, fittingly filled with parties of two, each at a table finished like the one in the window with tall white tapered candles and, yes, roses. Every touch is deliberate yet subtle; notice, for example, the interesting play of colorful light on the otherwise dark and muted paintings. The candlelight flickers on the crystal and on your faces and creates shadows on the wall of dancing roses and wine goblets. Melodious strains of Vivaldi and other classical composers fill the air. The unobtrusive yet attentive professional staff tends to your every need as your palate is treated to the finest French cuisine imaginable. Before the meal, we were tempted to take a bath in the steamy fragranced terry towel we were presented with. Following that, two yummy bite-sized treats "from the chef" gave new meaning to the word "appetizer." Then we bit into two hot fresh-baked soft rolls that we spread with pretty puffs of fresh butter in three colorful flavors — lingonberry rose, basil green, and sweet yellow. Generous portions of magnificent and beautiful food — extraordinary in color, flavor, arrangement, and texture — followed. This is almost impossible to do, but listen, save room for dessert. Nuf said.

TABLE D'HOTE   ❖ ❖ ❖ ❖
44 East 92nd Street *between Madison & Park Avenues*
(212) 348-8125
Moderate to Expensive
Reservations essential

Stand under a simple green awning and peek through the flowered half-curtains at nine antique bare wood tables. Decorated with painted china and baskets of dried flowers, this little French country bistro is picture perfect and simply irresistible. Two fans turn overhead. The redwood floors below are uneven. The walls are planks painted white. Scaled down like a comfortable dollhouse, everything here is miniature, except the innovative French-influenced food, which is large in portion and flavor. The service is relaxed but professional. The atmosphere is casual but special, altogether charming and delightful. People — mostly couples — tend to speak in hushed tones, so it's not bad even when crowded — which it understandably often is. Here in a sometimes overlooked revitalized neighborhood (the quietest!), you'll swear you're in Europe.

TARTINE RESTAURANT AND BISTRO
426A 7th Avenue *between 14th & 15th Streets*
Brooklyn
(718) 768-2769
Moderate

If driving, go over the Manhattan Bridge and continue up Flatbush Avenue. Turn right on 7th Avenue. The bistro will be one-and-a-half blocks away, on the right.

With fewer than ten tables, the owners have somehow managed to create a fairly bright and wide-open SoHo-like environment in a rather small space. This charming, casual bistro serves up some tantalizing food, rich in taste and beautifully presented. A screen door and window let you peek into the busy, clean, tiny kitchen — it's hard to believe they can prepare such delights in such a small kitchen. Piano music is piped in, soft and subtle. The ceiling fans turn over head as you enjoy a leisurely meal.

VANESSA'S
289 Bleecker Street *at Seventh Avenue*
(212) 243-4225
Expensive to Very Expensive

This is an invitingly elegant French restaurant with space for privacy and attentive service that is welcome and never intrusive. It was a warm, windy Sunday evening when we went (on a double date) and we all found this country Victorian dining room exceedingly romantic. Everyone gave high accolades to the service, and we praised the food with a chorus of oohs and aahs after each course.

Greek Kissing

PERIYALI   ◆ ◆
35 West 20th Street *between Madison & Fifth Avenues*
(212) 463-7890
Moderate to Expensive

The owner describes the cuisine here as "living Greek home-cooked." A blend of the old and the new in every way aptly describes the decor as well as the food, which emphasizes light tastes and low fat. Whatever you call it, though, if the lip ratings in this book referred to the food alone, this restaurant would carry four. Nothing is oily. Even the pastry crusts are light and flaky. This is truly a culinary experience of the first order.

Prior to our superior meal, we munched on garlicky olives at the tile-and-wood bar, where we sat on cushioned swivel bar seats beneath a series of hanging moonlike globes. The billowy "ceiling" and reflected lighting create a soft look in the small rooms. The happy rumbling of many people enjoying their meals never rose loud enough to be called noisy. Crowded yet intimate, somehow this genuinely European restaurant is both casual and elegant at the same time. The best tables for two are way in back. In summer, you may sit in the small open air garden with only three tables, but beware that it sometimes gets smoky back there.

Hungarian Kissing

CAFE BUDAPEST
221 East 58th Street *between Second & Third Avenues*
(212) 486-2022
Inexpensive to Moderate

In the mood for chicken paprikas, stuffed cabbage, or wiener schnitzel in a casual but warm and cozy setting? Then go to this delightful Hungarian restaurant where every evening but Monday you'll be serenaded by a pianist seated at a white piano. At other times, barely audible classical music sets the mood nicely. It's a small room done in warm neutral colors, with comfortable banquettes, and soft lighting. Tuxedoed waiters will serve you food that tastes just like mother used to make.

◆ *Romantic Warning:* The clientele varies widely and determines the romantic quotient of this very small restaurant. At any given moment, you're as likely to find a mother and child here, or an elderly gentleman dining alone, as you are a couple on a date. We recommend then, that instead of making a reservation, you peek your heads in and see if the tone speaks to you. If it doesn't, you'll be on a street with a dozen other excellent — albeit more expensive — options.

Indian Kissing

There is something mysterious and exotic about Indian cuisine. No matter where we've indulged our longing for tandoori, chapati, and lassi, we've always enjoyed the scents, sights, sounds, and samplings that are unique to this style of cooking. In addition to the intriguing menu, there always seems to be a ceremonious flourish in the way the waiters handle themselves, the diners, and the food.

AKBAR

256 East 49th Street *at Second Avenue*
(212) 755-9100
475 Park Avenue *between 57th & 58th Streets*
(212) 838-1717
Moderate to Expensive

Both of these locations are as pretty as they are elegant. If your tastebuds long for exotic spices in a classic New York environment, you will be delighted with either of these restaurants. Although the Park Avenue one has beautiful stained glass ceilings, we prefer the food at the Second Avenue Akbar.

BUKHARA

148 East 48th Street *between Lexington & Third Avenues*
(212) 838-1811
Moderate to Expensive

One of the most handsome and comfortable Indian restaurants in town. The solid, regal decor makes this the romantic's choice for a traditional Indian repast, but the formality ends with the setting. This is a robust eating experience. The tasty lamb and chicken dishes are meant to be eaten with your hands (or properly speaking, with one hand), but don't be concerned, hot towels are brought to your table before you start.

DARBAR

44 West 56th Street *at Madison Avenue*
(212) 432-7227
Moderate to Expensive

The perfectly prepared and presented Indian cuisine, the exotic atmosphere, and the warm service all combine to make this one of our favorites. Although the prices are higher here than at most Indian restaurants and some of the tables are close, we return again and again for more. The waiters are especially caring and attentive, with several assigned to each table.

MADRAS WOODLANDS — (See Restaurants, Kosher)

NIRVANA-ON-ROOFTOP
30 Central Park South *near Fifth Avenue*
(212) 486-5700
Moderate to Expensive

Sometimes when a special evening is at stake, a dramatic stroke may be required. One of the most dramatic settings possible is Nirvana. The unobstructed rooftop view of Central Park is what makes it nirvana. Up here everything is a shine above — even the food.

PASSAGE TO INDIA
308 East 6th Street *between First & Second Avenues*
(212) 529-5770
Moderate

Cozy is the word for this location, and given all the other Indian restaurants in this vicinity, that is quite a compliment. Tempting selections include moist and flavorful tandoori and fresh vegetarian creations. Candles lend an ethereal glow to the surroundings.

Irish Kissing

MORAN'S
19th Street and Tenth Avenue
(212) 627-3030
Moderate

Located in a dreary part of Chelsea, this old New York restaurant is sometimes empty when other places are crowded. The seafood is fresh and heavenly, and the desserts will make you fat just looking. As you enter, the kitchen is very much in evidence as is a real old-world wooden bar. Many of the rooms have fireplaces, and crystal lamps on the walls enhance the sparkle from the candlelit tables. From the kelly green lights to the fresh flowers to the nicest waitress, Irish hospitality and elegance have combined to create a truly warm kissing environment. And that's no blarney.

◆ **Romantic Note:** Many weddings take place here. hint. hint.

◆ **Romantic Option: Moran's** has another location at **103 Washington Street** between Rector and Carlisle. Before crossing the threshold of this former chapel, however, call **(212) 732-3020** to be sure that the upstairs room with its seashell chairs and blazing fireplace is open because downstairs you'll find a fairly typical (but good) Irish pub with the TV on.

Italian Kissing

I don't know about you, but to us almost anything Italian is lusciously romantic — art, clothes, movie stars, design, food — whatever it is, there is something profoundly arousing about everything reminiscent of this country. When we can't kiss in Italy, we do the next best thing: We kiss in Italian restaurants; bring on the pasta!

ABBRACCIAMENTO ON THE PIER
2200 Rockaway Parkway, Brooklyn
(718) 251-5517
Moderate to Expensive

From Manhattan, take the Brooklyn Bridge to the Brooklyn Queens Expressway West. Follow the Belt Parkway East to Exit 13 (Rockaway Parkway). Abbracciamento is just south of the Parkway, on the Canarsie Pier.

As you drive towards Abbracciamento, an array of twinkling lights begins to glitter across the bay. It's hard to believe a place this lovely could exist way out here in Canarsie. "It's a mini Windows On The World!" exclaimed my companion once we entered this charming, out of the way establishment and saw the city sparkling in the distance. Go for a romantic dinner on a warm evening. The generous wooden deck on Jamaica Bay has wrought-iron tables with a wonderful vista of sail-boats, sea, and sky. Views are great from indoors, too, because all the walls are made of glass. Even in winter, the semicircular restaurant, aglow with candles, is inviting. Spend an evening drifting to a deft piano player's romantic tunes.

◆ *Romantic Option:* Come by boat. Slips are available for customers.

◆ *Romantic Warning:* As with most places, it gets crowded on weekends and reservations become necessary.

ANTON'S
259 West 4th Street *at Perry Street*
(212) 675-5059
Moderate

This restaurant doesn't get loud because you wouldn't even think of speaking loudly in this candlelit room where jazz music dances softly through the air. This is a place to whisper. Done in quiet pinks with a single rose on every table, flowery banquettes, and pretty window treatments, the decor feels French, but the cuisine is very much Italian. The small menu is large with marvelous food.

◆ *Romantic Note:* The outside tables are especially appealing, situated as they are on such a quiet Village street, but unfortunately they can't always be reserved.

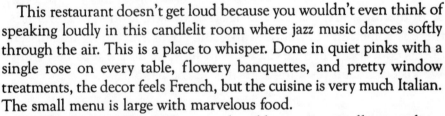

ARCOBALENO
21 East 9th Street *at University Place*
(212) 473-2215
Moderate

Take a walk through the Village till you find yourselves at Arcobaleno. The steps will take you down into a country setting with wood tables and tall framed windows that look out onto a garden veranda in the back. If you're in the neighborhood, walking along the street hand in hand, and the urge for pasta comes over you, indulge that craving here.

BONDINI'S RESTAURANT

62 West 9th Street *between Fifth & Sixth Avenues*
(212) 777-0670
Expensive

West 9th Street off Fifth Avenue is one of the prettiest tree-lined blocks in Greenwich Village. Tucked away in a brownstone a few steps below street level on West 9th Street is a surprise: Bondini's Restaurant. Enter and the curtain rises onto a Mediterranen scene. The walls and carpets are a cool sea-green and gray, and the ceilings are high. There are fresh roses set daily upon white linen tablecloths and artful arrangements of fruit and flowers throughout the restaurant. The cocktail area has a dreamy purple couch and comfortable sinkable chairs done in chintz. A perfect setting in which to listen to the piano player and to each other.

The restaurant specializes in Northern Italian cuisine, and the menu is as enticing as the decor. Among the starters on the menu is carpaccio, thin slices of raw succulent filet of beef topped with shaved Parmesan and sprinkled with arugula and mustard. An excellent main course is the perfectly textured crisp calamari. A sinful ending is the "tiramisu" which, loosely translated into Italian, means "pick me up." After this meal, they'll have to! But never mind; there's no hurry here. Sit awhile with your fine brewed coffee. Linger and be pampered by the caring staff.

◆ *Romantic Note:* In the spring and summer have a romantic tête-à-tête at the one outdoor table overlooking the street. More reminiscent of a bistro in Paris than a New York City scene.

CARMELLA'S VILLAGE GARDEN

49 Charles Street *at West 4th Street*
(212) 242-2155
Very Inexpensive

Carmella's is one of our favorite spots in the city. If you see a couple with a bottle of wine speeding through the village, you can bet they're headed here. The cluster of rooms is dark and handsome in winter, but from spring to late autumn, you must dine under the vines and awnings in the garden. This is one of the least expensive places in New York, and one of the most endearing.

CHELSEA PLACE
147 Eighth Avenue *between 18th & 19th Streets*
(212) 924-8413
Moderate

The setting of Chelsea Place exudes romantic vibrations. Its facade is an antiques store that showcases an armoire on the rear wall, a secret opening to the restaurant. The first room you see is a bar with loud live pop music and dancing. You may have to deal with a crowded bar as you make your way through to the main dining room, but when you get there, there will be no doubt that it was worth the effort. Once there, the room has an elegant, warm ambience, and all year round you can sit next to a duck pond. A large picture window overlooks a small pristine garden where ducks waddle and swim. In the rear there is another area enclosed in glass that has statues and sculptures. The whole place is conducive to sharing sweet nothings, along with rich Italian dishes.

Upstairs is the "Winter Dining Room," with a fireplace and a rock and tree garden enclosed in glass. There is also the Alex Room, with jazz and Broadway music Wednesday through Saturday, where you can have a pre- or apres-dinner drink. Without question this is a flawless, total evening package for the both of you.

♦ *Romantic Warning:* For weekend nights it's advisable to make a reservation a week in advance for the main dining room.

CUCINA DELLA FONTANA (Garden)
368 Bleecker Street *at Charles Street*
(212) 242-0636
Inexpensive
Cash Only

You'll say *bellisima* when you pass through the flowered screen, down the steps, past a fountain that looks like it was transported directly from a Roman piazza, and into a casual, urban leafy-green garden trattoria. Although you'll feel as if you're dining alfresco, you'll actually be encased within a climate-controlled greenhouse. In fact, this is the place to duck into for a hot meal and cuddles on a snowy, rainy, or cold day.

Note: The portions are huge, but the food is inconsistent. It helps if you know what to order. Try the Chicken Paesana for a hearty meal. The mixed salad is the best in town for the price.

◆ *Romantic Warning:* The best room — the garden — is also the smoking room. But the garden is large, the tables are far apart, and the fans keep the air moving, and so it isn't a problem unless you're super-sensitive to smoke. As an alternative, the adjoining grottolike non-smoking room painted in blues and pinks is sure to inspire a smooch or two, and the main restaurant upstairs is cozy and quaint, too.

◆ *Romantic Suggestion:* Off the garden, there's a tiny cabaret. If the evening's entertainment appeals to you, have a meal first, and then go there. It gets packed, however, and so reservations are necessary on the weekend.

DA SILVANO
260 Sixth Avenue *between Houston & Bleecker Streets*
(212) 982-0090
Moderate to Expensive

For some reason, while other places are bursting out at the seams with people, this casually elegant restaurant remains relatively quiet, and that doesn't make any sense at all. Here the food and atmosphere combine to form the recipe for a perfectly outstanding Italian meal any night of the week. Put together with creative Italian flair, the walls are exposed brick, gentle music plays, the service is genteel, and the food is out of this world. This is truly a place to be sated and satisfied. Doesn't that sound good?

ECCO
124 Chambers Street *at Church Street*
(212) 227-7074
Very Expensive

The neighborhood and this restaurant have absolutely nothing in common. Squeezed into a fairly shabby street scene is the magnificent Ecco which, with its high ceiling and carved wood paneling, immediately brings you into another world once you pass through the etched-glass doors. The food preparations are just as outstanding.

Note: Since this has, at times, been a see-and-be-seen spot, ask for an out of the way table. Or just direct your vision at each other and no one else in the room will matter anyway.

ERMINIA
250 East 83rd Street *between Second & Third Avenues*
(212) 879-4284
Very, very expensive
Reservations well in advance essential

Simply unheard of: an ivy-covered one story building in Manhattan. Entrancingly intimate, flower-filled, lantern-lit, barn-sided, and wood-beamed, complete with a parade of Rolls Royces and limos waiting patiently outside for the notables within. The celebrity testimonials on signed menus that decorate the wall proclaim this to have some of the finest Italian food in Manhattan. To tell you the truth, we have to take their word for it. Dinner was so astronomically high priced that we could hardly afford to look — and that's not even considering the cost of the new evening outfits we'd require. If you want a dining experience and can keep cool in the company of so many familiar faces who don't know you from Adam and Eve, this may be your cup of espresso.

◆ *Romantic Warning:* The small room is filled with many tables; thus, you may feel cramped, but you won't mind rubbing elbows with Gene Wilder or Jackie O, will you?

FELIDIA
243 East 58th Street *between Second & Third Avenues*
(212) 758-1479
Expensive to Very Expensive

Just as the name, Felidia, evokes the splendor, fragrance, and joy of fresh flowers, so too does the ambience in this very lovely dining establishment. Felidia's charms are evident even before you enter. The front window with its frosted etched glass scene of two seated figures with a cornucopia provides only a hint of what's inside. Inviting and unusual, yet tasteful in every way, from the warm wood bar area in front to the bi-level solarium in back, Felidia defies comparison. It's more casual than elegant with hanging copper pots and terra-cotta floors, but you won't feel out of place dressing up in the evening. The restaurant's bright warmth is brought about by a profusion of plants, flowers, colorful cushioned chairs, an elaborate production of exposed brick, brightly colored plaster walls, and a temptingly visible collection of wine. Amazingly enough, the perfection of the food surpasses the setting. Perfectly prepared and lovingly presented at a slow and comfortable pace, you shouldn't go home hungry for anything — except more kisses.

◆ **Romantic Warning:** We enjoy lunch at Felidia, but it is difficult to kiss unobtrusively here at that time, as the business crowd far outnumbers couples. For maximum enjoyment, try to go when it's least crowded.

FIORI
4 Park Avenue *at 33th Street*
(212) 686-0226
Moderate

Beautifully arched tiled ceilings, classic murals, and terra-cotta floors reminiscent of an Italian villa (it was built as a private train station for the Vanderbilt mansion once upon a time) is the lofty setting for this premier New York restaurant. Perhaps it's a bit too noisy during lunch hours, but the popularity only attests to the quality. The dinner crowd is smaller, so you can actually see the lovely surroundings. The food is simple — pasta, pizza, and seafood — and delicious.

THE GRAND TICINO   ◆◆
228 Thompson Street *near 3rd Street*
(212) 777-5922
Moderate
Reservations suggested

The restaurant scene in *Moonstruck* was filmed here because the director thinks this small, dark green room is "terribly romantic." I don't know why, but it is. Lots of couples come here with twinkles in their eyes, and their smiles are contagious. The waiters are friendly and helpful and will go out of their way to make sure you have a dining experience. You should, too, because this is some of the best Italian food this side of Italy.

GRAZIELLA'S
2 Bank Street *at Greenwich Avenue*
(212) 924-9450
Moderate

An elegant place, Graziella's is a place everyone seems to miss. It's a bit out of the way, but this small, angled room is serene and unhurried. We spent a memorable evening here once, when we watched the room fill up and empty out again. I think it's one of the handsomest of the Italian spots with perfect atmosphere and luscious food.

IL MULINO
86 West 3rd Street *between Sullivan & Thompson Streets*
(212) 673-3783

This Italian restaurant is passionate about living up to its reputation of preparing some of the best pasta dishes you'll ever taste. The warm Italian waiters will tease you with heavenly appetizers as they stand tableside and perform culinary wonders. The small interior, filled with flowers and rich wood paneling has an inviting feel. As you listen to the soft Italian music playing in the background and savor the aromas of fresh pasta and seafood (the lobster defies description), you can whisper amore between courses.

IL PONTE VECCHIO
206 Thompson Street *between Wooster & Bleecker Streets*
(212) 228-7701
Moderate

If you've ever been to Florence, you'll want to reminisce about it here. Reproductions of Da Vinci and Michelangelo drawings fill the walls as do many prints portraying every angle of the Ponte Vecchio. The room is small, but it's quiet only when it's not crowded — which is almost never because the food is so good. Ah, Firenze.

IL TINELLO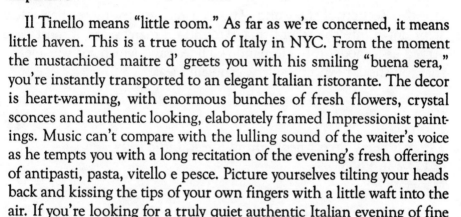
16 West 56th Street *between Fifth & Sixth Avenues*
(212) 245-4388
Expensive

Il Tinello means "little room." As far as we're concerned, it means little haven. This is a true touch of Italy in NYC. From the moment the mustachioed maitre d' greets you with his smiling "buena sera," you're instantly transported to an elegant Italian ristorante. The decor is heart-warming, with enormous bunches of fresh flowers, crystal sconces and authentic looking, elaborately framed Impressionist paintings. Music can't compare with the lulling sound of the waiter's voice as he tempts you with a long recitation of the evening's fresh offerings of antipasti, pasta, vitello e pesce. Picture yourselves tilting your heads back and kissing the tips of your own fingers with a little waft into the air. If you're looking for a truly quiet authentic Italian evening of fine food, wine, and conversation, try Il Tinello. Buon appetito.

LITTLE ITALY
Mulberry Street
Very Inexpensive to Very Expensive

We should warn you that there's not so much Italy left in Little Italy anymore. The old neighborhood has retreated to Mulberry Street and branched off a bit onto a few nearby arteries. What hasn't changed is that there are restaurants lining the streets that will exceed your wildest Italian fantasies. If you have the time, you can shop for the one to your liking by simply browsing the windows and menus that grace each doorway. Here's a hint: Try one where no one is smoking (unless you smoke), and antipasti in the window make your hearts pound. Or just come for cappuccino and dessert; cafes are almost as numerous as the restaurants.

Grotto Azzurra
387 Broome *at Mulberry Street, Little Italy*
(212) 925-8775
Moderate

A very private time can be afforded here in an otherwise overly crowded section of the world. This is a real grotto, more then a few steps down into the terra firma. Around for many years, it must have served as a model for "Hernando's Hideaway," which for you means that you should expect a sultry, candlelit meal.

Paolucci's
149 Mulberry Street *near Grand Street, Little Italy*
(212) 226-9653
Moderate

This is one of the classic choices in Little Italy. Here, an informal atmosphere and good humored (very Italian) service and fresh food can accent a memorable evening. One waiter told us: "Sometimes they are in love, and sometimes they are not so much in love. The food and me, we try to help."

MARCHI'S
251 East 31st Street *between Second & Third Avenues*
(212) 679-2494
Moderate

Strolling down this quiet street lined with small townhouses, a church and some brownstones, it's easy to miss Marchi's. When we first stumbled upon this restaurant, we felt like explorers making a discovery. We happened to glance down through the lace-covered windows of what we thought was a lovely ground floor apartment and we noticed a table filled with well-dressed people dining grandly in a jovial atmosphere. The room was carpeted in a rich red plush with elaborate flower arrangements and oil paintings. It felt as if we were observing a private party in a Victorian dining room. This was New York, wasn't it? And what was this place, a private club? No awning or sign was evident. After a thorough search we found the entrance and we went inside. And a fabulous Italian feast followed, highlighted by impeccable service, a unique prix fixe, set five-course meal (no ordering) which never varies, except in the smallest way. The handout they give you describing the meal strictly states that the Marchi's have very definite ideas on how a fine meal should be served and it is for this reason you will not be served butter; "butter leads to bread and too much bread and butter would only spoil your appetite." We didn't miss the butter. The foods are sensual and fresh, from the antipasto to the lasagna to the appetizer, chicken, veal, fresh cheeses, dessert, Cristoli (fried sugar twists) and demitasse. This is a meal that will please the heart and soul.

Note: Reservations are suggested and jackets are required.

PAOLA'S   ◆◀
347 East 85th Street *between First & Second Avenues*
(212) 794-1890
Moderate
Reservations Really Required

Have you really never sat inside a peach? Well, here you'll have your chance. The restaurant looks like a kiss. Its lushness will draw you in. Many antique mirrors in this ultra small room enhance the peachy warmth of the walls and tin ceiling; the soft lighting pulls it all together. Yes, the ambience is sublime, and so is the pasta.

◆ *Romantic Warning:* The tiny popular room seats just 32 people right on top of one other. To enjoy it, you'll have to plan very carefully or be very lucky. Go on an off-night in August, very early, or very late.

PICCOLO MONDO
1269 First Avenue *between 68th & 69th Streets*
(212) 249-3141
Expensive

Of all the Italian restaurants in New York (and there are almost as many as stars in the sky) this is one of the great ones. It is a place where romantics flock when they want to be left to themselves and their pasta.

ROMA DI NOTTE
137 East 55th Street *between Lexington & Third Avenues*
(212) 832-1128
Moderate to Expensive

Roma di Notte epitomizes romance with its spacious marble dance floor, danceable music, hidden intimate dining nooks, and strolling singers with rich Italian voices. You'll find the food, if you ever get around to eating, to be excellent. It is one of the more reasonably priced places to dance and dine in the city.

SAVOY
70 Prince Street *at West Broadway*
(212) 219-8570
Moderate
Reservations recommended

From a distance, Savoy looks something like an old-fashioned diner in the true silver-sardine-can sense of the word. As you get closer and can see in, you may wonder why a diner would display wine bottles. Soon you'll spy some flowers and greenery, and before long you'll realize that this is no diner — not in any sense. It is not until you step inside, however, that you will learn the truth. This is a serious and intimate modern Italian restaurant. The immaculate kitchen is visible through glass doors. A fireplace blazes in winter. Most of the tables are close but a few are set apart. Done in chic country-deco with sculpted paper sconces and a copper mesh ceiling and serving food par excellence, Savoy is a joy.

SFUZZI ◆◆◆
58 West 65th Street, *near Lincoln Center*
(212) 873-3700
Moderate to Expensive

The Pompeiian "ruins" decor of this treasure belies its civility. This restaurant is very large and understandably popular. Come very, very early or at 8:00 p.m. when people spill out of the restaurants to head for the theater, and you can expect close attention from a professional staff. When in Sfuzzi, do as the Sfuzzians (unless you don't drink) and start with a Frozen Sfuzzi, which is actually a frozen bellini, a frothy concoction of sparkling wine and fresh peach juice. Then proceed to linger over an amazingly large and deliciously Italian prix fixe meal. The easy jazz piano melodies of the early hours turn into piano or classical guitar at the dinner hour. The music is strong enough to appreciate but quiet enough to promote soft conversation.

◆ ***Romantic Note:*** If possible, choose to sit side by side on the comfortable banquettes that line the upper tier. The corner banquette table is especially inviting.

VIVOLO ◆◆◆
222 East 74th Street *between Lexington & Park Avenues*
(212) 737-3533
Moderate

With fresh flowers on every table and fireplaces upstairs and down, the atmosphere can best be described as rusticly elegant. You'll see that all the men here tend to wear jackets even though it's not required. You'll have your choice of romantic environments. A small front room with four tables is sunny and private. The main dining room downstairs is cozy and dark with mahogany walls. A beautiful long bar flounced by wall candles dominates this room but does not get crowded. Upstairs has the feel of a stately manor. Whatever the mood, if it's romantic, it's here.

VUCCIRIA
422 West Broadway *between Prince & Spring Streets*
(212) 941-5811
Moderate

It's easy to get comfortable in this SoHo Sicilian charmer. The casual decor is both beautiful and fun. Overhead is a faux catwalk that evokes dreams of pleasant strolls through Shangri-la. The ceiling is painted like a blue sky with puffs of white clouds. An entire wall of exposed brick covered with old photographs completes the picture. Top it all off with warm and friendly professional service and top-notch moderately priced pastas, salads, meats, and fish, and the result is a restaurant we could be happy eating in every day. It's a small room, but the seating allows you to have distance. Big tables that could seat four are happily offered to groups of two.

◆ *Romantic Warning:* The small room does get noisy when it's crowded, so it's worth making an effort to go during an off-time. The music can be romantic, but sometimes it's raucous. However, they make an effort to play a nice mix in order to appeal to everyone.

ZINNO
126 West 13th Street *at Sixth Avenue*
(212) 924-5182
Expensive

Several small rooms that wind their way to the back of this restaurant, located on the ground floor of a brownstone, give many opportunities for dining in what could only be called intimate surroundings. The food is exceptional and the service impeccable. All you have to do is supply the words of love to set the right mood.

Japanese Kissing

There are two types of people. The first gets the craving and feels an overwhelming need to sample those sculpted mosaics of seaweed and raw fish. Such a person sometimes condescends to dine with a companion just to be polite; whether you're there isn't so important— as long as the chef is. The other type doesn't eat raw fish. Do not expect a romantic evening if you are of two minds on this.

◆ *Romantic Warning:* Sushi and sashimi have been getting a lot of bad press lately. If you're concerned, our recommendation is to check with the New York Board of Health to see what their latest information is on the subject of eating raw fish, but don't forget that there are many other wonderful Japanese delicacies to order besides sushi and sashimi. I know for some of you that may be hard to believe, but it's true.

EDO GARDEN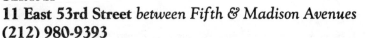
104 Washington Street *between Carlisle and Rector Streets*
(212) 344-2583
Moderate

This Japanese delight is on a little traveled — by New York standards — cobblestoned street. Upon entering, you'll be greeted by a pool and fishtank filled with very cute fish. On the left is a dimly lit bar. Because it's authentically Japanese in every way, you must remove your shoes to go to the tables in back. There are seven very private tatani rooms and one hibachi room. Four of the tatani rooms are for private groups of two. Sit barefoot at the low tables and touch toes (who'll know?). Magnificent Japanese woodcuts decorate the walls and lush and fragrant flower arrangements abound.

SERYNA
11 East 53rd Street *between Fifth & Madison Avenues*
(212) 980-9393
Very, Very Expensive

This is as seriously Japanese as it is extremely expensive, but it is also refined, authentic, and delicious. Because of the superior Japanese dining to which this restaurant is dedicated, it will be an experience that your pocketbook and hearts will remember.

Kosher Kissing

With all due respect to those of the Jewish faith who are Orthodox and eat strictly kosher, I know that in regard to the etiquette of modesty, you are not likely to find any demonstrative affectionate behavior taking place in public. But that is not to say that there isn't romance to be achieved through long discussions, long stares, and long dinners out during the week or after Sabbath on Saturday night. The pleasure of eating, the pleasure of good company, the pleasure of loving conversation and a reliable *hashgachah** can make an evening out a *simcha** all on its own with just the two of you. And, if you are out on a first or second date, with the need for more *shiduchim,** and the atmosphere can help, why not?

***Definitions:** *Hashgachah:* A Hebrew word that refers to the rabbinic authority who verifies that a restaurant or food product is indeed glatt (really) kosher. *Simcha:* A Hebrew word meaning joyous occasion. *Shiduchim:* A Hebrew word for matchmaking.

CHANTILLY'S
1105 Kings Highway, Brooklyn
(718) 627-7865
Inexpensive

Right in the middle of one of the least romantic areas of Brooklyn I can think of is this confectionery shop that serves coffee and kosher chocolates. The neighborhood may not be perfect, but for sweet words over very sweet delicacies, in a dainty atmosphere, you can't do much better than this.

MADRAS WOODLANDS
308 East 49th Street *between First & Second Avenues*
(212) 759-2440
Moderate

Here you'll find a genteel (not gentile) dining room with attentive waiters that are gracious and very polite. The food isn't what we would call traditional Jewish fare; rather it is exotic, gourmet vegetarian cuisine, with unforgettably delightful fresh tastes and aromas. The tables are well spaced and the simple pink and gray decor is relaxing. Those with adventurous tastes will find this to be a unique dining experience for sure.

MY MOST FAVORITE DESSERT COMPANY
1165 Madison Avenue *at 86th Street*
(212) 517-5222
Inexpensive to Moderate

Dessert lovers that we are, even if this place weren't a classic cafe with marble tabletops designed for two in a sweet unruffled atmosphere, we would still be fans. Desserts here are outrageous examples of how sugar can be used to torment tastebuds to excess. They make fresh quiches and excellent salads and pastas, too, but one glimpse of the bakery items, and all else is forgotten.

TEVERE "84"
184 East 84th Street *between Second & Third Avenues*
(212) 744-0210
Glatt Kosher Italian Restaurant; No Dairy
Expensive

The lace window curtains serve the double purpose of screening the interior from gawking admirers while providing a richly dark and cozy sanctuary within. Enter under a brick arch into the single tiny candlelit room. Roman oil paintings and lovely flower arrangements complete this very Italian, very wonderful Kosher Italian picture. Talk is kept to a hush and the romantic notes of Pavarotti and Domingo provide the backdrop to an evening of fine Italian dining. Tuxedoed waiters will fill your beautifully set linened table with the most delicious "classic Cuisine of the Roman Jews." There is a little nook near the window that seats just two couples, and it may be reserved. Once you've seen Tevere "84" you'll realize that Kosher and Romance can be a match made in heaven. Go for lunch, brunch, or dinner.

VA BENE

1589 Second Avenue *between 82nd & 83rd Streets*
(212) 517-4448
Moderate to Expensive Italian

Kosher restaurants in Manhattan have an elegance and style that is welcomed by those who have wanted more than pizza or a pastrami sandwich for an evening repast. Though perhaps a bit too noisy for true affectionate consideration, this soft but brightly lit *milchig* (dairy only) restaurant has an inviting decor. The coral/peach lighting is recessed in the burnished mahogany ceiling, and the effect is rich, warm, and interesting. The small, formal dining room is attended by tuxedoed waiters, who are both patient and courteous. The food is mostly good, but there are some inconsistencies: The lightly breaded sole was remarkable and the tempting desserts worth saving room for, but the cheesy lasagna was a bit disappointing. Nevertheless, "va bene" means going well, and if you're looking for kosher kissing, you'd do well to go there.

Lebanese Kissing

AL BUSTAN
827 Third Avenue *between 50th & 51st Streets*
(212) 759-5933
Moderate to Expensive

The soft lighting, soothing watercolors, and eggshell colored walls of this very small room make you feel as if you're encased in a delicate egg. If you're lucky enough to have this restaurant to yourselves, you should have a magical time. On the other hand, loud voices of large parties sometimes present a distraction in this small room, even though the tables are spaced well apart. Considering the soothing decor, the acoustics here are unfortunate. The food, however, is distractingly delicious and should make any discomforts seem minor. Al Bustan means "the orchard," and the restaurant prides itself on being a garden of plenty, with fresh vegetables offered right away for healthful munching along with impossibly good pita bread and two kinds of wonderful olives. The restaurant's logo describes both the atmosphere and the bounty: it is a mystical double symbol, one part being a fruit cut in half to reveal the seed, the other a sun and moon. The ambience is so soothing when it's not crowded that you will feel as if you are part of the watercolors on the wall. And the service is superior. This is the first time we were ever asked if we wanted more dessert!

Spanish / Mexican Kissing

For the most part, Spanish and, even more so, Mexican restaurants are casual, fun, carefree kinds of places for beer and margarita drinking, chip-dipping, and loud conversation. That's all well and good; but for the purpose of this book, we really did our research to find those places that attend to the palate as well as your *muy grande* heart. We found a handful of romantic spots where, in between appetizers (tapas), you can enjoy a kiss to cool off the spices and peppers.

HARLEQUIN
569 Hudson Street *at West 11th Street*
(212) 255-4950
Moderate to Expensive

An exquisite location with a menu to match. The Spanish cuisine is well served here, and this is one of our favorite quiet spots in the city. The decor is classic with exotic touches, and the service is attentive and helpful.

MAXIMILLIANO
208 East 52nd Street *at Third Avenue*
(212) 759-7373
Expensive

This is one of those places we kept passing on the way to work but never stopped at. It was right under our noses and we never knew what treats waited for us inside. The interior is elegant and the service formal but gracious. Two unique appetizers were a generous meal by themselves, but the main course was divine. For a lunchtime get away, even if it wasn't right around the corner, we would return again and again.

ROSA MEXICANA
1063 First Avenue *at 58th Street*
(212) 753-7407
Moderate

When my friend showed me this place she said, just look and tell me if it's not wonderfully romantic. As usual, she was right. The back dining area was truly lovely. There is a stone fountain in the center overflowing with flowers. The room is softly lit. Rose-colored stucco walls create a pretty hue all about and huge floor vases are filled with even more flowers. This is considered one of the prettiest and best Mexican restaurants in town. It also seems to be one of the best for couples who want to share the city's most superb guacamole and a sensational margarita with two straws.

SOLERA
216 East 53rd Street *between Second & Third Avenues*
(212) 644-1166
Expensive prix fixe

With a pleasant attention to detail, this restaurant is a study in extravagant simplicity. From the interestingly constructed bar in front to the latticed indoor garden room in back, every inch is attractive. Despite its elegance, somehow it is always comfortable and homey here. One reason is the warm design of the small and separate rooms. Another is the caring attention paid by the staff. And last, but not least, is the food. We didn't know Spanish cuisine could be so light yet filling — so sensually subtle. This is a new restaurant that will surely be around for a long time.

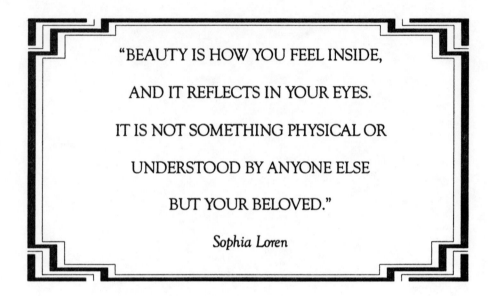

"BEAUTY IS HOW YOU FEEL INSIDE,

AND IT REFLECTS IN YOUR EYES.

IT IS NOT SOMETHING PHYSICAL OR

UNDERSTOOD BY ANYONE ELSE

BUT YOUR BELOVED."

Sophia Loren

◆ Cabaret and Lounge Kissing ◆

Remember those late-night movies in black-and-white from the '40s where hearts were lost, found, broken, and mended all at a quiet table in the corner of a jazz club or piano bar? There was always music in the background that would swell just in time for the lovers to engage in a tearful embrace. As cliched as it sounds, those romantic moments are alive and well in New York City. Music lovers here know there are almost too many nightlife possibilities to choose from. Our list is only for those with tender thoughts. You won't find hard rock emporiums or wild disco scenes listed here. Regardless of taste, your modus operandi should be to check the *Village Voice* or the *Times* to see who's playing where and make a reservation.

Note: Cabarets usually impose a cover or music charge, which can range from about $10–$25 per person, along with a two-drink minimum. In some rooms dinner is available, but even a very expensive cabaret (if you don't dine) can prove more financially manageable than a moderate restaurant for an evening out. (The price ratings are based on a comparison of costs of all the places listed.)

THE BALLROOM   ◆◆◆
253 West 28th Street *between Seventh & Eighth Avenues*
(212) 244-3005
Expensive

There is no ballroom at The Ballroom, but there is incredible music, excellent food, and a suitable atmosphere for cuddling. This is the well-known Spanish restaurant that is credited with starting the tapas revolution. It is also one of the finest cabarets in New York. Their headliners know how to render a love song designed for those in love to understand.

BRADLEY'S   ◆◆
70 University Place *between East 10th & 11th Streets*
(212) 228-6440
Dinner plus music charge = Expensive

A small and dark old New York cabaret, with a long bar, tin ceilings, a grand piano, and many big round close tables, this is where Tony Bennett keeps his heart when he's not in San Francisco. (He doesn't sing here, he listens.) He knows, as do the many regulars, that this is a place for serious jazz listening. The music begins around 10:30, and talking stops. Sway arm in arm to the sounds of the world's best live jazz and kiss quietly.

◆ ***Romantic Warning:*** This — like most jazz clubs — is not the place for you if smoke gets in your eyes.

THE CAFE CARLYLE — (See The Carlyle Restaurant, Restaurants, Continental)

CHUMLEY'S
86 Bedford Street or 58 Barrow *(back entrance)*
(212) 675-4449
Moderate

Think crowded, pubby, smoky, dark, TV-always-on-at-the bar. So why Chumley's? You'll know when you walk down a silent residential street and you have no clue whatsoever that you're in the vicinity of a raucous establishment. Feeling adventurous? Go ahead, open the big, heavy wooden door at 86 Bedford (if you can find it). There's no sign, but it's not a private residence. Even when you know it's there, you'll be surprised to discover Chumley's — an authentic 1920's SPEAK-EASY! There is a menu, but unless the crazy, cramped atmosphere talks to you, have a quick drink and leave through the back entrance on Barrow where another small surprise awaits you. . . .

◆ ***Romantic Note:*** The "5" is missing from the 58 on the Barrow Street entrance door. This is probably deliberate.

DANNY'S GRAND SEA PALACE – (See Restaurants, Broadway)

EIGHTY-EIGHTS
228 West 10th Street *at Bleecker Street*
(212) 924-0088
Inexpensive

This is an intimate art deco room big enough for two handfuls of couples to cozy up to the piano and listen to some wonderful melodies and well-turned songs.

◆ *Romantic Warning:* We recommend you reserve a table at the upstairs Cabaret Room, unless you prefer the raucous piano sing-alongs downstairs.

THE GRAND BAY HOTEL LOBBY LOUNGE
152 West 51st Street *between Seventh Avenue & Broadway*
(212) 765-1900
Inexpensive

City life can provide many things for many people, but the accessibility of cozy corners that are private and nurturing can be difficult, if not impossible, to find, inside or out. What New York City doesn't lack even a little are those places suited to "power" eating. All of that is fine and good, particularly if Wall Street turns you on, but if you're in the mood for appreciative eye-gazing, your choices are limited. The Grand Bay Hotel, in spite of its power location, lacks a grandiose lobby area and, therefore, has just the right prerequisites for an intimate repose. This quiet, calm corner of the city, painted in pale tones of tan and heather, with velvety sofas and snuggly chairs, is an inviting spot that most times of day will provide a tender backdrop for your rendezvous before or after anything you're about to do.

GREENE STREET CAFE
101 Greene Street *at Spring Street*
(212) 925-2415
Expensive

This is a cabaret that calls itself a cafe, which is really stretching things. No one would mistake it for anything other than a high-brow, formal restaurant in the truest sense of the words. It is perhaps too slick to be romantic, but the extremely high ceiling, large wicker chairs, spot-lit trees, a really excellent (very pricey) menu and (what makes it all worthwhile) the entertaining contemporary jazz sounds make this place totally irresistible. Greene's has a cabaret at 105 Greene Street on the top floor, Friday and Saturday nights only.

THE HUNT BAR at the HELMSLEY PALACE HOTEL
455 Madison Avenue *at 50th Street*
(212) 888-7000
Inexpensive

We don't want to give Leona Helmsley any more press than she already buys for herself, but the truth of it is that the Hunt Bar is one of the most intimate, handsome bars in New York and it happens to be located at the lavish Helmsley Palace Hotel. This is a genuinely exquisite setting to ren-dezvous in before, during, or after a busy day. There are only a handful of seats. Sit side by side on damask-covered stools at the rich wood bar or on the satin striped sofas within view of the carved fireplace. The paneled walls and ceiling are superb examples of brilliant craftsmanship and detail-ing. When you're there, you'll feel esconced in another era.

J's
2581 Broadway *at 97th Street*
(212) 666-3600
Inexpensive to Moderate

An out of the way (no street level entrance or sign), extremely cozy, reasonably priced cabaret (nominal food charge; no cover), J's serves up excellent Continental cuisine and entertainment. This ought to put you in a New York state of mind.

L'OMNIBUS CAFE
680 Madison Avenue *at 61st Street*
(212) 751-5111
Expensive to Very Expensive (for dinner only)

Few venues in New York can claim as seductive a Parisian setting. The room is lit by candles in flowered sconces, and murals depicting femmes fatales in alluring haute couture set the mood. Attention is centered on the two or three shows nightly, offering cafe-society piano renditions of classic songs (Cole Porter, George Gershwin, etc.) performed by first-rate entertainers.

Supper is available, but drinks or coffee and dessert are equally appropriate and will help keep the tab within reason. If you're there for the latter, try some of the outstanding French patisserie displayed on a dessert cart. Service is unusally cordial for a place so *chi chi*, and they'll even sing happy anniversary if you request it. Reservations are advisable. Save this one for a very special occasion.

Note: The cover charge is on the high side, and there's no minimum.

◆ *Romantic Option:* Upstairs at the sensual, dazzling **Maxim's** restaurant you'll find another charming place to rendezvous, with dining and dancing to a five-piece orchestra — that's arm in arm, close, hip guiding, rhythmic dancing, the way it should be done.

THE MARK BAR
25 East 77th Street *at Madison Avenue*
(212) 744-4300
Moderate

Located in the luxurious old-world Mark Hotel, this is one of our favorite street level bars for a quick kiss. We love to spend an hour on the little round cushioned chairs, clustered couches, and plush loveseats in the dimly lit room with its warm wood faux columns on dark green walls. The low sounds of quiet jazz play in the background (on an excellent sound system). Candlelit and flower-filled, this is very much like a private parlor in an English country manor. The decor is small, sweet and intimate, and not at all intimidating. Somehow it is suitable for business or pleasure — or both.

MICHAEL'S PUB
211 East 55th Street *between Second & Third Avenues*
(212) 758-2272
Expensive

Good food and great singers make this a sure bet for a wonderful night out. If you're looking for something truly memorable on the East Side, you've come to the right spot. (Yes, this is where Woody Allen unofficially plays clarinet on Monday nights.)

MOSTLY MAGIC
55 Carmine Street *between Bedford and Bleecker Streets*
(212) 924-1472
Entertainment Cover; Moderately priced food available

Put a little youthful magic back in your romance and try something different. Come to a place somewhere over the rainbow where coins disappear behind ears, people sip from little umbrellaed drinks, children laugh (in the earlier hours), gentle jazz piano melodies sway, and talented comedians and magicians pull rabbits from hats. A small, three-tiered nightclub done in pink and black, this is New York's magic mainstay — Tuesday through Sunday.

◆ *Romantic Warning:* Mostly Magic allows children to attend the shows. For mostly adults and mostly excellent entertainment, choose the weekend late shows.

THE OAK ROOM at the ALGONQUIN HOTEL
59 West 44th Street *between Fifth & Sixth Avenues*
(212) 840-6800
Expensive

Those who know the New York cabaret scene know that this is the place. Aesthetically and amorously, the best of the best is the Oak Room. The dark wood paneling and gracious, intimate atmosphere help to create lasting memories. You can get very cozy sitting side by side on the long banquette, lining the sides of the room.

ONE FIFTH – (See Marylou's, Restaurants, American)

PIER 17 at the SOUTH STREET SEAPORT – (See Miscellaneous Kissing)

THE RAINBOW ROOM – (See Restaurants, Continental)

ROMA di NOTTE – (See Restaurants, Italian)

TOP OF THE TOWER
3 Mitchell Place *at 49th Street & First Avenue*
(in the Beekman Tower Hotel)
(212) 355-7300
Inexpensive

New York is probably the most romantic when you're high above it gazing down at those things that are usually bothersome when you're in the thick of it. Bumper-to-bumper honking cars, neon lights from building after monolithic building, and the endless promenade of people soften and take on an ethereal quality when considered from heights reserved for birds and those with penthouse views. In terms of kissing places with this attraction, there are many scattered in the skyscrapers that make up this city's lofty, dense personality, but none is as secluded and quintessentially romantic as the cocktail lounge at the top of the Beekman Tower Hotel.

The Top of the Tower has a spectacular 360-degree view of Midtown's East Side. Nestled against the outside perimeter, a few well-spaced tables, designed mostly for two, make a circle around the tower. Each table has only a small candle for light (thus reducing glare) and a ringside view. The open-air balcony is available in good weather (although those suffering from vertigo might want to reconsider). Gentle, unobtrusive piano music begins after 9 p.m.

Note: There is no cover charge, but the drinks are on the high side.

◆ *Romantic Warning:* It is strongly advised to call before going lest a private party to which you haven't been invited has closed the tower for the evening.

WINDOWS ON THE WORLD HORS D'OEUVRERIE
One World Trade Center
(212) 938-1111
Moderate to Expensive
Jackets Required

Although this is the perfect place to go spontaneously, you must choose the night carefully. If it's rainy, cloudy, foggy, or overcast, get thee to a dark nightclub and not to this breathtaking cocktail lounge perched 107 floors above the sparkly city. On the other hand, if the evening is about to descend on a clear day, there may be no more enchanting place to witness the event than the Hors D'Oeuvrerie (as captivating as it is difficult to spell).

The room is perfectly lit. The sometimes noisy bar is tucked away behind swinging saloon doors. All you'll hear are the melodic sounds of a keyboard in the background. There are abundant tables for two beside the omnipresent windows. All that alone would be enough to enhance a loving tryst, but as you may already know, the appeal of the Hors D'Oeuvrerie doesn't stop there. Looking west from that height as the buildings change from their daytime business dress to their elegant evening wear, you'll remember that sunsets really do exist.

Note: Weekdays are significantly less crowded here than weekends. Sunday brunch is an extravagant, excellent choice. Breakfast is available every day, but the atmosphere tends to be more business-oriented. Never mind, the view will help you create your own atmosphere.

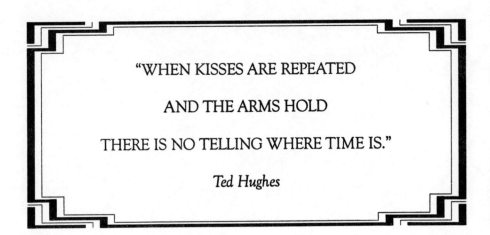

"WHEN KISSES ARE REPEATED

AND THE ARMS HOLD

THERE IS NO TELLING WHERE TIME IS."

Ted Hughes

◆ Outdoor Kissing ◆

**BATTERY PARK CITY PROMENADE
and the WORLD FINANCIAL CENTER**
West Street *between the World Trade Center
& the Hudson River & Vesey & Liberty Streets*
(212) 945-0505

Easy access by taxi or car via Liberty Street and South End Avenue or by subway: A, C, E or PATH to Chambers Street/World Trade Center or 1, 9, R or N to Cortlandt Street/World Trade Center.

This is one of the few places in New York that is a desirable spot day or night, and in every season and every type of weather, although it is most enchanting on a breezy summer day. **The Winter Garden (between 2 and 3 World Financial Center)**, with its soaring arched ceiling and exalted marble staircase is the centerpiece of the World Financial Center. Although new and modern, it has an opulence you rarely see these days. Link arms and proceed from here to take it all in. When you've had your fill of shops and Godiva chocolate, step outside and take a walk along the water past the yachts and sculpture gardens to the very end of the Battery Park City Promenade, stopping to sit whenever the mood seems right. People will skate by; children may play by; lovers will stroll by. This is one of the best places in New York to be at sunset, when the city behind you is shining, and the water takes on a coppery glow. At twilight the southern end of the promenade twinkles with tiny bright blue lights.

◆ *Romantic Suggestion:* Day or night, at some point, all that walking arm in arm is sure to make you hungry. Turn around. **Pipeline, 2 World Financial Center (212) 945-2755,** has inexpensively to moderately priced hamburgers, salads, sandwiches, soups, chili, chicken, pastas, desserts, and the like. What it lacks is atmosphere. Don't go there. At least, don't take a table there. Try this: First, notice the unappealing thronging crowds and lines at Pipeline's outdoor tables. You don't want to join that, do you? Of course not. Now notice that cluster of fairly empty public tables right next to Pipeline with the same view. See them? Good, 'cause you can get take-out from Pipeline and eat there. No crowds, no wait, a few trees, a little breeze, great food, and each other: what could be better?

◆ *Romantic Option:* On a cold or rainy day, bring your picnic indoors to the great marble steps of the Winter Garden or dine beneath tall palm trees in the **Winter Garden Cafe, 2 World Financial Center, (212) 945-7200,** or choose any of the other many restaurants. Or sip a Caribbean drink from two straws as you listen to a concert. It's the next best thing to an island vacation.

BROOKLYN BOTANIC GARDENS
1000 Washington Avenue, Brooklyn
(718) 622-4433

From Manhattan, take the Manhattan Bridge, go straight on Flatbush Avenue to Grand Army Plaza, then follow Eastern Parkway to a right on Washington Avenue. Or take the 2 or 3 train to Eastern Parkway Station.

These gardens are a 50-acre oasis of pastoral splendor and tranquillity in the midst of the bustling borough of Brooklyn. Bring a special someone and dreams to share as you discover the winding and secluded paths, throw pennies into sparkling fountains, stretch out on the grass while gazing upward at a full blue sky, or listen to the rush of a rocky stream. The Garden itself is comprised of many smaller gardens within a forest, and so you are sure to find a special, always to be remembered spot, just for the two of you.

On a grand scale, the **Cranford Rose Garden**, with formal walkways leading to a latticed white portico at one end, is, in the months of June and September, an elegantly wondrous tribute to romance's own true flower. In April and May the **Cherry Esplanade**, with its rows of wildly pink blossoms, cheerfully heralds the spring. Smaller, more intimate spaces include the **Shakespeare Garden**, an English country cottage setting for the collection of flowers mentioned in Will's plays and sonnets, and the **Fragrance Garden**, beds of flowers that can be savored by the senses of smell and vision. And there's so much more: the **Rock Garden**, the **Iris Garden**, and **Daffodil Hill,** all surrounded by dogwoods, rhododendrons, ash trees and honey-suckle, willow and witch hazel, snowdrops and conifers, stately oaks and beeches. There is also **Steinhardt Conservatory,** a miracle of urban architecture and horticultural design. The glass pavilions allow you to pass through a steamy tropical forest, a Mediterranean hillside, and a scorching desert. Around the world in an afternoon, smack dab in the middle of Brooklyn.

Perhaps the most beautiful location is the **Japanese Hill** and **Pond Garden.** When you pass through the bamboo gates, you enter a world of timeless harmony and craftsmanship. Once inside, winding, narrow pathways take you around the reflecting lake, toward vantage points high and low, past Japanese lanterns, over small stone bridges and up a grassy, secluded hill to a Buddhist shrine. Here everything is appropriately symbolic: Tall pines suggest longevity, and the rock formations signify strength; even the shape of the lake represents the Japanese symbol for heart and mind.

Note: The Brooklyn Botanic Gardens are very popular at cherry blossom time and on high-summer weekends. However, the enforcement of strict noise and recreational restrictions, as well as many out of the way spaces and less traveled byways, mean that romantic interludes are rarely, if ever, hard to come by.

◆ *Romantic Suggestion:* The **Patio Restaurant** (Inexpensive), overlooking the Fragrance Garden, offers refreshment in spring and summer.

THE BROOKLYN BRIDGE

The bridge spans the East River joining Manhattan and Brooklyn. Leave the car and take the subway. To reach the Manhattan side of the bridge take the 4, 5 or 6 to the Brooklyn Bridge, or the 1, 2 or 3.

This isn't the longest bridge in the city, but it's certainly the most beautiful. Walking over the venerable Brooklyn Bridge is an exhilarating experience. Here you can feel the impact of the city in the air, neither encumbered nor fenced in by buildings. Here you can walk above it all and take in the astonishingly spectacular view at the same time.

Probably the most convenient and provocative way to enjoy your own trek across the span is to start at **City Hall Park.** The park is pleasant anytime, but in the warm months its gardens are in full bloom and the serene, white fountain cools the area with a light refreshing spray. From here, you can't miss the bridge towering above you. Cross Park Row and find the kiosk labeled "Bridge Footpath." Then go down the steps. Once on the footpath, you'll have a clear view up to the middle point of the bridge's bow shape. As you're lifted high above the city streets, be sure to look down at the canyons of Wall Street and the forest of masts on the tall ships of South Street Seaport. From the middle of the bridge, look upward toward the Manhattan skyline, and don't forget to remind each other to breathe. There are benches along the way where you can snuggle in the breeze and, depending on the time of day, you'll have the pathway all to yourselves. Early in the morning or toward twilight, the glistening waters of the harbor and the proud silhouette of the Statue of Liberty are unforgettable.

◆ *Romantic Warning:* There's a reason it took 250 years for New Yorkers to build a bridge over the river: It's a long way! The walk takes about 30 to 45 minutes.

BROOKLYN HEIGHTS PROMENADE – (See River Cafe, Restaurants, American)

CARL SCHURZ PARK
East End Avenue *from 84th to 89th Street*

Tucked away next to the East River on the very edge of upper Manhattan, this quiet little park has been a haven for lovers for as long as we can remember. Walk up the semicircular stairway at 86th Street to the promenade. To the north, you'll see the twinkling strands of lights which mark the Triboro Bridge and, far away to the south, the Queensboro Bridge. In the trees behind you, flocks of birds provide a musical background to your walk.

In winter, walk hand in hand along the wide curving promenade overlooking the water and witness the change of day across the sky. In spring, the flower beds are full of tulips and daffodils, and the entry to this park is lined with cherry trees abloom in pink. In fall, the autumn air is crisp and the leaves are as colorful as any you'll see this far south of New England. In summer, the benches are a great place for a picnic as you watch the movement of ships along the river. At the south end of the park there is a playing field and a playground; both are sometimes used for summer evening concerts.

◆ *Romantic Warning:* On warm, sunny days, especially in spring and summer, everybody in the neighborhood comes out to get a tan or play. Though Carl Schurz is still a fun place under these circumstances, "quiet" would no longer describe it.

CENTRAL PARK

Between 59th & 110th Streets
& Fifth Avenue & Central Park West
Visitor Center: (212) 397-3156

For those who know how to safely handle this vast acreage of city park, it can be as if Central Park and romance are, themselves, a loving couple. The aroma of chestnuts, the sight of couples huddled warmly in horse-drawn carriages or strolling hand in hand by the sailboat pond amidst the blossoming cherry trees, the sounds of the carousel's piping calliope, or the feeling of just being part of the theatrical celebration that overflows from almost every corner — such things make Central Park a unique year-round treasure. There is so much to see; lakes and broad lawns, quaint wrought-iron street lamps alongside curving walks, lofty hardwood trees, granite outcroppings, and the electric atmosphere of cosmopolitan Manhattan nearby. When you experience the park's endless varied sensations — watching street performers at **Bethesda Terrace (mid-park at 72nd)**, or hearing the Philharmonic on the **Great Lawn (mid-park at 81st)**, or taking in sunshine wherever it feels the most comfortable — you will most assuredly have your prelude to romance.

What could be more enlivening on a frosty day than to glide together at the **Wollman Ice Rink** and then share a steaming hot chocolate while watching the colorful parade of the graceful and the clumsy pass by? Or on a fragrantly warm and sunny day, you could rent a boat at **Loeb Boathouse**, or stop for lunch at the **Boathouse Cafe**, in the park near **72nd Street and Fifth Avenue (212) 517-4723**. Paddle out onto the lake and then drift along under the formidable stone and wooden bridges, or along the shore by the languid willows, catching a glimpse of the distant buildings through the green drooping leaves. There are many modes of transportation in Central Park besides boats, skates, or hansom cabs; you can also try a bicycle built-for-two available for rent at Loeb Boathouse. Roughly near 100th Street, there is a cut-through for cyclists between the East and West Drives, with a lawn that slopes down toward a lovely wooded glen.

The Conservatory Garden is another special, quiet place in the park just off **Fifth Avenue at 105th Street**. It is the only formal garden here, and actually is three separately designed plantings — one has the Untermeyer fountain as its centerpiece, another is dotted with statues of storybook characters, and the third is flanked by two stately, trellised archways covered in aromatic wisteria vines. This section of Central Park is truly one of the magical spots of the city.

Note: The numerous attractions and activities offered in Central Park are far more than can be listed here. Call the Visitor Center to find out the day's happenings.

CITY ISLAND, Bronx

Take the Triboro Bridge towards the Bronx. Follow Bruckner Expressway (Route 278) north. Exit at 8B: Orchard Beach/City Island. Follow the road, bearing right at the traffic light. Well-marked signs point the way to City Island. About 30–45 minutes from Manhattan.

From October through April, we occasionally like to take a mini-holiday afternoon to this sunny island locale — an unpretentious New England whaling village off the coast of the Bronx. Here you can take your time looking at sailboats, water, and soothing scenery. City Island is tiny, about a mile long and very narrow. You can easily walk or bike the length of City Island Avenue, from the bridge to the mainland, all the way to Long Island Sound. If you love boats, this is paradise. Old and new marine gear abounds and the area is lined with boat yards and shops. The village even has a sailmaker.

Quiet residential streets run east and west off City Island Avenue. With the bridge behind you, turn right on any byway. Every street ends at a private (warning: private means private) beach facing the Manhattan skyline, across Eastchester Bay.

◆ **Romantic Suggestion:** Restaurants line City Island Avenue. For lunch, try **Anna's Harbor Restaurant, 565 City Island Avenue, (212) 885-1373** (Moderate), with its huge, glass-enclosed dining area jutting into the bay. Filled with plants, it has the feel of a greenhouse on a harbor. Eat lunch and watch the boats, or come for an early dinner and see the sunset.

◆ **Romantic Warning:** If you head for City Island in summer, expect traffic, crowds, and limited parking spaces. Off-season is definitely the more romantic time to visit here. Also, don't bother going to City Island unless you plan to eat a meal — a seafood meal that is.

◆ **Second Romantic Warning:** City Island is interesting, quaint, different and, sometimes, delicious, but if you go expecting Bermuda or San Juan Island, you'll be disappointed. This is City Island. Its main appeal is its proximity to the city.

CLOISTERS/FORT TRYON PARK
192nd Street *between Riverside Drive & Fort Washington Avenue*
(212) 923-3700

The most romantic thing about the Cloisters is not the Cloisters, which officially refers to the Cloisters Museum, the medieval branch of the Metropolitan Museum of Art. (The museum has been assembled stone by stone from European monasteries and closely resembles the real thing. It is beautiful and interesting but a little too austere and religious to be defined as a smooching location.) Rather, the romance is to be found in Fort Tryon Park, the giant sprawling home to the museum. With its hours of meandering river and wood trails, chirping birds, (yes, there are birds that chirp in Manhattan), panoramic vistas, towering trees, herb gardens and, in the springtime, flowers, flowers, flowers, it is a New York fairy tale.

Upon entering the park at the very end of Fort Washington Avenue, you'll be immediately confronted with a difficult choice: which beckoning path to take. Why not take both? First, linger around the short surreal garden path that will be directly in front of you. It is difficult to tell where the colors of the leaves and flowers end and the Hudson River Palisades backdrop begins. Next, take the river route by following the stone wall around toward the left. In a few minutes, you will see the Cloisters museum in the distance. When you get there, stop in and see the famous Unicorn tapestries and rest in the central open-air garden courts, the lower court featuring herbs and the upper a plethora of flowers. Then, take the woodsy route back past the **Unicorn Cafe**, which on a balmy day is kind of a sweet place to sojourn over a cup of coffee. If you take the circular route, you will eventually find yourself reluctantly back at the entrance.

◆ *Romantic Option:* If you keep walking north past the Cloisters, you will come to Inwood Park, and there are trails that will take you down to the river.

◆ *Romantic Warning:* This is a city park. If you look too closely you will see signs of wildlife: graffiti, litter, and minor vandalism. And, although after many years of exploring this park I've never observed any problems, a park warning is part and parcel of New York life. But don't let that stop you; keep to areas where people are concentrated.

COLUMBIA UNIVERSITY
Main Gate, 116th Street & Broadway

Those who make it a rule never to wander above 100th Street are missing out on something special and should consider breaking tradition. For the young, the young at heart, and those who wholeheartedly cherished their college years, long forgotten memories of campus life are certain to return as you ramble through the ivory towers of Columbia University. Replete with history and echoes of the classical past, this hallowed institution offers appealing architecture, wide-open grounds to picnic on, great student-watching, and a few hidden corners in which to indulge a kiss or two. Depending on the season, there's no telling what activities you'll stumble across on campus: perhaps a concert of ethnic music, a crafts fair or, believe it or not, a political demonstration. There are always Frisbee games of various skill levels going on, the foolish frolicking of students, and sun lovers stretched out soaking up the warmth whenever the skies are clear. Why not join them? You're only young for the rest of your lives.

◆ *Romantic Option:* **Riverside Church Bell Tower and Observatory, Riverside Drive between 120th and 122nd Streets**, is the ideal place to go with someone who is passionate about celestial views and heavenly music. From the 20th floor, you'll climb 147 steps (trust me, it's worth it) through a 74-bell carillon where hypnotically beautiful concerts are performed every Sunday. An observation deck provides a 360-degree panorama where you can pause for an elevated kiss, but don't neglect the spectacular views in all directions.

FOREST HILLS GARDENS, Queens

Take Interborough Parkway east to the Forest Hills exit north into Forest Hills.

Although I'm not the type who usually recommends ogling homes of people who are more likely to speak of the number of wings on their residences than the number of rooms, once you swallow your envy, a brisk or lazy walk through the estates of this neighborhood can be an enticing pleasure. After cruising the web of twisting roads that lace through the astonishing architecture, together you can easily stroll from the gardens into the nearby park, where the overlook is a favorite place to kiss. After all that walking, ice cream, cappuccino, or a bite to eat is certain to appeal, and I enthusiastically recommend a detour to the **Metro Soda Fountain, 116-02 Metropolitan Avenue (718) 846-8787** (Inexpensive). The Fountain has been fastidiously restored to its original detail, complete with etched glass, art deco molding, and pressed tin ceilings. The lighting is warm and rosy, the music is vintage 1940s. Tasty sandwiches and salads are served here, but the soda fountain's most distinguishing feature is its ice cream menu. Dig into peanut butter sundaes, or share a traditional banana split.

FRANCIS LEWIS PARK, Queens

Take the Whitestone Expressway (678) to the last exit before the toll. After the exit, turn right on 3rd Avenue which dead ends at the park.

Not what anyone would call a comely park, but for those who love searching out classic views of Manhattan, this one should not be missed. It is rarely crowded and is, for a city spot, beautiful. The

Whitestone looms overhead, and the sound of the cars racing by resembles the sound of ocean surf. The lawn sweeps down to water's edge where a few park benches are scattered about here and there at discreet distances from one another. And then there's the view of the city, a vibrant living sculpture that is impossible to describe adequately. But after you've seen it, you'll never forget it.

JAMAICA BAY WILDLIFE REFUGE
Cross Bay Boulevard, Queens
(718) 474-0613

From Manhattan, follow the Belt Parkway to Exit 17. Cross Bay Boulevard and head south toward Rockaway across the North Channel Bridge. The Refuge is one mile past the bridge on the right.

This is one of the great hidden gems of New York City: an island of greenery in a sea of concrete. Although it is hard to be entirely alone here, somehow the company of egrets, ospreys, owls, woodpeckers, herons, and swans (to name a few) isn't terribly intrusive. Even the Audubon loyalists who flock here won't disturb your privacy because there are plenty of secret escapes just off the main trail. Following the two-mile West Pond Trail down toward the water, where it winds between the bay and a manmade freshwater pond, you can watch the continual shift of the horizon. Around one bend the Verrazano Bridge comes into view and, around another the Twin Towers and the Empire State Building suddenly loom large. Near the end of the loop a sign points back to the visitor center. If you turn off the main trail at that point, you'll find a spider web of small paths that meander through birch groves and holly bushes, where few visitors venture and the privacy is yours alone.

The mood of the Refuge changes with the season, but it retains a romantic spell all year round. Spring and fall are a bird watcher's delight, when feathered friends are migrating between breeding grounds high in the Canadian Arctic and winter hideaways in Central and South America. When the winter seems to go on endlessly, urban-weary New Yorkers can find solace in nature's stark beauty. And in summertime, when hot feels like an understatement, there is comfort here in the cooling sea breezes that blow gently across the countryside.

◆ *Romantic Option:* If an Irish coffee or a spirit-warming cognac sounds like it would hit the spot after your day at the Refuge, you can meet that need plus enjoy a full tempting seafood dinner at **Pier 92 Restaurant, 377 Beach 92nd Street, Rockaway Beach, (718) 945-2200** (Moderate to Expensive). Head south down Cross Bay Boulevard and onto Rockaway Peninsula in search of this place. No signs mark the restaurant, but insiders look for the McDonald's next door as a landmark. The Pier sports a crackling fire during the winter, outdoor tables in the summer and, at all times, spectacular views across Jamaica Bay to Kennedy Airport.

LONG ISLAND CITY WATERFRONT, Queens

Driving from Manhattan, take the upper roadway of the Queensboro Bridge to 21st Street exit. Turn left on 21st and then right on 44th Drive to the end. From Queens and points east, follow any major Queens artery westward, avoiding entrances to bridges and tunnels, to Vernon Boulevard which parallels the shoreline.

Those definitive, intensely romantic views of the mid-Manhattan skyline and the Queensboro Bridge common to a score of movies you've surely seen dozens of times are best captured in person here. In the background, the wondrous shapes of steel, the world center of commerce and culture, expressed in soaring architecture; in the foreground, the East River and, by day, the Gothic ruins of Roosevelt Island. After dark, the buildings' dimensions and textures yield to a mesmerizing light show — the formal dress of the city: The Chrysler in art deco elegance, the Empire State with its tricolor personality, Citicorp's signature statement, the Bridge wearing a sparkling diamond necklace. A place to take it all in and yet be very much alone.

Two favorite outdoor locations provide marvelous vantage points with considerable privacy. The cement pier at the foot of 44 Drive juts over the water for the most spectacular view. About a half-mile to the north, Queens Bridge Park is a more pastoral setting with overwhelming close-ups of the bridge.

◆ *Romantic Suggestion:* **The Water's Edge, East River Yacht Club, East River and 44th Drive, Long Island City, Queens (718) 482-0033** (Expensive), adjacent to the pier, is lavishly appointed and offers an expensive, mostly seafood, Continental menu. Live piano music, experienced, professional service, outdoor garden seating when weather permits, and the view of Manhattan as the backyard can assist anyone's romantic plans. You can drive here or come by a boat that leaves every hour from the pier north of the 34th Street Heliport. For a more moderate choice, **East River Grill, 44th Avenue and Vernon Boulevard, (718) 937-3001** (Inexpensive to Moderate), a long block north of the pier, is part of the East River Tennis Club complex. It is mostly business-oriented during the day. Go during the long steamy summer evenings. When the sun bathes the city in a warm embrace, dinner is served outdoors and features American grilled food. The Club becomes a friendly, easygoing Long Island retreat, grass-carpeted down to the river with the urban mecca glistening across the water. A perfect spot for a sunset.

Note: Weather permitting, the East River Grill sponsors disco dancing every summer Saturday under the stars, but be warned that the restaurant closes on rainy days in summer. Call first.

NEW YORK BOTANICAL GARDENS
Southern Blvd. & 200th Street, Bronx
(212) 220-8777

Located in Bronx Park, which they share with the zoo, the Gardens are neighbors with Fordham University, where Mosholu and Pelham Parkways and Fordham Road come together. Metro North Station from Manhattan runs a special from Grand Central Station which includes admission to the Conservatory.

The Gardens make a brilliant backdrop for romance when they blaze with their unending variety of flowers, but thanks to the steamy Conservatory, Mother Nature and sonny boy Cupid, they can be visited all year round. From the first daffodils of April, through the red roses of late September, the warmer months are the best time to take your dreams to this earthly paradise. Whether your flower-madness compels you and your beloved to sniff away at the tens of thousands of blooms, or your wanderlust leads you over the green knolls and meadows, or your gentler sentiments incline you to find a shady tree, the Gardens have something for both of you.

You might want to know that it's not all carefully cultivated dahlias and dogwood here: Nature primeval is also to be found. The only virgin forest left in New York City stands here by the gorge that the rapid Bronx River has cut through the rocks over the course of centuries. Right near the dramatic falls of the river, you can dine at the Old Mill and feel that you're in a quaint New England town miles away from city life.

◆ *Romantic Options:* You can easily stroll across Fordham Road to visit either the university (don't miss the Chapel, whose bells inspired Edgar Allen Poe to write "Annabelle Lee" — their cottage stands nearby) or the zoo, officially the **New York Zoological Gardens (212) 367-1010** — one of the largest zoos in the world and one of the best. You shouldn't underestimate the charms of the animal kingdom. The zoo's two nature rides, one called Skyfari, provide some quiet moments complete with *Out of Africa* scenery and soundtrack. You won't be the only ones here, particularly when summer vacation is in effect. But once you've started your trek around this paradise, all you'll see are the animals and each other.

◆ *Romantic Suggestion:* When you've finished, if you have a car, you must drive back over Fordham Road and turn left to the **Arthur Avenue Historic District** to dine at some of the best Italian restaurants in the city.

THE PETREL
Southeast corner of Battery Park
(212) 825-1976

If you tend to get seasick, sailing and kissing are totally out of the question. For those with stronger constitutions, this watery tour of the harbor on a 1938 classic, 70-foot, full sail vessel is an essential ingredient for a quick out-of-city excursion. May through October, bask in the summer sun and breezes on the wooden deck of this well maintained boat. From this vantage point you can catch a glimpse of Ellis Island

and the Statue of Liberty as you glide by. There are afternoon and evening sails. The afternoon is quieter, and therefore, more romantic. On the other hand, the evening sail makes sunset look like a spectacular Broadway performance. Either way, *bon voyage*.

QUEENS BOTANICAL GARDEN
43-50 Main Street, Flushing, Queens
(718) 886-3800

Take the Long Island Expressway westbound to Exit 23 (Main Street). Turn right at the light after you exit which will put you on to Main Street. The street will dead end at the garden's fence. Follow this around to your left till you reach Dahlia Avenue, which is the gate into the garden.

Queens Botanical Garden packs a remarkable amount into its 39 sublime acres. In addition to its **Rose Garden**, which is the largest in the Northeast, the garden is home to a series of individual pocket gardens, including a rock garden, a backyard garden, an herb garden, and even a bee garden, a perfect way to spend an uninterrupted afternoon. Walkways lead past statues, a fountain encircled by tulips, and a multitude of fragrant flower beds. The sundial near the entrance bears an appropriate message engraved onto its face: "Grow old with me, the best is yet to be."

◆ *Romantic Suggestion:* If you like to daydream, have a look at the **Wedding Garden**. Entrance is permitted only to private parties who rent the space, but you can peer through the picket fence and see everything. A gazebo, a wooden chair-swing, and flowing willow trees all evoke the Victorian era. A brook meanders under a small footbridge, feeding the exotic goldfish-stocked pond. Can you imagine 100 friends and relatives milling around here just for your special occasion?

Note: Main Street, Flushing has become one of New York City's greatest melting pots. Be sure to walk the few blocks from the Garden and allow time to savor the Indian spice shops, browse through Chinese groceries, and perhaps stop for an Afghani or Japanese lunch. The best stuff is sometimes just off Main Street, and so detours are encouraged.

RIVERSIDE PARK

The park borders the Hudson River to the west of Riverside Drive from 72nd Street to 145th Street.

Longer than Central Park, closer to what nature had originally intended and with a more dramatic setting, Riverside Park is often overlooked by those searching for a place to stroll. This park is actually a superb option for a romantic hour, simply because it is less popular and hectic than its more famous neighbor; and if you're coming from Broadway, you're closer to Riverside, anyway. This area is prime leisure territory, away from the madding crowd. The towering trees and hilly meadows form the right setting for a relaxing country afternoon a few minutes from the very epitome of civilization. Besides having spectacular vistas, the park is also dotted with monuments to local and far-flung heroes from Ulysses Grant to Joan of Arc. This generous use of marble, perhaps, gives the park its Parisian air.

◆ *Romantic Option:* If you'd like to cater yourself a scrumptious picnic, stop in at **Zabar's, Broadway at 80th Street, (212) 787-2000**, before you set out. From there, it's about a two-minute walk to this unexpected acreage.

◆ *Second Romantic Option:* **The 79th Street Boat Basin, at 79th Street on the Hudson River**, is one of the great projects of builder Robert Moses and is an ideal locale for pretending to escape to an island getaway and a simpler way of life, even if just for a moment or two. The 125-slip marina, on the western edge of Riverside Park, is the year-round home of some 150 people, whose houseboats range in size and design from simple to grandiose. Sit awhile on a tree-shaded bench watching the boats rock gently in the water and feel the cool relief of Hudson River breezes. Come down on an early summer evening to see the sun set over the New Jersey Palisades. Barges and sailboats float by regularly, and low-flying private planes pass overhead while the sea gulls drift by in the distance.

◆ *Romantic Warning:* If you don't know your way around the city, we recommend that you not go farther north in the park than Grant's Tomb. If you exit the park up here, the Morningside Heights neighborhood can provide you with shops, bookstores, restaurants, and some nice walks of its own.

SHORE ROAD WALK in Bay Ridge, Brooklyn

Take the Brooklyn Bridge Brooklyn-Queens Expressway (278) south to Bay Ridge. Exit at Bay Ridge Parkway heading east. The road dead ends at Shore Road.

This is one of the most beautiful walks in the city. Shore Road snakes around the entire western edge of Bay Ridge. This small corner of Brooklyn is blessed by a majestic 180-degree view of the Narrows, Verrazano Bridge, Staten Island, and the land beyond. The area and view is so perfect it can easily motivate avid feelings of the heart.

As you follow the shoreline, you will notice large grassy areas, playgrounds, playfields, and more grassy areas that seem to go on forever and forever. Somewhere here is your private area of the world to, sit and watch the sun make its daily exit.

SNUG HARBOR, Staten Island
1000 Richmond Terrace
(718) 448-2500

From the Brooklyn Queens Expressway, take the Verrazano Bridge to the Staten Island Expressway (Route 278) to the Clove Road exit. Turn right on Clove Road and go about a mile to Bard Avenue, and make a sharp right onto it. Go several miles to the end of the Bard Avenue and then turn right onto Richmond Terrace. On your right you will see the entrance to Snug Harbor Cultural Center.

Snug Harbor is very appropriately named. An excursion to this fetching cultural center with its lush setting is a peaceful contrast to Manhattan business and nightlife. The center is an 80-acre complex with Greek Revival buildings that are about 150 years old and are being restored. Originally a haven for sailors, the area now houses museums and theatres. There you can wander through the botanic gardens, nuzzle close in the gazebo, or relax on the grounds near the duck pond.

On the grounds is an art museum called the **Newhouse Gallery**, which exhibits contemporary paintings and sculpture (it's open daily from 12 p.m. to 5 p.m. except Monday and Tuesday; admission is free). Despite its small size, it is international in scope and shows the works of well-known artists. The center also offers a wide range of entertainment: plays, films, dance, and musical concerts under the stars, some featuring top-name performers.

◆ *Romantic Suggestion:* To top off a day spent at Snug Harbor you can dine at **R.H. Tugs, 1115 Richmond Terrace, (718) 447-6369** (Moderate), a waterfront restaurant across the street from the harbor. Although decorated with tin ceilings and whirling fans, its main romantic appeal is the water, aglow with shimmering lights in the evening. Moonbeams bouncing off the water's surface are hypnotically entrancing. Processions of tugboats will entertain you as they make their way across the industrially scenic Kill Van Kull. In warm weather you can get even closer to the water; drinks, hors d'oeuvres, and barbecued dishes are served on the patio, where there is more privacy and the rhythmic sounds of the gulls and water becalm you. By the way, the food at Tugs is outstanding. Be sure not to miss the Tug Boat ice cream pie.

WASHINGTON MEWS
North of Washington Square Park
between University & Fifth Avenues

Tired of pocket parks? Here's something a bit unusual: a short cobblestoned street where some NYU faculty members are lucky enough to live. The quiet gated lane just beckons to be strolled on. Window boxes filled with flowers and flowering ivy decorate the front of these quaint European two-story maisons. It's easy to pretend you're in France here.

◆ *Romantic Note:* Washington Mews is closed to pedestrian traffic from 11 p.m. to 7 a.m. and always closed to public traffic. The few cars on the street belong to faculty who use their keys to enter and park.

WAVE HILL, Bronx
Independence Avenue & 249th Street
(212) 549-3200

Take the Henry Hudson Parkway northbound to the 246th-250th Streets exit or southbound to the 254th Street exit. Follow the signs to the entry gate, which is two blocks west of the Parkway.

In late March when Midtown Manhattan hints only uncertainly of spring, Riverdale's Wave Hill estate, a mere fifteen minutes' drive north, is already munificent with the pleasures of the season. The verdant grounds overlook the Hudson glistening in the welcome sunshine and the stately Palisades spread before you in the distance. Hundreds of trees, representative of the earth's far corners, are budding, while purple "Glory of the Snow" festoon the hillsides. Workers tend the young gardens, which promise more delight in the months ahead when ripe herbs will diffuse their heady perfumes and exotic flowers will exhibit a riot of color. Even now the greenhouse is radiant with cacti in bloom, delicate orchids, and calendulas of startling yellow and orange.

Built more than 150 years ago for attorney William Morris, Wave Hill House has seen a succession of notables in residence. Donated to the city in 1960, the estate is now the setting for a variety of cultural offerings. Art and photography exhibits fill the mansion's galleries, and dance highlights the summer schedule. The auditorium, with its hand-carved ceilings, armor collection, and panoramic river view, makes a distinguished backdrop for Sunday afternoon chamber music concerts. Call for a calendar of events. Or come up on the spur of the moment for nature's ongoing staged spectacles. On the woodland trails and rolling meadows, settle back, hold hands, and let the birds and butterflies go on with the show.

POCKET PARKS

We introduced this book with a romantic quote that speaks directly to the major problem New Yorkers face when it comes to romance (one of the more interesting problems for anyone who lives in a big city):

"As usual with most lovers in the city — they were troubled by the lack of that essential need of love — a meeting place." Hopefully that is what you're finding in these pages, but this particular section speaks to that dilemma most directly. The pocket parks contain prodigious amounts of greenery, privacy, views, singing birds, and walking room inside a near-countrylike space. Most important, they provide a meeting place where the two of you can get to know one another a little better than you did before.

Damrosch Park
Between the New York State Theatre
& the Metropolitan Opera House at Lincoln Center

This park is a surprisingly colorful corner of Manhattan that somehow escapes all the tourist traffic. You could certainly create a picnic outing from any of the delis on Broadway and camp here for the afternoon. It's very cozy under the trees, and if you think "music be the food of love," then stay for one of the free summer concerts. This one is worth a special visit. Even the corresponding space formed by Avery Fisher Hall, the Opera House, and the Juilliard School is, with its pool and trees, one of the most elegant squares in New York.

Ford Foundation
320 East 43rd Street *between First & Second Avenues*
(212) 573-5000

The abundant greenery hidden within this modern skyscraper is a sight for tired city eyes. Though not exactly a traditional pocket park by New York standards, there is a profound peacefulness here that is hard to find elsewhere in Manhattan. The entire center of the Ford Foundation building is an enclosed atrium with floor to ceiling windows. Inside is a forest of trees and exotic blooming plants. Brick paths lead you around and through the foliage, and there is a sunlit sitting wall where you can listen to the gentle bubbling of the still-water pool. You may find the atmosphere more like a library than a park; it is that quiet. No food is allowed, and the office traffic is sparse. Here you may relax, forget about the world at large and concentrate on each other.

Greenacre Park
221 East 51st Street *between Second & Third Avenues*

What people think of when they hear the term "vest-pocket parks" is captured at this particular city oasis. Literally nestled between thick granite walls, this qualifies nicely as a refuge from the assaults of urban life. The small tables and chairs (as opposed to the common fixed benches) and the crystal-clear waterfall rushing over large stones and rocks give this spot a true European flavor. You can sidle your chair right up to your companion's, and commence with the matters of the heart. There is even a small refreshment stand inside the gate. **Note:** Closed for two months in the winter.

Paley Plaza
3 East 53rd Street *between Fifth & Madison Avenues*

Perhaps too small to even be considered a pocket park, this is a small change of scenery where you least expect it. It is a reprieve from the world at large, breathing space where the sounds of a waterfall replace the traffic noise, and the cooling spray on a hot summer day will revitalize you for more exploration.

Sutton Place Park
East 57th Street & Sutton Place

If the evening is pleasant and there's romance in the air, stroll over to Sutton Place Park at the eastern end of 57th Street. After dark, the river is aglow with reflections of light from the opposite shore, and the stately Queensboro Bridge is handsomely outlined with its own necklace of illumination. Most couples linger by the railing a while, watching the tugs and tankers silently ply the waters. The park offers an ample number of benches for snuggling, a fair amount of privacy, and is in one of the city's safest neighborhoods. What's more, you can enjoy this hideaway until closing time at 1:00 a.m.

◆ **Romantic Warning:** This is strictly an after-dark venue for the amorous. During the day, the park is overrun by toddlers and their nannies doing everything but the things you would call romantic.

St. Paul's Chapel
Broadway at Vesey Street

A very peaceful oasis in the city, the charm of the 18th-century church and the old shade trees shelter you from the surrounding streets. Many romances of Old New York can be traced by reading the stones and the information plaques provided. **Note:** Open all year round during church hours.

Washington Market Square
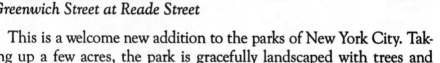
Greenwich Street at Reade Street

This is a welcome new addition to the parks of New York City. Taking up a few acres, the park is gracefully landscaped with trees and flower beds. In the summer, it's overrun by office workers from the surrounding stock brokerage houses (although, for some the crowds do not impede romance), but in the morning or early evening, you'll have a bench under the trees all to yourselves. This is a great place to rendezvous before dinner at one of the many restaurants in Tribeca. **Note:** Open all year from approximately 8 a.m. to dusk.

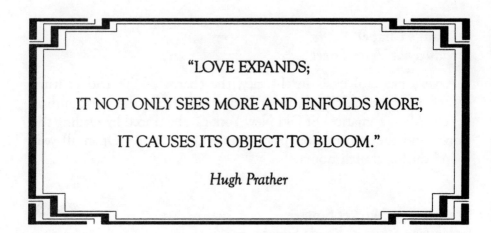

"LOVE EXPANDS;

IT NOT ONLY SEES MORE AND ENFOLDS MORE,

IT CAUSES ITS OBJECT TO BLOOM."

Hugh Prather

◆ Miscellaneous Kissing ◆

CORNER BILLIARDS
85 Fourth Avenue *at 11th Street*
(212) 995-1314
Inexpensive to Moderate

A pool hall where you can get a sturgeon-caviar platter or a filet mignon sandwich? Yup. No wonder the *New York Times* calls this the "Waldorf of pool halls." It's not seedy! But come during the week when the crowds are light and you won't be bumping behinds with too many men. Let Bruce Springstein and Van Morrison define the mood as you whiz the stripes and solids around the smooth green felt and pretend to let each other win.

◆ *Romantic Note:* They have 28 tables and a no-smoking section.

F.A.O. SCHWARZ Toy Store
767 Fifth Avenue *at 59th Street*
(212) 644-9400

F.A.O. Schwarz is not a place for just anyone. You have to have a strong yearning to wander among rows and rows of the most adorable snugly stuffed animals; a need to play with toys, computerized and otherwise, frivolous or serious; and be willing to be about six, seven, eight, or nine for at least an hour or two. This maze of a toy store is for those couples who really know how to have fun and laugh out loud, the way you did when you were children and your parents let you loose at a carnival or in a toy store. Actually, it's a shame F.A.O. Schwarz doesn't have hours exclusively for big children like us. (We wrote the management a letter suggesting that, but they haven't responded yet; it must be their nap time.)

What makes any of that romantic? Well, if you have to ask, then don't bother with this selection; go on to the others instead. For those who know what we're talking about, enjoy!

THE GRAND CENTRAL CATWALK
Grand Central Station

Enter this palatial structure from Vanderbilt Avenue and 44th Street. Behind the late 19th-century Commuter Bistro, on your left as you come in, you will find an elevator that will take you to the catwalk entrance on the top floor.

Four stories over the amphitheaterlike waiting room of Grand Central Station there is an old catwalk that spans the width of the building. Nowadays, it is hardly used (except by romantic adventurists such as yourselves) even though it provides an unusual perspective of one of New York's most outstanding pieces of architecture. Out in the middle of the walk, romantically inclined couples will feel like they are suspended in space, riding in a balloon high above the constellations twinkling against the pale blue ceiling of Grand Central. Below, arriving and departing passengers pace the marble floor, oblivious that they are extras in your movie.

◆ ***Romantic Option:*** Just outside the famous Oyster Bar is a set of arches where you can whisper sweet nothings to each other from across a crowded room. Stand in diagonally opposite corners and whisper into the wall; your voice will carry across the ceiling to your mate who will be the only one able to hear you.

A HANSOM CAB RIDE THROUGH CENTRAL PARK

The hansom cabs are parked along Central Park South between Fifth & Seventh Avenues.

My husband thought this would be great; I insisted it would be bumpy and ridiculous, but in the name of romantic research, I relented.

Early on a clear March morning, with the brisk air swirling around us and the sun warming our faces, we briefly discussed prices with our coachman. The only thing we wanted for our money was a romantic excursion, nothing more and nothing less. We climbed into the cab and settled under the heavy wool blanket. For some reason, we both started laughing. As the park opened up before us and the sounds of the city quieted, we found ourselves being lulled by the clip-clop of the horse's hooves striking the ground. About twenty minutes into the ride my husband nudged me with a smile. All right, so I was wrong. Don't rub it in.

Note: Although, as with taxi cabs, there are set prices for hansoms (they're licensed by Consumer Affairs, 212-487-4444, but even if you call to inquire what they are, it's unlikely that anyone will know). In any case, the art of bartering with a hansom cab driver can be part of the whole escapade. As a rule, do not expect a bargain on a Friday or Saturday night when the weather is clear, warm, and beautiful. On the other hand, when cabs are more plentiful than riders, you can give bargain-hunting your best shot.

PIER 17 at the SOUTH STREET SEAPORT
89 South Street *at Fulton Street*
(212) 732-7678

This one may be a bit too popular and consumer oriented for some lovers' tastes, but the calming, aquatic ringside view of the city is, well, perfect, and on a sunny day, on weekends or bright evenings during any season, everyone else in the city seems to know that, too. What you can do is find the romance in the off-hours or when the weather isn't to everyone else's liking. A foggy day can showcase the skyline in a slightly opaque, mysterious cover that you will probably be able to enjoy in relative seclusion. Or you can risk approaching the area on a balmy day or evening, past the cobblestoned, cafe-lined Fulton Street, which will be overflowing with energized, anxious singles seeking companions. If you've already found yours, so much the better; the carnival flavor can still be exhilarating.

Pier 17 is a multilevel panoply of shops and restaurants overlooking the East River. There's a selection of upscale watering-holes facing all directions, each vying for the most glorious panorama. From the bar or the terrace of **Harbour Lights, (212) 227-2800** (Expensive), three gleaming bridges highlight the landscape. Opposite, beyond the handsome interior of **Flutie's, (212) 693-0777** (Expensive), rests an impressive array of sailing vessels. As you sip drinks in the water-borne breezes, the feel is more a like a Mediterranean outpost than the clogged financial caldron across the road.

You can also take one of the many cruises which leave the Seaport most evenings during the warmer months. Call **Seaport Cruises at (212) 608-9840** for the schedule. The cruises won't float you much beyond lower Manhattan, but the sunset views of the Statue of Liberty and the skyscrapers along the shore are not to be missed. The rock 'n' roll cruise is particularly festive. Experience New Year's Eve any time of the year: a band plays the perennial soul favorites for dancing, and the deck vibrates to the rhythm of two-stepping couples. By the time you return to dock, you may not know that the music has stopped.

◆ *Romantic Note:* Most all of the restaurants at Pier 17 offer nighttime entertainment. This is just one special, vibrant face of the Seaport. If it sounds like an excess of gaiety, remember, visit in the off-hours or during inclement weather. The beauty can still be relished but with more cordial, quiet delight.

◆ *Second Romantic Note:* In the summer months, almost all of the restaurants at the Pier offer Sunday brunch with terrace seating. If you can get through the crowds or arrive early (10 a.m.) it is a wonderful place to start off summer mornings on the right soothing note.

◆ *Possible Romantic Option:* **Caroline's, (212) 233-4900** (Expensive), at the Seaport, is a well-known night spot that features some of the best comedy this town has to offer as you dine on very decent seafood and Continental cuisine. It may not be romantic, but it's definitely fun, and fun can be a nice accent to almost anything else you choose to do together.

RICHMONDTOWN RESTORATION
441 Clarke Avenue, Staten Island
(718) 351-1617

From the Verrazano-Narrows Bridge follow the signs for New Jersey west to the Richmond Road/Clove Road exit, turning left at the second traffic light after you exit onto Richmond Road. About five miles ahead, turn left onto St. Patrick's Place and follow signs to Richmondtown Parking.

Think of this as Williamsburg North. In the middle of Staten Island, you can explore the colonial way of life by wandering through the inviting grounds and well-preserved buildings of this unexpected historical oasis. Nestle by the pond and feed the ducks, watch demonstrations of old-fashioned crafts by costumed artisans, or go on a guided tour inside the fourteen handsomely restored buildings. Traveling to a restoration may sound like an academic exercise; yet, each time we stroll from the parking lot to the re-created village, we know every step draws us into a bygone era, and our fantasies and imaginations are fueled for a long time to come.

At Richmondtown, everything is people-oriented, rather than technology-centered. Sensual pleasures include the smell of bread baking in colonial brick ovens, richly detailed handmade furniture, and a gentle landscape that encourages meandering. You can even learn 18th- and 19th-century ballroom dance or hearthside cooking, and you can attend a quilting bee. For us, the most romantic events are the Friday and Saturday night concerts in the candlelit tavern, presenting folk music of the period in a rustic setting. In winter, a very real fireplace creates authentic warmth for both shows. To stay in the Early American frame of mind, have dinner before or a snack after the concert at **M. Bennett's Restaurant, (718) 979-5258**, a colonial bistro next door to the tavern. The tavern and restaurant are small, and so reservations are a must. The concerts are seasonal, ending some time in June and starting again in the fall.

ROOSEVELT ISLAND TRAMWAY
Second Avenue *at 59th Street*
(212) 832-4540

Amusement park aficionados will enjoy kissing on the Roosevelt Island Tramway. It *almost* feels like someplace else; a place where the smells of cotton candy and sounds of twisting rides permeate the atmosphere. *Almost.* Instead, the view is the East River, the 59th Street Bridge and the residential island known as Roosevelt. The thrill is yours for the price of a token (purchased at the tramway).

SKATE-A-DATE – (See American Festival Cafe, Restaurants, American)

STATEN ISLAND FERRY
Whitehall Street *at Battery Park*
(718) 390-5253

Yes, the Staten Island ferry is basically a commuter boat. But for
starry-eyed romantics, it's the love boat: a romantic cruise past some of
this city's most famous scenery. Grab an outside bench for the best
view: the majestic World Trade Towers; the inspiring Statue of Liberty;
the historic Ellis Island. The ferry is one of the best kept secrets in New
York. For less than the price of a subway token, the panoramic Manhattan skyline is yours for the night. Stand by the railing and take it all
in: the sounds of the water gently lapping against the boat, the salt air,
the light wind. Plan ahead by packing a small picnic to enjoy with the
scenery — nothing fancy, just paper cups, champagne, cheese and crackers.

◆ *Romantic Note:* Go at dusk for the most inspiring view: On
the way out of Manhattan, the skyline is set against pastel shades of
pinks and purples. The return trip sets a different mood: the postcard-
perfect view of the city's twinkling lights. Ferries leave every half hour
on weekdays; every hour on weekends.

◆ *Romantic Warning:* The best views are seen from outside the
enclosed seating area so plan your trip in nice weather. If it starts to
rain, there are seats inside. Also, keep in mind that this *is* a commuter
ship, so if you go at rush hour, it will be crowded.

WORLD YACHT CRUISE
Pier 62, West 23rd Street *at the Hudson River*
(212) 929-7090
Very Expensive
Reservations and proper dress required

We must begin by warning you that our opinion of the World Yacht
Cruise may be prejudiced by the fact that we went on the most delightful summer night of the year. Having said that, this is what it was like:
We walked across the parking lot to a gigantic cruise ship, the *New
Yorker*. We, of course, searched out the romantic seats. Had we arrived
earlier, we would have requested a window, but perhaps the seat we
took on the second level beside the rail proved to be even better as it

commanded views of both sides of the ship and the dance floor, while allowing us some measure of privacy. Soft piano music played until the 10-piece band started up and the ship left port. The music began softly with such classic favorites as "Isn't it Romantic?" but as the drinks flowed and the crowd warmed up, it became a rock and roll free-for-all by the end of the evening. The food was better than expected Continental cuisine (don't order anything too fancy or difficult to prepare). We ordered simply and were not disappointed. In fact, we were pleasantly surprised.

The crowd represented a beautiful melting pot of New Yorkers and tourists. There were some larger parties, a few older children, but mostly we were couples of every age, race, and ethnic persuasion. The outside sun deck (not to be missed because it is the best kissing spot "around" Manhattan) was alive with electric jubilation as the sweeping views of Manhattan washed past on one side and Lady Liberty practically touched us from the other. The presence of other people — many witnessing this for the first time — actually enhanced the thrill, and the bright orange sunset was the icing on the cake.

◆ *First Romantic Note:* We were on the largest vessel, but depending on the size of the crowd and, presumably, the time of the year, smaller boats are also used for the dinner cruise.

◆ *Second Romantic Note:* Lunch, brunch, and kosher cruises are also available.

◆ *Third Romantic Note:* Paid parking is available and recommended because it may be hard to find a cab afterward.

◆ *First Romantic Warning:* Expect to stand on lines to get your boarding pass and to be seated. After that, it's smooth sailing. Nevertheless, be patient and come early (15 minutes before boarding starts to get the best seats). We recommend the upper level.

◆ *Second Romantic Warning:* The price is even higher than what you'll be quoted because although the rate includes a three-course meal, all drinks and even coffee cost extra — a lot extra! Tips are not included in the price either.

◆ *Third Romantic Warning:* There are little tacky touches; for example, a photographer snaps your picture and then tries to sell it to you for $10. If that kind of thing is going to bother you, don't take this cruise, which is what it is, a three-hour cruise.

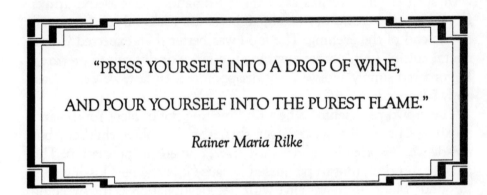

"PRESS YOURSELF INTO A DROP OF WINE,

AND POUR YOURSELF INTO THE PUREST FLAME."

Rainer Maria Rilke

◆ Museum Kissing ◆

The objects of beauty, creativity, and history in the museums of New York City can evoke such emotion that if you don't have a someone with you to embrace, you are likely to kiss a security guard. All the feelings you can imagine, and some you haven't thought of yet, are possible in this setting. If the two of you are art lovers, you'll find ecstasy in many of the museums; don't, however, expect to see everything; by the time you get through even one museum, many of the exhibits will have changed and you'll have to start all over again. There are worse things.

AMERICAN MUSEUM OF THE MOVING IMAGE
35th Avenue *at 36th Street, Astoria, Queens*
(718) 784-0077

From Manhattan take the R train to Steinway Street Station. Or call for driving directions.

For those who are passionate about Greta Garbo, Alan Ladd, Cecile B. De Mille, D.W. Griffith, Marilyn Monroe, Jimmy Stewart, and the history of Hollywood in general — this place is paradise. The exhibits are interesting and fun. Many allow the two of you to participate, but the real highlight is that your inexpensive ticket will let you see an entire day of films. Lights! Camera! Action!

FRICK COLLECTION
1 East 70th Street *at Fifth Avenue*
(212) 288-0700

If the Frick weren't always so crowded, we might go here every day. The mansion itself is remarkable, as are the many portraits by such famed artists as Van Dyck and Whistler. Roaming around such magnificence and then resting a while in the glass-ceilinged courtyard is a guaranteed heart-stirring outing, regardless of the presence of others.

THE HAYDEN PLANETARIUM
American Museum of Natural History
81st Street *at Central Park West*
(212) 769-5920
Inexpensive

Talk about great places to smooch in the dark. This ranks among the best. It may not be a starry night outside but inside it's a different story: romantic, cool (even on a hot summer's day), and quiet. A long and, best of all for our purposes, dark, hallway to the right of the entrance takes you deep into the night's mystery: experience a total eclipse of the sun; then get up-close-and-personal with fiery planets and bewitching meteorites. Welcome to the Outer Space Black Light Gallery where seducing stars fool even the foolhardy into thinking it's actually night. Or better yet, another galaxy. Go ahead; have your first kiss here. After all, Woody Allen and Diane Keaton did in the movie *Manhattan*. (You may want to rent it again after your visit: It makes you relive the moment.)

The gallery exhibit is only one of the many opportunities here for stealing private kisses. We practically guarantee no one will see you nuzzling in The Guggenheim Auditorium (next to the gallery).

The theater is one big open space surrounded by screens. Again: one big *dark* open space: much better than a movie theater! Plop on the floor cross-legged and comfortable, lean against one of the poles (or against one another) and . . . well . . . we don't have to tell you what to do. The show varies but generally deals with astronomy and space. It only lasts about five minutes so don't get too comfortable.

Where you can get comfortable is upstairs in the planetarium. For a mere $5 entrance fee, there are comfortable seats that recline towards the skies; an interesting 45-minute light show and real twinkling stars. Snatch a seat toward the back (there are no bad seats since the theater is round), sit back and enjoy the show — your own or theirs.

Note: Show times are 1:30 and 3:30, Monday through Friday, October through June; 11 a.m., 1, 2, 3, 4 and 5 p.m. on Saturdays; 1, 2, 3, 4 and 5 p.m. on Sundays. July through September shows run at 1:30, 2:30, and 3:30 during the week; 1, 2, 3 and 4 p.m. on weekends. There's a special schedule for holiday weeks.

◆ *Romantic Option:* There are other interesting exhibits surrounding the planetarium in the Hall of the Sun. Our favorite: finding out what your weight would be on other planets. Hop on the moon, Venus, Mars, Jupiter, or the sun. Better yet: Stand on the scales together and watch it tip past the 300-mark. Two heavenly bodies are definitely better than one.

THE METROPOLITAN MUSEUM OF ART
Fifth Avenue *at 82nd Street*
(212) 535-7710

Don't let the noisy, casually clad bodies sitting on the steps distract you from an incomparable romantic stroll. This place is not only magnificent but huge, taking up over four city blocks on four separate floors. Be assured that the bodies thin out as you proceed to the various galleries. When you get to the less well known exhibits you will have left the crowds far behind. After you've wandered through several of the hidden wings and observed the display of colors and design that have spanned the centuries, be sure to visit the **American Garden Court**, one of the most comfortable and beautiful areas in the museum — or in the city, for that matter. You can sit and discuss your impressions in this spacious, glass-enclosed courtyard replete with wrought-iron benches, trees, sculpture, and a surrounding balcony. At some point, make your way over to the lofty white **Petrie European Sculpture Court**. Perch yourselves among the sensually dramatic and moving limestone statues, or gaze out through the window at Central Park.

Whatever else you do, do not miss taking the elevator up to the outdoor roof garden, formally called the **Iris and B. Gerald Cantor Roof Garden**. Open May through October, this is a singular sight in Manhattan. The museum is not very tall, and thus the garden is not too high up. It hovers like a bird amongst the tree tops of Central Park. Here the park is a clean, green, quiet quilt, with Manhattan's panorama of silver skyscrapers just beyond. Here Rodin's sculptures breath in the open air (every year the exhibit changes). On a sunny day, we could spend all day here in romantic bliss.

◆ *Romantic Note:* Many people don't realize that the museum is open late on Friday and Saturday evenings. Go at those times, and it's all yours. Don't say we never gave you anything.

MUSEUM OF MODERN ART
11 West 53rd Street *between Fifth & Sixth Avenues*
(212) 708-9480

Not everyone appreciates modern art, but if modern art is your cup of tea, the Museum of Modern Art is your kettle of tea. From Dali to Picasso to Van Gogh here you'll find an unrivaled display. We dare you to gaze together for ten minutes at *Starry Night* and not kiss! But even if you have no interest whatsoever in modern art, you'll enjoy drinking tea (and coffee), discussing your opinions, and of course kissing, in the museum's outdoor **Sculpture Garden Cafe.**

WHITNEY MUSEUM OF AMERICAN ART
945 Madison Avenue *at 75th Street*
(212) 570-3600

An eclectic American art museum, the spacious Whitney now has an added treat: **Sarabeth's at the Whitney.** Here American food and American art go hand and hand: a simple tall dining room for contemplation and an exchange of creative ideas that a walk through the many galleries of the museum will elicit; a place to dine on savory afternoon tea, lunch, or the scrumptious brunch that Sarabeth's has made famous. In good weather, dine outdoors beside a giant ball of twine in the sculpture garden courtyard.

◆ *Romantic Note:* When touring the different levels of the museum, don't take the elevators or you'll miss some great kissing opportunities on the stairs. **Note:** The museum opens at 11:00 on Saturdays and Sundays and closes a half hour after the restaurant. Restaurant hours: Tuesday 1–7:30; Wednesday through Friday 11:00–4:30; Saturday 10:00–4:30; Sunday 10:00–5:30; Closed Monday.

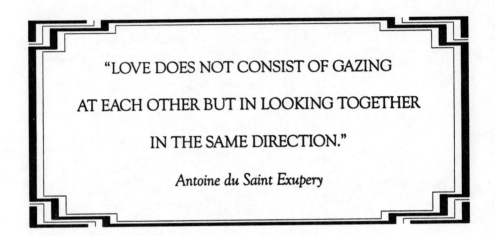

"LOVE DOES NOT CONSIST OF GAZING

AT EACH OTHER BUT IN LOOKING TOGETHER

IN THE SAME DIRECTION."

Antoine du Saint Exupery

Worth The Trip

◆ Connecticut ◆

BERTRAND'S RESTAURANT FRANCAIS
253 Greenwich Avenue, Greenwich
(203) 661-4618
Expensive to Very Expensive French Cuisine

The restaurant is in the center of town, but call for directions to be safe.

As you pass through the door of Bertrand's coral stucco exterior you will immediately be taken by the elegance and grandeur of this three-level restaurant, glowing beneath a unique tile-and-glass dome ceiling. The peach brick walls and the light radiating from above add to the bright, chic atmosphere. The tables overlooking the front windows are a particularly romantic spot where you can enjoy the atmosphere but keep your privacy as well.

Bertrand's prides itself on its feats of culinary excellence. The aromas emanating from the kitchen add a certain panache to your entire evening. If you are looking for truly authentic, four-star French cuisine, Bertrand's is surely the place. And if you happen to be in Greenwich on Thursdays, there is a prix fixe menu that highlights a particular region of France.

◆ *Romantic Option:* **Jean Louis, 61 Lewis Street, (203) 622-8450,** is a small and cozy French restaurant just around the corner from Bertrand's. The coral stucco motif of the exterior continues inside with coral wallpaper. There are only a handful of tables, and there is a decidedly less impressive atmosphere here than at the neighboring Bertrand's, but the menu more than makes up for any stylistic gaps.

THE COTSWOLD INN

76 Myrtle Avenue, Westport
(203) 226-3766
Very Expensive

Call for directions.

The Cotswold Inn is a beautiful bed & breakfast that is both authentic and charming. It is a plush place to immerse yourself for the weekend. The house is extremely comfortable with exquisite antique furniture and four-poster beds. One room even has a working fireplace. The bedrooms are quite private and are decorated with fine prints and fabrics. Breakfast is a deluxe Continental presentation of fresh muffins and pastries, and complimentary wine and snacks are available in the early evening. Although more expensive than most bed & breakfasts in the area, The Cotswold provides a romantic ambience that the others lack.

THE HOMESTEAD INN

20 Field Point Road, Greenwich
(203) 869-7500
Moderate

Take I-95 to Exit 3 in Greenwich. Turn left at the bottom of the exit and proceed to the second light where you turn left onto Horse Neck Lane. At the end of Horse Neck Lane, turn left onto Field Point Road. The inn is one-quarter mile down on your right.

The Homestead is a traditional Connecticut farmhouse built in 1799. With its setting of trees and tranquil sloping lawns it would be hard to ignore the seclusion this place has to offer. The rooms in the main house were not our favorites, the furnishings in several of them seemed a bit second-hand instead of antique, and the televisions seem out of place in all of them. The most charming rooms by far are in the wing called the Independent House. Each suite is outfitted with a canopy bed, bright fabrics, and large windows that open onto a deck with white wicker furniture where you can enjoy the view and peace of a summer evening.

All the rooms have private baths, and a delightful breakfast is served in the elegant dining room.

The inn's appeal is greatly enhanced by **La Grange**, the restaurant located in the main house. The chef here will dazzle you with his classic French cuisine while you indulge yourself in the relaxed, elegant country setting.

◆ *Romantic Alternative:* **The Stanton House Inn, 76 Maple Avenue, (203) 869-2110**, (Inexpensive), is a white farmhouse built in 1840 and now part of a bustling Greenwich neighborhood. Although the hallways are plain and a bit rundown, the rooms are actually rather bright and inviting. Each room has a wetbar and most have private baths. The service is extremely friendly and welcoming. Breakfast is a complimentary Continental buffet. Although the Stanton House is located in town and does not offer the seclusion of The Homestead, its simple warmth can provide a great stay.

◆ *Romantic Option:* **Brett's Restaurant and Bar, (203) 629-1114**, (Inexpensive), is an option for dinner if you are in the mood for a more casual dining experience. It has a friendly, warm atmosphere that is stylish and potentially romantic, as well as good Italian cuisine (pasta, interesting pizzas, etc.) that is more than reasonably priced. Most evenings they have live music. It changes nightly, and so you can expect anything from country to jazz.

THE INN AT LONGSHORE **Dining Room**   ◆
260 South Compo Road, Westport
(203) 226-3316
Expensive Continental Cuisine

From the Connecticut Turnpike take Exit 17 to Saugatuck. Continue straight through two traffic lights to the first stop sign and then turn left on Riverside Avenue. Turn right over the bridge onto Route 136. At the next light turn right again on Compo Road South and continue for one-half mile to the the inn.

The restaurant here, surrounded by a premiere golf course, is a refreshing place to enjoy a drink or dinner together, regardless of your handicap. The dining room faces a beautiful vantage point overlooking the Connecticut shoreline where boaters and windsurfers whisk by in the summer, and the quiet is all about in the winter. You can eat on the terrace just inches above the water. There is a fine selection of seafood and pasta and, though not exceptional, the food is good and consistent.

◆ *Romantic Note:* If you are a jazz lover, the inn has live music every Friday and Saturday night, but this also attracts quite a crowd. If you are looking for quiet, intimate dining, perhaps earlier in the week is your best bet. But for the view, this spot is perfect at any time.

ROGER SHERMAN INN Restaurant
195 Oenoke Ridge, New Canaan
(203) 966-4541
Very Expensive French Cuisine

Call for directions.

The dining room at the Roger Sherman Inn is one of the most engaging places we've encountered. The coral walls, floral tapestry draped chairs, soft lighting, radiating fireplaces, and outdoor terrace at this refurbished country mansion all combine to create an elegant and inviting setting. Traditional French cuisine, featuring such delights as duck with pear-and-Cassis sauce and Grand Marnier souffle, is expertly prepared and served. Out here in the hills of Connecticut, immerse yourselves in a sumptuous evening for two.

STONEHENGE INN AND RESTAURANT
Route 7, Ridgefield
(203) 438-6511
Moderate to Expensive

From the Merritt Parkway, exit onto Route 7 and look for the sign to Stonehenge on the left side of the road.

Stonehenge Inn is a stately white country farmhouse with green shutters and doors, nestled into a forested backdrop, set upon ten acres of grounds that are centered around a pond dotted with geese and swans. The main inn emanates a warmth that continues into the restaurant on the lower level. The dining area is framed by floor-to-ceiling French doors and has a canopied terrace overlooking the aforementioned pond. Although the atmosphere is somewhat country-clubbish (the tables are all situated in the center of one room), the view is still pleasant and the food quite good. Perhaps after dinner you'll consider a walk through the lovely grounds to complete your country escape.

If you decide to spend the night, which would be a wonderfully romantic decision, the rooms are nicely furnished and comfortable, particularly the suites. All the rooms have private baths and air-conditioning. Each is ideal for those who need a weekend of solitude. There is an in-ground swimming pool for guests in the summer, and hiking trails. In the morning, breakfast is served either in your room or on the terrace.

WEST LANE INN
22 West Lane, Ridgefield
(203) 438-7323
Moderate to Expensive

From New York take Route 684, or, in Connecticut take Route 7 off the Merritt Parkway. Exit on Route 35. Continue to the town of Ridgefield. The inn is on Route 35 at the south end of town.

This is an impressive B&B. There are two handsome buildings here; one is a formal Victorian mansion, the other is a newer addition that rests on an immaculate lawn scattered with trees. The rooms are quite large and nicely done, particularly in the main house, although most are rather simple and more like a hotel than what you might expect to find at a country inn. A simple Continental breakfast is served on the porch arranged with wicker chairs and glass tables.

◆ *Romantic Note:* Unfortunately, we were 15 minutes late for breakfast which meant we were charged for what we ate; we thought this was a rather strict policy for a B&B, but it wouldn't stop us from coming back.

◆ *Romantic Suggestion:* We stayed at the West Lane Inn primarily because we didn't want to drive back to the city after dining at **The Inn at Ridgefield,** next door at **20 West Lane, (203) 438-8282,** (Expensive). If you like and can afford fine dining, don't go to Ridgefield without sharing a delicious evening here, where Continental food is apparently prepared by angels and served in gorgeous New England style. Whether your meal includes rack of lamb or succulent Dover sole, finish it off with flaming crepes suzettes.

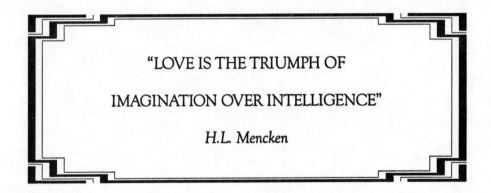

"LOVE IS THE TRIUMPH OF

IMAGINATION OVER INTELLIGENCE"

H.L. Mencken

◆ Long Island ◆

Note: *The descriptions that follow are loosely arranged from west to east heading away from Manhattan.*

Traveling to Long Island is an unconditional romantic must, because, to put it simply, there is everything here two people in love could want to share. Part of the island is a series of cosmopolitan towns that feed directly into New York City. As the miles take you farther east, most memories of modern civilization are left far behind. This is one huge land mass, resplendent with forest, quaint fishing villages, mile upon mile of winding roads, sandy white beaches, explosive ocean surf, and acre after acre of very exclusive, prime east coast real estate.

The variety of terrain and culture may make it difficult for you to decide where to go first. The North and the South Shores have very different characters, but which one to visit will often come down to a coin toss. Whether you're looking for a day trip or a long lazy weekend, Long Island has what you want — except for an abundance of romantic overnight accommodations. They are not plentiful in Nassau County or the western parts of Suffolk, although there is always a place to stay. Sometimes you may have to settle for a standard motor lodge or hotel, that is, until you get close to the Hamptons and Montauk.

SANDS POINT NATURE PRESERVE
Middleneck Road, Port Washington
(516) 883-1612
Hours and tours change throughout the year. Call for current information.

Straight from Manhattan, take the Midtown Tunnel to the Long Island Expressway (495) to Searingtown Road (Exit 36N). Go north on Searingtown Road which first becomes Port Washington Boulevard and then becomes Middleneck Road. Follow signs to Sands Point Nature Preserve. It's on the right on Middleneck Road, just north of the village of Port Washington and six miles north of the LIE.

This 216-acre preserve successfully conspires to seduce nature lovers with trails, ponds, nature walks and talks, mansions, a castle, and many bunny rabbits. The preserve's brochure might sound like heavenly Greek to tired New Yorkers: "Around the pond, large shrub honeysuckles, fast-growing trees like black cherry, ailanthus and black locust, and thick bittersweet, wisteria, grape, and Japanese honeysuckle vines combine to form a dense protective underbrush . . . warblers migrating in the spring and fall . . . cedar waxwings, scarlet tanagers, and robins . . . the northern waterthrush . . . eastern kingbird, various flycatchers, belted kingfisher, mallard, black duck, and Canada goose. Between the pond and the shoreline is a meadow filled with wildflowers including soapwort, yarrow, wild parsnip, goldenrod, trumpet creeper, milkweed, moth mullein, heath aster, and muliflora. Thick sumac and bramble patches provide both food and cover for wildlife including rabbits, pheasants, catbirds and song sparrows."

Many, but not all, of the trails are self-guided. Be sure to take the one that puts you on the beach (#5 Shoreline Trail). Hidden by brush, you're not even aware you're near a beach when you're walking on the grounds. Note that this is not a swimming beach, but the beachcombing can't be beat. The pond trail, too, is not to be missed. We don't usually go in for guided tours, but we throughly enjoyed the one we took of Falaise, an ornate Normandy-style manor house built as a home on the bluff in 1923 by Harry F. Guggenheim. Stand on the deck overlooking the water and imagine what it's like to live in such a place. In the back there are gardens and a pool. What are you waiting for? While you're sitting here, all that is waiting for you!

◆ *Romantic Suggestions:* Leave in time to take a sidetrip to **Shore Road in Port Washington** where you'll find much activity and some fine restaurants. Stop at the **North Hempstead Town Harbor** and walk on the dock. Right beside it is the aptly named **Sunset Park** with benches facing west over the water where boats come, go, and stay, and swans glide ceremoniously around them. Less than a mile north on Shore Road is **Baxter Pond Park**, a little duck pond with short walks through the woods. Somewhat farther north, overlooking scenic Mill Pond, is a most excellent and reasonably priced Indian restaurant: **Diwan at 37 Shore Road, Port Washington, (516) 767-7878**. The decor at this giant, green, pink-walled house is interesting and exotic, but the main attraction is the artfully prepared food.

ROSLYN and the ROSLYN DUCK POND

Twenty miles northeast of Manhattan. Take the Long Island Expressway (495) to Exit 37 north. Once on the service road, pass Willis Avenue and proceed to Roslyn Road where you'll turn left. This becomes Main Street. Watch for the signs indicating Roslyn Park which will direct you through the village center and straight to the Duck Pond.

Well-known and dutifully visited for generations, the Roslyn Duck Pond in **Roslyn Park** somehow has retained a serenity that will have you falling in love all over again. We were first there about 30 years ago when Roslyn was far less developed and there were not quite as many ducks (perhaps they have come to find it romantic, too), but surprisingly, the town feels even more pristine and lovely than we remember. The handsome rolling lawn is nibbled neat and trim by resident aquatic birds who often provide great natural entertainment. There is plenty of room for couples to wander in, a 1744 paper mill to amble through, and a small bandstand pagoda and wooden footbridge spanning the channeled stream that leads to the three levels of the pond, before you reach Hempstead Harbor on the outskirts of town.

The park is in a valley nestled between two well-timbered hills; in the valley, stone dwellings dating from 1690 coexist with inspired contemporary homes. All of Roslyn is steeped in history, and a stroll through the town park can help unburden your thoughts so that you can dwell on the matter at hand; to wit, each other. The town itself is as entrancing as it was years ago, and Main Street has a handful of dining options that allow for a brief respite from your journey.

◆ *Romantic Warning:* There are benches and picnic tables at the Duck Pond, but even more plentiful are trees to shelter you from the sun and heat. However, beware of territorial geese that have been known to try and claim their land back from those visiting their part of the world. And, although no dogs are allowed in the park, the birds themselves contribute noticeable enrichment to the soil. That's probably why everything is so green, but watch where you sit and walk.

◆ *Romantic Option:* A very lovely afternoon can be spent at the **Nassau County Fine Arts Center**, which features a **Museum of Fine Arts** and the **William Cullen Bryant Preserve**. The Center/Museum is located just to the east and north of Roslyn, off Northern Boulevard (Route 25A). Here, find the **Frick Estate**, a Georgian mansion with art galleries and 145 acres of well-manicured lawns, meadows, ponds, and glens. The grounds are also home to outdoor sculpture and formal gardens, but what is most remarkable about the site is that it has retained the character of perpetual leisure that the landed gentry so enjoyed in a more loving, less hasty time.

THE CHALET
One Railroad Avenue, Roslyn
(516) 621-7975
Moderate

Twenty miles northeast of Manhattan. Take the Long Island Expressway (495) to Exit 37. Once on the service road, pass Willis Avenue and proceed to Roslyn Road and turn left. In fewer than one-and-a-half miles, turn left immediately after passing under the railroad bridge. The restaurant is a few yards up the hill on the right.

Not many restaurants have it all. The Chalet comes close. Its greatest virtue is its intimate warmth. Unaffected and unpretentious and set on a wooded hillside, the Chalet has a deserved reputation as that rare dining spot with food, service, decor and location that add up to a desirable evening out. The Chalet's building is a storybook creation, dating from the 1800's, of stone and brick with gingerbreadlike details. Inside is uncluttered Victoriana of mirrors, quilts, hanging antiques, and bentwood chairs. In warmer months, the second-floor outdoor balcony opens to extra seating for dining under the trees and stars, and out here there are plenty of both. The Chalet is not fancy, but the elements meld, surpassing all of your out-of-town romantic expectations.

The service is attentive — which means they attend to your privacy as well as your dining; they're friendly without being intrusive. Classical or light jazz background music adds nicely to your sentimental feelings. The menu offers the familiar, blended tastefully with the imaginative; a recent appetizer of smoked venison sausage slices with a spicy black bean sauce topped by red peppers, scallions and sour cream, was fabulous. You may be tempted to try one or many of the other restaurants in Roslyn and nearby. Some are better decorated. Some are quite famous and expensive, and a number boast historical locations or harbor views; but none treats your heart as well as does the Chalet.

◆ *Romantic Option:* After dinner, walk through the historic preservation district of Roslyn, down the hill and past the Roslyn Duck Pond, to window shop, and have a drink at the **George Washington Manor, 1305 Old Northern Boulevard, (516) 621-1200** (the 1753 Onderdonk House where George really did spend the night). There you can tarry most romantically on the sublime outdoor patio, which features yet another Roslyn pond, where swim three ducks named Moe, Larry, and Curly.

GARDEN CITY HOTEL
7th Street, Garden City
(516) 747-3000
Very, Very Expensive

Take the Midtown tunnel to the Long Island Expressway (495) east to exit 34 south (New Hyde Park Road). Turn right and continue three miles to Stewart Avenue. Turn left on Stewart and go three miles to the end. Make a quick right and then a left into the parking lot.

Picture this suite: two large separate rooms with two *completely* private terraces with lounge chairs, two marble baths, a fully stocked wet bar area, cushy couches, a fireplace, a fully stocked kitchen, every amenity, terry robes on request, antique furniture, and a modest amount of pink neon lighting. Sound inviting? It is. The problem? The price for such an affair goes off the scale. The two of you can fly to Bermuda and back for the standard rate. A merely very expensive room is very much like a typical Hilton or Hyatt hotel room — very nice but nothing special. There are a few junior suites that fall somewhere in between, but they are very expensive as well. Weekend and special packages are possible for some rooms. So let's say that in the affordable range, this can be a great weekend escape for people looking to get away from the kids for a night.

The hotel, however, has a score of appealing offerings for active couples: a very decent restaurant, a health club with Jacuzzi and pool (massages available), an outdoor sun deck, a club for disco dancing, a piano in the lounge, tennis and golf nearby, two leisure passes for access to Long Island county parks (such as nearby **Eisenhower Park**). This is opulence Long Island style.

Note: Their **Polo Grill** is famous for its bountiful Sunday brunch with ice sculptures. Their very elegant Giorgio's restaurant has temporarily closed. Hopefully, it will reopen sometime soon.

OLD WESTBURY GARDENS
Old Westbury Road
(516) 333-0048

Take the Long Island Expressway (495) to Glen Cove Road (Exit 39 south). Follow the service road eastbound for a little over a mile. Turn right onto Old Westbury Road. Continue one-quarter mile to the Gardens.

"Let's take some time to smell the roses," urged my mate, reminding us we needed respite from workaholic New York City life. He knew just the place for restoration: Old Westbury Gardens. This hundred-acre haven is a typical English country estate, plunked improbably in the middle of Nassau County. And lucky for us! At Old Westbury, we not only smelled the roses, but reveled in the scent and sensation of walking through the woods on a carpet of pine needles while watching the swans glide on the lake and fat geese waddle on thick emerald lawns. There's a grove of wooden tables in this sylvan setting for bring-your-own picnics. For the less prepared a snack bar provides light fare.

Built at the turn of the century as a private residence, the Gardens are home to a stately mansion surrounded by sculpted gardens and woodlands. The interior of the house, with its 18th-century antiques and fine paintings by Gainsborough, Constable, Sargent, and others, is well worth the tour. But the grounds and walkways dotted with benches and a profusion of flora is the romantic part. Settle onto a bench at the **Temple of Love,** among its fluted stone columns beneath a lacy wrought-iron canopy, and gaze like we did at the swans and ducks on the lake.

The Gardens are open Wednesday through Sunday, from late April through October. There is also a series of **Picnic Pops Concerts** during these months, beginning at 7 p.m., for a charge of $6.00.

PLANTING FIELDS ARBORETUM

Planting Fields Road, Oyster Bay
(516) 922-9201 or (516) 922-9206

From New York City take the Long Island Expressway (495) to exit 39 North (Glen Cove Road). Go north on Glen Cove Road to 25A (Northern Boulevard). Turn right, heading east on 25A. Turn left (north) onto Wolver Hollow Road. At the end, turn right onto Chicken Valley Road. The iron gate entrance to the Arboretum is about one mile on the right. Pay a nominal admission charge at the gate.

I wouldn't go out with anybody who wouldn't enjoy going here for a date. This just may be the most romantic place you'll ever see. Your first reaction will be to call this vast acreage a park, albeit an idyllic park, but it's not really a park at all; an arboretum now, it is the former baronial estate of a man named Coe. What makes it so sublime is the picture-perfect landscape. Surrounded by imposing iron fences, the grounds are filled with trails and nature walks, every kind of exotic tree from around the world, flower gardens, shrubs of every imaginable variety, spouting fountains, shimmering pools, and rolling hills where displays of radiant native and exotic flowers cover the area in a kaleidoscope of colors. This is an unparalleled collection of the best Mother Nature, and mother architecture, have to offer. The arboretum is so large that it is almost impossible not to wander into at least one secluded area, even at the peak of summer.

The winter months may send send snowy blasts across their windows, but like a giant, lush Garden of Eden, the many greenhouses at the Planting Fields are a world where the mysteries of color and life do not cease. Every turn of the head will bring something spellbinding into view. **Note:** The fragrant orchids and lilies are in bloom from December to mid-March.

The mansion itself, **Coe Hall**, one of the nation's finest, hosts concerts and other special events. Call **(516) 922-0479** for the schedule of events.

SEA CLIFF

From either the Long Island Expressway (495) or Northern State Parkway, take the Glen Cove Road exit north. Continue on Glen Cove Road past 25A (Northern Boulevard) for about another five miles until you see the Sea Cliff sign. Bear right there and make an immediate left (at the first light) onto Sea Cliff Avenue. Follow this for a little over two miles – up the hill, beyond the Long Island Railroad tracks into the town itself.

Sea Cliff is a small town where the atmosphere has been the same for generations, where people warm themselves by the same hearths as did their grandparents. Replete with many small intimate streets, it is a place for walking. There is something different at every turn — flowers tumbling over wooden fences, wildflower gardens, and salty ocean views.

Stop in the town for a leisurely afternoon of browsing and antiques shopping along Sea Cliff Avenue. You can have lunch at **Once Upon A Moose** at the corner of **Sea Cliff Avenue and Central Avenue, (516) 676-9304**, (Inexpensive), or, kitty-cornered from it, load up for your picnic at **Arata's, (516) 671-0290**, and head off for the beach. You could stop at **Prospect Park** at the end of town. It's known for a spectacular view of the harbor with the Connecticut shoreline in the distance and unsurpassed sunsets where the blaze of the passing day sets the water on fire. Or turn right on Prospect and then left down the hill on Cliff Way, all the while overlooking the water, to the benches of **Sea Cliff Park** — just a few feet from the shoreline.

COLD SPRING HARBOR

(Not to be confused with Cold Spring, New York.) Follow the directions to Sea Cliff, then drive south on Sea Cliff Avenue to the end, making a short right and left onto Glen Cove Road. This will take you to 25A (Northern Boulevard). Turn east for 13 miles from the Glen Cove intersection where 25A descends towards the waters of Cold Spring Harbor.

The drive to Cold Spring Harbor is a wonderful excursion into a countrified serene world. As you head east, you'll drive past fine old houses, woods, nurseries, horse farms, winding side roads, and rural land. The town itself, or rather Main Street, is a small-shop-browser's heaven. Many of the houses in Cold Spring Harbor were built during the prime of an 1850s whaling boom. The harbor is the frame for the entire setting, and it has an aura of languid beauty. After filling yourselves with the sights and sounds of this town and cruising through the many crafts, antiques, and crystal shops, there is something to be said for stopping in at Merrill Lynch Realty and laying hands on some of this fabulous property — or at least thinking about it.

◆ *Romantic Note:* **The Country Kitchen, 55 Main Street, (516) 692-5655,** (Inexpensive), has been a luncheon favorite for decades and **The Old Whaler Restaurant, 105 Harbor Road, (516) 367-3166,** (Moderate), across from the harbor, has withstood the test of years.

NORTHPORT

Follow the directions to Cold Spring Harbor. Another eight miles eastward on 25A (Northern Boulevard) will bring you to Northport. Make a left at Woodbine Road, which will bring you to the foot of Main Street.

On your way to Northport, depending on how much time you have, you may want to stop along the way at Huntington or Centerport, perhaps for some sightseeing at the planetarium or the **Vanderbilt Estate.** Otherwise, the scenic drive to Northport has some visual pleasures of its own and, given that you can't do everything, one destination at a time is not unreasonable. **Cow Park,** in the center of town, is picturesquely situated on the harbor where sailboats rest peacefully in the water. You can lounge on the grass and take in a summer concert at the gazebo.

To really put the glow on this excursion you need to go the extra mile(s) and drive past **Main Street on Woodbine,** past some exquisite beachside Victorian mansions, turning right up the James Street hill and left on Ocean Avenue to the end where you head left and down to the village of **Asharoken.** Here is an extraordinary drive along a road separating the Long Island Sound from Huntington Bay — a breath-taking and tranquil stretch with beach houses and sea birds and cool ocean breezes. Drive on past the Coast Guard Station road and follow the signs to the beach. **Hobart Beach** is a sandy finger protecting a tiny harbor and pointing out between the bay and the sound. Shed your shoes and take that long rejuvenating walk amid the beach grasses and jetty boulders and finish out a rare, unspoiled day in relative privacy together in your own corner of the world.

THE JOHN PEEL ROOM at the ISLAND INN
Old Country Road at *Roosevelt Raceway, Westbury*
(516) 228-9500
Moderate to Expensive Dinner
Moderate Brunch

Take the Long Island Expressway (495) to Exit 38 heading south to the North-ern State Parkway. Take Exit 31A heading south until you reach Old Country Road, turning east. The inn will be on your right.

Brunch at the John Peel Room is a delightful way to transform an ordinary Sunday brunch into an enchanting Victorian dining experi-ence. As you enter the large dining room, you will be greeted by the plaintive strumming of live harp music. The decor is warm and New England cozy, the high-back chairs wide and comfortable, and the paintings all about help to create the aura that is so inviting and so very romantic. In the middle of the first dining area are large floral center-pieces, and at the rear is an open hearth where one can see the diligent workings of the kitchen.

Before you even embark on your meal, you can sit in the lounge on cushy couches in front of a glowing fireplace. Once the meal begins, sit back and together watch the parade of pastries, fluffy gourmet omelets, giant apple pancakes with lingonberries, quiches and crepes served courteously all around. Choosing is the only difficult part of being here. If you do nothing else (besides kiss in between courses) save room for dessert. If you are a chocolate lover, you'll find the triple chocolate cake irresistible, but we prefer the tipsy sherry trifle, usually served in one big, creamy bowl if two or more order it.

Note: Dinner here is a treat as well as brunch.

◆ **Romantic Suggestion:** If you want to turn this morning event into an evening getaway, the adjoining **Island Inn** has many lovely rooms.

CORAL HOUSE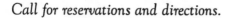
70 Milburn Avenue
Baldwin, NY
(516) 223-6500
Moderate American/Continental

Call for reservations and directions.

The window seats provide a pretty lakeside view complete with ducks, geese, and weeping willow trees. These are obtained on a first come first served basis, and it's worth making a special effort to get one. With its clean country decor, wood paneling, many skylights, fresh flowers, tables set with pink linen and candles, old photos and walls of books, the Coral House is a fine Long Island kissing locale. Order turkey and you'll think it's Thanksgiving for two — all year round.

Note: Do not imagine that "Scenic Milburn Lake," bordered on one side by a heavily trafficked road, is a romantic destination separate from the restaurant. It is extremely scenic when viewed from the restaurant, but it is far less so up close. Although we like to take a stroll around the lake before or after dinner, be warned that you may have to avert your eyes from some unappetizing collections of pollution. Also, depending on your taste, the following is either a promise or a warning: They play light FM music in the background.

◆ **Romantic Warning:** Many weddings and other events take place at the Coral House. Unless you're an invited guest, it's not advisable to visit the restaurant when there is a noisy celebration in progress. Call ahead and ask when you make reservations. During the week is the best time.

NAUTICAL MILE
Freeport

*Take the Long Island Expressway (495) east to the Cross Island Parkway
south. Exit at the Southern State Parkway east to the Meadowbrook Parkway
south. Follow the Meadowbrook to exit M9 Merrick Road going west. Drive
one mile and turn left on Guy Lombardo Avenue. Turn right at the fifth traffic
light (Front Street). Go one block and make a left on Woodcleft Avenue. Visit
the whole length of Woodcleft Avenue.*

Considering that Long Island really is an island, you'd expect to see
more sea shanty atmosphere everywhere, but it all seems to be all
concentrated here on the Nautical Mile. A rough and ready place to
visit after a day at Jones Beach, this is Long Island's more rustic version
of City Island — an authentic waterfront with fishing boats coming and
going all day. The main charm of the Nautical Mile is that it was not
designed to attract tourists. Real seafarers come here to buy yachts, to
buy parts for them, to have them serviced, to dock them, and to dry-
dock them. The main drag, therefore, is not always aesthetically pleasing, but it gets nicer and nicer as the sun goes down, and there are
many gregarious waterside restaurants on this one-mile stretch of land.
Most of the boats you'll see are serious fishing boats packed almost
exclusively with burly men, but every third boat or so is an excursion
boat filled with couples and other fun-loving folk. If the sea calls to
you, you can sign up for a scenic boat ride, a sunset cruise, a moonlight
boat ride with dancing, or a brunch or dinner cruise on the **Poop Deck
Dock (Sunset Cruises, 23 Woodcleft Avenue, 516-623-5712).**
   Note: Contrary to our usual advice to avoid the crowds, the Nautical
Mile is at its salty best on Saturday nights in the summer. If you're
prepared to have fun sipping cocktails as you wait for your outdoor
picnic table, you'll find that mingling with the crowd is part of the fun.

Michael's Ristorante
301 Woodcleft Avenue, Nautical Mile
(516) 867-2121
Moderately priced Italian

For some saucy Italian food in a pretty environment, try Michael's. It's less family oriented than many of the other eateries on the Nautical Mile. Done all in pink, the inside is a romantic and quiet spot to share a meal. The waterview tables, unfortunately, are built for parties of four, which makes this a good place for double-dating. Outside is a pleasant and quiet, no-frills covered deck with white patio tables and plastic chairs, and of course, that same pretty view. If you want to experience a few places on the Nautical Mile, have drinks and appetizers on Michael's patio, and then go for dinner at Otto's. See the next entry.

Note: Light FM music plays inside and out.

Otto's Sea Grill
271 Woodcleft Avenue, Nautical Mile
(516) 378-9480
Moderate Seafood (Expensive if you order lobster)
Cash Only

Lighten up and take a breather. Whoever said romance had to be candlelight and waiters in tuxedos never saw Otto's, where balmy nights and summer fun go hand in hand. Very casual, noisy, and crowded, Otto's is our favorite eatery on the stretch. Just your basic seafood, it's moderately priced and pretty good. But the real attraction is the experience of being at Otto's. We love to dine outside in the summer surrounded by geraniums on the sun deck and listen to the talented guitarist sing and strum James Taylor and Jonathan Edwards songs ("Lay around the shanty barn and put a good buzz on") in the visible but separate bar area — a real bar scene. Well, blow me down. Is that Popeye and Olyve Oyl at the next table? The tumultuous fun is countered by the quiet of the docked boats behind us rocking gently in the wake of the many passing party boats, fishing boats, sightseeing cruises, and private yachts.

Note: Come in the summer and sit as close to the water as they'll put you (you can't reserve special tables; seating is first come, first served). Live soft music plays inside (and it's kind of nice, but not nearly as nice as sitting outside). Weekdays are much quieter, but go on the weekend for the whole experience. Don't eat dessert. See the next entry.

Sea Cream Cafe
147A Woodcleft Avenue, Nautical Mile
(516) 867-2232

This looks like an ordinary take-out gourmet ice cream storefront, but my dears, there's a surprise awaiting you out back — a tiny garden cafe overlooking the water. Sea Cream does serve tasty meals if you're in the mood for an inexpensive sandwich, burger or fish fry, but don't miss coming here after dinner. This is THE place for ice cream, cappuccino, and late night snacks.

THE WEST WINDS YACHT CLUB
104 East Bedell Street, Freeport
(516) 546-4545
Moderate to Expensive Continental, specializing in seafood

Take the Long Island Expressway (495) to the Meadowbrook Parkway south to Merrick Road west (Exit M-9). Turn left on to Mill Road to the end. Make a left on to South Main Street and continue one-half mile. Turn left at the first stop sign on to East Bedell Street straight to waterfront.

Here's a place to go if you get to the Nautical Mile and it's much too crowded or it just doesn't suit your mood or taste. The only thing is, it's very important to go here only when there's no wedding or party going on. We love going to weddings as much as the next person, but there's nothing romantic about sipping soup while "Jeremiah Was a Bullfrog" blasts in your ears — even if you are in a very charming room with a very pretty view.

ROBERT MOSES STATE PARK

Almost fifty miles from Manhattan. Take the Long Island Expressway (495) to Exit 53, which is the Sagtikos Parkway, south to Robert Moses Causeway. Before reaching the Causeway, you will actually be on the westbound Southern State Parkway for about one mile; it will then intersect with the Causeway. Don't let this confuse you; just follow the signs.

For more than nine months of the year, the parking lots at Long Island's beaches — not to mention the beaches themselves — are virtually empty. Perhaps people don't realize that the ocean operates year round. It's to your romance's great advantage, though, that the masses seem to find surf and sand suitable only for swimming and sunning. Throughout the year, excepting those hot and beach-perfect days in July and August, and on occasion June, couples can find virtually complete privacy — for miles — under an enormous sky untouched by concrete and commercialism.

The approach to the park is a sight to behold. Three bridges, one an authentic drawbridge, must be crossed before reaching the entrance on the western end of Fire Island. On a clear day, the view is vast. There is an abundance of everything restless surf lovers could want. The spectrum of blues ebb and flow into each other as the waves undulate on the horizon. The shore line seems to go on forever, and its creative uses are many: hunt for shells, walk along the water's edge, build castles, bury your feet in the cool damp sand, or just sit and talk — or not, the ocean can speak for both of you most eloquently. Don't leave without taking it all in — the skittering birds, the salty fresh air, and the constant, raging rhythm of the waves. The footprints you leave will always be there, even after the waters and wind have washed over them.

◆ ***Romantic Note:*** Robert Moses State Park is less well known, less developed, and half the size (it covers a mere 1,000 acres) of the more popular Captree, Gilgo, and Jones Beach state parks, fifteen miles due west. Robert Moses State Park offers the same fine ocean sand, colorful shells, and turbulent surf Long Island is famous for, but the fact that it is on rustic, roadless Fire Island lends this acreage a great deal of privacy. In fact, most people who know of Robert Moses Park realize it is on Fire Island and incorrectly assume it to be accessible only by the seasonal passenger-only ferry that carries sun worshippers to summer rentals. Of course, many ocean lovers choose to visit Jones Beach just because it is developed and provides more things for the kids to do. But we understand that's not what you are looking for. . . .

◆ *Romantic Option:* If you want to hike through salt marshland in a somewhat more secluded and composed setting, visit **Tobay Beach Bird & Game Sanctuary**, which is on **Ocean Parkway** (on the bay side) nine miles west of the Causeway.

BAYARD CUTTING ARBORETUM
Montauk Highway, Oakdale
(516) 581-1002

Fifty miles from Manhattan. Take the Long Island Expressway (495) to Exit 53 (Sagtikos Parkway) south, to Southern State Parkway east, to Exit 45E (Route 27A). The Arboretum is less than one mile beyond the exit ramp.

This oasis of beauty and quiet can feel like your own private retreat while you explore its carefully planned and meticulously maintained grounds. The area projects a European flavor with its setting on the cliffs of the pastoral Connetquot River. Graceful shade trees rise from the banks of its mirrored surface and black-faced swans float languidly by. There are plentiful, handsomely crafted wrought-iron benches overlooking all of it. There are six marked walks you may take, although you'll no doubt prefer to stroll about casually, turning here and there on any whim or impulse. In the spring, flowers line the way.

◆ *Romantic Suggestion:* "A walk back in time" correctly describes, but does not even hint at, the romance to be found on a visit to **the Mews in Oakdale**, a short drive from the Arboretum. Here you will find an unusual collection of quaint buildings that forms a sort of walled village. This is a sweet haven of white picket fences, brick and gravel drives, copper pipes and flashings, cupolas, wishing wells, and patiently tended gardens, all on shady one-way lanes. To reach the Mews from the Arboretum, take 27A east to 27 east and stay right, exiting immediately at County Road 85

(Montauk Highway). At the first traffic light (Idlehour Boulevard) turn right. Continue about one mile to Hollywood Drive. The Tower Mews arch is just ahead. Park on Hollywood or Idlehour, as no parking is allowed in the Mews.

STONY BROOK

Sixty miles from Manhattan. Take the Long Island Expressway (495) to Exit 62 North (Nicolls Road) to left on 25A (westbound). Pass the Long Island Railroad station and turn right on Main Street. At this light, 25A continues to the right. Follow this into Stony Brook.

Stony Brook is one of a handful of villages on Long Island's North Shore that have evolved into a blend of authentic rural, historical pretty, and highly sophisticated. To take advantage of all the potential romance that abounds in these parts, it is probably necessary to stay at least one night. Meander through this village and the surrounding neighboring areas. It is all as enchanting as you could imagine.

Along **Main Street** is a jewel of a dewy pond framed by wooded nesting areas and frequented by graceful swans. The **Mill Pond**, which feeds the brook (the town's namesake), turns the waterwheel of the adjacent mill (circa 1699). The brook leads into Stony Brook Harbor to an expansive sandy beach, passing the Hercules figurehead salvaged from the **USS Ohio** (launched in 1820). Going the short distance from the pond to the beach, you'll pass terraced, ivy-covered walls, colonial houses, and a handsome Federal-style business district. Endless country vistas, ancient trees, a secluded harbor, and the nearby ocean surf all lend a sleepy air to this somewhat remote part of the world.

◆ *Romantic Suggestion:* Be sure to walk up **Harbor Road** (between the Mill Pond and the Grist Mill itself) into the head of the harbor area. The hilly, winding roads lead past homes and farms set in rolling meadows, woods, and thickets. From some spots, you can see the harbor and beyond to Smithtown Bay (in Long Island Sound). If you can walk at least as far as the breathtaking mansion on the hill, with its own idyllic pond (less then two miles on the right), you'll feel like you're in Switzerland.

◆ *Romantic Option:* The **John Christopher Gallery, 131 Main Street, (516) 689-1601,** is proof that a gift shop can provide a loving interlude. A browse through this shop is special, not only for the quality craftworks beautifully displayed, but for the gentle and evocative music being played. Many of the stores here (which include designer names) call themselves "shoppes," but unlike many stores who give themselves this appellation, the shoppes here in Stony Brook warrant the extra letters.

◆ *Romantic Warning:* Watch those "no parking" signs — they are strictly enforced. Also, note postings of private property. Trespassers are not tolerated.

Three Village Inn
150 Main Street, Stony Brook
(516) 751-0555
Inn: Moderate
Restaurant: Moderate to Expensive

Take the Long Island Expressway (495) to Exit 56, Route 111 north, and follow the signs carefully, continuing to the end, where it runs into Route 25A eastbound (at a large intersection in Smithtown). The inn is one-and-a-half miles farther down 25A.

Rambling and sedate, this positively charming inn dates back to 1751 and was the home of Long Island's first millionaire. The country colonial decor complements a natural maple floor and low-beamed ceiling, and it occupies a site very close to Stony Brook's harbor. The rooms in the main building are quite pleasant and large; all have private baths and look out onto lovely grounds. There are six private cottages facing the water, some with fireplaces.

In the excellent restaurant, servers in appropriate colonial garb offer hot-baked breads and fresh, beautifully prepared seafood. A fire is often roaring on cool evenings, and on weekends a pianist adds a few more sparks. The balmy harbor is visible from many tables.

MIRABELLE

404 North Country Road (Route 25A), St. James
(516) 584-5999
Expensive

About one mile west of Moriches Road and 25A junction. Just east of the light at the intersection of Edgewood, Woodlawn, and 50 Acre roads.

Mirabelle is that miracle of a dream come true: Classically trained French chef and savvy gourmet writer marry; they open an exquisite restaurant in a simple 19th-century farmhouse in the country, and they sate the palates and spirits of fortunate like-minded souls. The owners here really know what they're doing, and what they do is quite remarkable. They have created a romantic dining haven without relying on the appurtenances we usually think of as requisite for blissful eating. What they've done is kept the decor simple, elegant, and understated. The staff is friendly but not familiar, formal but not stuffy. Wall sconces and votives in crystal holders provide subdued lighting; fresh flowers are in abundance, and a large portion of the tables are set for two. In warm weather the outdoor terrace is a charming garden site for a drink, and although the restaurant is quite close to the road, its red gravel-and-brick walkways and casual landscape keep the outside world comfortably distant. What really makes the Mirabelle's heart tick is the food. We had a brilliant meal there, and we knew after finishing that we would return to this find again and again.

PORT JEFFERSON

Sixty-five miles from Manhattan, using the Long Island Expressway (495) to Exit 63, heading north on County Road 83 (North Ocean Avenue, also known as Patchogue-Mount Sinai Road). Turn left at the junction with Route 112 five miles down the road, which eventually becomes Main Street and Route 25A westbound, and leads straight into town.

Port Jefferson, first settled in 1682, was a bustling harbor community until just about a decade ago, when it became gentrified and cosmopolitan and better known as an historic seaport. Now a walk along Main Street, crowded with tourists during the sun-soaked summer months but practically empty off-season, takes you into a beguiling harbor with views across the water to Connecticut. Even when you can't see quite that far across, the blue of Long Island Sound is inspiring. You'll feel as if civilization has just washed away and you are here alone with each other, away from it all. Your city ears will hear mysterious sounds: your footsteps as you walk on the dock's reverberating boards and the adrift-at-sea lull in the slap of the water on the boats and moorings.

◆ *Romantic Suggestion:* As lunchtime approaches here, one takes to wandering about town. Our favorite place to wander is **Moore's Gourmet Market, 225 Main Street, (516) 928-1443**, where we usually choose an exquisite picnic. Everything from caviar to temptingly rich desserts is available. To enjoy your feast get back in your car and drive about two miles west from the blinking light at the foot of Main Street on 25A to Setauket, where there are at least three glorious semi-rural spots to lay out a blanket away from everyone and dine elegantly, alfresco. The spot we always head for is the beach area in the **Dyer's Neck Historic District.**

◆ *Romantic Alternative:* If eating indoors is your preferred style of dining, you can do that in superb style at Danford's Inn at Bayles Dock,- complete with a water view and fresh seafood (see next listing). For good food in a more casual atmosphere, **The Printer's Devil, 106 Wynne Lane, Port Jefferson, (516) 928-7171**, (Reasonable) with its stained glass, rich oak detailing, and contemporary accents is a friendly, casual, publike dining alternative.

Danford's Inn   ◆◆◆◆
25 East Broadway, Port Jefferson
(516) 928-5200
Inn: Moderate
Restaurant: Moderate

Take the Long Island Expressway (495) to Exit 63 (North Ocean Avenue) and turn north (left) at the first light after you exit. Proceed to Route 112 and turn left again. This will take you straight into Port Jefferson and will become Route

25A westbound as well as Main Street, which ends at the harbor where you make a right onto East Broadway. Danford's is a few yards farther.

Imagine having your own balcony overlooking the harbor with an unhindered water view. At dawn, dusk, or midday the sun across Port Jefferson harbor will undoubtedly create the backdrop for one of the special moments of your stay here. Danford's rooms can give you all of that and more. The suites themselves, most of them recently built, are studiously designed in 18th- and 19th-century motifs that are a refreshing change from the sterile uniformity that newer constructions usually project. Modern convenience is well-blended with the abundant heritage at this inn, and the restaurant and common areas all follow this tradition with great care and respect. The lobby is a warm and rich space with a crackling fireplace casting an amber glow all around. Speaking of fireplaces, a few suites and parlors have their own. In addition to the daily Continental breakfast, a hearty breakfast buffet is served on weekends.

We appreciate that the Danford's Inn restaurant doesn't overdo its nautical theme. It is lovely to dine on one of the glass-enclosed porches overlooking the harbor. Watch the ferryboat dock, the sailboats tack across the water, or just watch the water ripple. The mood here is comfortable but not overly casual. The interior has a refreshingly bright air, even at night in the subdued light . . . all very relaxing and civilized and satisfying.

WILDWOOD STATE PARK
North Country Road, Wading River
(516) 929-4314

About 75 miles from Manhattan. Take the Long Island Expressway (495) to Exit 68 north (William Floyd Parkway), to Route 25A (Sound Avenue) east, to Hulse Landing Road, and then north to the park.

There are places to kiss and there are places you wish you could kiss in. On Long Island, many of the best places to kiss seem to be privately owned. Not so at Wildwood State Park. This is one of the few camping locations on the island. In my opinion it's the only camping facility worth pitching a tent at. As for pitching woo, this can be done anywhere, but here at Wildwood it can be done with great effect.

The park sits on Long Island Sound in the midst of acres serenely devoted to agricultural use. But the cultivated flat plain you cross as you approach and enter the park soon becomes well-treed and then thickly wooded as the land starts to roll with little hills and valleys. Suddenly, the land ends — a sheer bluff drops to the beach and a tranquil body of water laps at the shoreline. The steep paths to the beachfront are themselves fun to traverse; as the two of you make your way down to the shore, through breaks in the trees you can see the watery horizon.

The beach here is quite unique. In one large area, where one would expect to find sand, there is an immense track of pebbles, tumbled smooth and oval by the force of waves. Some boulders in the water are good perches when the tide is out. Campgrounds are not on the beach but set back a little in the hills. You shouldn't have much trouble finding a secluded glen in which to set up camp.

◆ *Romantic Warning:* The first time we camped here, it was in very hot weather and we set up our tent without paying attention to orientation. When we awoke in the morning, we found the sun had turned our tent into a hot and humid greenhouse. Plan ahead, or ask the rangers for their suggestions.

SAG HARBOR

About 100 miles from Manhattan. Take the Long Island Expressway (495) to Exit 70, head south on Route 111 to Route 27 east, which becomes Montauk Highway after Southampton, to Bridgehampton. Turn left onto County Road 79 (Bridgehampton-Sag Harbor Turnpike) at War Monument Obelisk. This road leads directly into Sag Harbor.

There's an irony to the making of great romantic places. Take New York City and Sag Harbor, for instance. Two hundred years ago, the two were the fledgling United States' official ports of entry. Today they have, to say the least, nothing in common, perhaps except for well-deserved reputations (and some residents who maintain homes in each). Unlike the well-known, well-developed Hamptons on the South Shore of Long Island, which are on the water's edge, Sag Harbor has retained its intimate haven status mostly because it is a few miles farther inland. It is off the beaten track, and its tranquillity and scenic beauty are transcendent.

Romance abounds in Sag Harbor. There's a languid feel to the air, the stately lichen-covered trees, dense ivy and rose bowers, and the flow of ocean water all around. This area is essentially peninsular, with an intricate coastline defined by many small coves and inlets. The water views are spectacular. There are thousands of vistas that change continually with the passing day and the mood of the skies. A thick, misty evening can be as electrifying here as a bright sunny day. The harbor is a sailor's mecca during the summer, when tall masts and full sails gamboling in the distance will arouse a sense of marvel, elemental freedom, and joyful abandon in even the most dug-in-at-the-heels landlubbing couple. You will have no choice but to gasp with wonderment and embrace.

◆ *Romantic Note:* Bicycles are available for rent here, or bring your own. There is so much to see and be a part of that biking is really the best mode of transportation for taking it all in.

◆ *Second Romantic Option:* Don't miss going to the nearest ocean beach which is **Mecox Beach** (in the town of Southampton). Nonresidents pay a hefty parking fee, but its really a bargain, considering what you get: white silky sand dunes, the entire Atlantic Ocean, and each other.

The American Hotel   ◆◆◆◆
Main Street, Sag Harbor
(516) 725-3535
Hotel: Off-season: Inexpensive, In-season: Expensive
Restaurant: Very Expensive

Take the Long Island Expressway (495) to Exit 70. Go south on Route 111 to Route 27 east to Bridgehampton. Make a left onto County Road 79, which leads straight into Sag Harbor and Main Street. The American Hotel is on the right, the last block of Main Street (before the traffic circle and the harbor's Long Wharf).

Calling this a hotel is like calling Versailles a home. There are only eight rooms here and the owner cares for this bed & breakfast hotel and restaurant as if it were a delicate flower. His dotage is not unwarranted. The eclectically decorated rooms are all oversized. The furnishings are genuine antiques with some deco pieces thrown in, and the mood is an elegant mixture of Victoriana and Americana. All is refined and stylish, with decorative touches of whimsy. Everything is fastidiously maintained. Even though so much of it is old, it all seems as if it were finished yesterday, from the stripped doors, exposed brick walls and vintage fixtures to the wood detailing. Each room occupies a corner with windows on two walls, and so all are bright. One has a loft bedroom and beamed ceilings. Views are the only thing lacking at the American Hotel, but you're only a block away from everything there is to see.

The dining room is well known and, in a word, superb. The style is elegance applied to a casual, unaffected self-assuredness. Tall tapers on the tables softly brighten the dark wood of the room, and they glimmer off the abundant crystal. Luncheon is served on weekends, and this is particularly enjoyable in the sun-filled, glass-topped atrium. The menu is Continental, highlighted by such exotic dishes as pheasant mousse.

◆ ***Romantic Option:*** If being near the ocean is not enough for you, and the sound of the surf at night is a romantic must, then the **Sag Harbor Inn, West Water Street, Sag Harbor, (516) 725-2949**, (Off-season: Inexpensive, In-season: Expensive), can fit that requirement. Unremarkable in most every way, this inn is more like a motor lodge. It is newly built and well constructed but lacks any sense of character or style. On the other hand, there is a pool and there are private balconies, lounges and terraces, a third floor promenade deck and, of course, the ocean, which is the only reason you would make a reservation.

SHELTER ISLAND

*Via ferry from Sag Harbor and North Haven on Long Island's South Fork:
The Greenport Ferry, (516) 749-0139, takes about ten minutes; The North
Haven Ferry, (516) 749-1200, crosses to the island in a mere three minutes.*

Shelter Island really is an island, which may not mean much in this
part of the world where everything is an island: Manhattan, Long
Island, Staten Island, City Island, Roosevelt Island, even Rikers is an
island — but Shelter Island is of another age and genre. It embraces you
with its feeling of remoteness and privacy because no bridges connect
it to anything else. The only way to get there is by boat. This is a
timeless place of unhurried quiet, a tattered oak leaf of land caught
between the tines of Long Island's forked east end.

First settled in 1652, the island with its steep wooded hills and bluffs
has a New England aura of permanence. The coastline is quite intricate,
with elusive coves and spits of sand, narrow fingers of land with deserted, impeccable white beaches. Here is an endless scenic adventure,
with frequent water views framed by lush green forests. The roads turn
under large stands of oak, past distinguished Victorian homes, creeks,
and ponds along the varied shoreline. This dollop of land achieves
perfection in its informal amalgam of country and seaside life. If you
can, get intimately acquainted with the island by bike, boat, or both.
And at some point be sure to get to Shore Road in Dering Harbor. On
the land you'll see fine, sedate homes; on the water, a fleet that is a
veritable boat show. Of course the most important attractions are the
misty morning fog, the bright midday sun, the sounds and smells of
the sea, the sunrise, the sunset, and the moon glimmering on the water
at night. Yes, romantic perfection if I do say so myself.

◆ ***Romantic Option:*** Since you came to Shelter Island on one of two
ferries (unless you sailed your own boat), take the other ferry and visit the
sites to the north or south. If you came through Greenport, take the South
Ferry to North Haven and go to Sag Harbor, the Hamptons, and Montauk.
If you came from Sag Harbor and North Haven, take the North Ferry to
Greenport and explore that village and Orient Point and take in the sur-
viving rural character of the North Fork.

◆ *Romantic Suggestion:* **Mashomack Preserve on Shelter Island, (516) 749-1001,** is a breathtakingly beautiful sanctuary owned by the Nature Conservancy. It is a place unlike most any other in the world, a rare landscape of salt marshes, tidal creeks, fields, woodlands, and sandy coastline that is essentially an awesome museum of life in process. The Preserve occupies an entire peninsula of Shelter Island and there are four secluded loop trails of varied length and terrain for the two of you to explore. **Note:** Mashomack is closed on Tuesdays.

◆ *Romantic Warning:* Unfortunately, this is a warning that one must heed nowadays in remote areas all over the country: Forested areas are filled with ticks that carry Lyme disease. Take all advised precautions, but don't let this stop you from visiting and hiking.

Ram's Head Inn
Shelter Island Heights, Shelter Island
(516) 749-0811
Inn: Inexpensive to Moderate
Restaurant: Moderate to Expensive

Follow directions to Shelter Island. Once on the island, from the South Ferry take Route 114 north to the fork, going straight on Cartright Road to the stop sign. Turn right on Ram Island Drive over the causeway to the inn on your right; from the North Ferry, take Route 114 south, pass the Mobil station and make a left on Winthrop Road, then right onto Cobbets Lane to the dead end. Then take the first left and the next right over the causeway to the inn.

On the surface, this is a simple, gracious country inn sitting atop a hill on a pretty little thumbprint of land stretching into Gardiner's Bay in the pincers end of Long Island. Big Ram Island is connected, actually, to Shelter Island by a narrow stretch of land, but in spite of this, or because of it, the Ram's Head Inn is two world's removed from the everyday. The 1927 center hall colonial-style structure that the inn occupies is not overwrought with designer touches. Its manner is understated, so that the place feels familiar without being cloying, and formal without being stuffy. The seventeen rooms and suites have either private or shared baths and all are on the second floor, where the sounds of the rustling leaves and branches of the magnificent oaks that cloak the inn is all the music you may need during your stay. Here the best things are outdoors; the area is surrounded by sweeping lawns and flowering shrubs, and the view from the dining area, covered terrace, flagstone patio, and lounge descends across the yard to the harbor for spectacular sunsets. There are two sloops for guest use, 800 feet of private beachfront, a tennis court, hammocks, boat moorings, and a dock. Continental breakfast is included, and the large dining room and lounge are subtly lit. In chilly weather the fireplaces provide more than enough warmth, and the country French menu is wonderful.

◆ *Romantic Option:* **The Dering Harbor Inn, 13 Winthrop Road, Shelter Island, (516) 749-0900**, (Expensive to Very Expensive), has a wonderful location overlooking the harbor and is actually, and I quote a very romantic source, "quite exquisite." It was closed when we were there for a visit, but from all appearances, it met all of our criteria for a romantic location.

MONTAUK and THE SOUTH FORK

Take the Triboro Bridge out of Manhattan and follow the signs to Eastern Long Island. You can choose the Long Island Expressway (495), the Southern State Parkway or the Northern State Parkway. Eventually you'll wind up on Route 27 which takes you directly into Montauk.

Like most natives, after time in and around New York, your hearts will have the need to escape to a deserted beach. You've heard about the fabulous, intoxicating eastern coast: white, wide, awesome, sandy beaches designed for hand in hand walks. Well, the South Fork provides all of that and more. Besides, the idea of being on the edge of the world together New York-style, is not to be missed for any reason.

The four (or more) hour trip to the very tip of Long Island where Montauk is to be found, is a historical potpourri, as well as an archaeological treat (and retreat). Any one of the towns along the way: Westhampton, Quogue, Hampton Bays, Southampton, Bridgehampton, East Hampton, Amagansett (among others), and finally Montauk, can provide everything a city-weary couples could ask for. Each of the towns has its own flavor as do the beaches that grace them. You might leave the main road at **Westhampton** and find the gazebo on the green or the town marina behind Main Street; both are perfect places for a picnic or a stroll. After lunch you could follow the signs to the beach and discover the miles of fabulous new homes facing the sea on Dune Road. This road runs along the beach all the way to viewing distance of Southampton. There you can see the results of the 1937 hurricane, **Shinnecock Inlet**, and have access to a beach of extraordinary beauty. Next you could take the bridge back to the mainland and head in to Southampton to experience **Job's Lane**, the oldest street in all of New York State, filled with fine shops. Or follow the signs to the beach where you'll find great and grand houses in yesterday's design and style. (The road to follow through Southampton is Route 27A. Continue on this road all the way to the outskirts of Montauk, where you'll have a choice of 27A or Old Montauk Highway. Whichever one you take, use the other on the way home.)

Once you reach Montauk and pass all the previous locales, the road becomes more of a lane running alongside the ocean and sand cliffs. At the end of this peaceful stretch of road lie the remote outreaches of the town. Void of all the conventions of life back in the Hamptons, there is only you and the very best nature has to offer for miles around. This is a place where you learn how to just be together because, besides from that, there isn't much else to do.

◆ *Romantic Suggestion:* **The Old Post House Inn, 136 Main Street, Southampton, (516) 283-1717,** (Off-season: Inexpensive, In-season: Very Expensive), is an authentic country inn that has been part of the Southampton scene since the original farmhouse was built in 1684. The Long Island Railroad came in the 1850s and brought the first tourists and the first romantic couples to the inn to bask in the comforts of country living. There are seven rooms, all with their own private baths. The common rooms have the original beamed ceilings and glowing fireplaces. Next door to the inn is the **Old Post House** restaurant, **(516) 283-9696,** (Moderate to Expensive). This is a perfect romantic spot for dining anytime. There are two fireplaces, the ceilings are low, candles are lit, tablecloths are appropriately lacy, and the food is wonderful. Piano music fills the air on Wednesday,

Fridays, and Saturdays. (They're open all year round, every day, for lunch and dinner.)

◆ *Second Romantic Suggestion:* **East Hampton** is one of the most beautiful of the towns with this same last name. The village itself begins with a pond and ends with a windmill. Park your car and walk about. Let yourselves get conveniently lost for a while as you discover the 17th-century houses tucked in between the more modern ones. If you're in need of refreshment, in the old town hall you'll find the **Barefoot Contessa**, a fresh-food emporium that will weaken your dietary resolve. Whatever you select, it will taste even better when you get to the beach and share it. If you want to stay overnight, there are really only two choices. The first is the **1770 House, 143 Main Street, East Hampton, (516) 324-1770**, (Off-season: Moderate, In-season: Expensive). The seven rooms are beautifully designed with loving detail and an aesthetic flair. Breakfast is served in the dining room that is as handsomely decorated as the rest of the home. Besides your morning meal (included in the price of the room), there is a prix fixe dinner menu (Expensive) that features diligently prepared international cuisine every evening. **The Hedges Inn, 74 James Lane, East Hampton, (516) 324-7100**, (Off-season: Reasonable, In-season: Moderate) is your other option. It is a classic bed & breakfast with private baths, some rooms with fireplaces, and a very pretty dining room that serves a fresh Continental breakfast in the morning and offers American-Italian food in the evening (Moderate to Expensive).

◆ *Third Romantic Suggestion:* There are many options for lodgings in Montauk: **Gurney's Inn Resort and Spa, Old Montauk Highway, (516) 668-2345**, (a good choice for a special dinner, too); **Montauk Yacht Club and Inn, Star Island Road, (516) 668-3100**; and the **Panoramic View, Old Montauk Highway, (516) 668-3000**, to name the three best. They are indeed beautiful, but they are also fairly popular, massive, and more ritzy than quaint. If it weren't for the ocean and surf on this remote point, you wouldn't necessarily know you had left the city behind.

◆ *Romantic Warning:* Even in our fantasy world where there's no traffic, Montauk would be a good four-hour drive from Manhattan; moreover, except for seaplanes and other private charter flights, the infamous Long Island Expressway is, unfortunately, the most direct way to get to the east end of the island. Well-known for its bumper-to-bumper traffic at peak hours, the Long Island Expressway must be approached with awareness or you'll get off to a most unromantic start. In high season, in traffic, it's not uncommon for the trip to take six hours or more. Since summer weekends start at the end of the workday on Friday and end Sunday evening, make your trip as pleasant as possible by leaving the city well before or well after the rush. Leaving on Thursday and staying until Monday is the most appealing idea all around.

"THE GREATEST HEROES ARE THOSE WHOSE

NAMES ARE WRITTEN ON OUR HEARTS."

Flavia

◆ New Jersey ◆

ARTHUR'S LANDING
Pershing Circle at Port Imperial, Weehawken
(201) 867-0777
Moderate to Expensive Continental Cuisine
Jackets Required

Through the Lincoln Tunnel, stay right through the Hoboken Tunnel. Once through the tunnel, turn left and then left again at the next light. Follow the road around to Boulevard East. Take Boulevard East to 48th Street. Make a right just after the restaurant onto Pershing Road to Arthur's Landing. Or, better, take one of the frequent Port Imperial Ferries from 38th Street and 12th Avenue in Manhattan. Call (201) 902-8850 for ferry information.

This restaurant was recommended to us by the maitre d' at the Rainbow Room, and we'd like to thank him. Here in this lofty two-level glass greenhouse restaurant, you have a choice: You can have drinks or a light dinner in the noisy but fun bar area where you can seat yourselves at granite tables or you can dine formally by candlelight. Whatever you choose, as you gaze out at the beautiful lights of Manhattan with the moon perched above it, you can't help but be in love. There is live piano music on Friday and Saturday nights at 8:00 p.m.

◆ *Romantic Note:* If you do choose to dine in the restaurant, you'll find that the upstairs is quieter and much more romantic. You'll probably have to wait for a seat up there, but it's worth it, and window seats are not guaranteed.

◆ *Romantic Option:* If you're going to a Broadway show, call Arthur's Landing to find out about their **Port Imperial Theater Package** which includes a ferry ride, bus connections, and a pre-theater three-course dinner.

BINGHAMTON'S
725 River Road, Edgewater
(201) 941-2300
Inexpensive

From Manhattan, drive through the Lincoln Tunnel and exit at Boulevard East, Weehawken. Turn right onto 60th Street, which becomes River Road.

For 62 years, the Binghamton carried passengers and automobiles across the Hudson from Hoboken to lower Manhattan and back again. The ferry trade sputtered out in the 1960s, but the historic ship has since been painstakingly restored and reopened as a restaurant. If you're seeking an unusual hideaway spot where you can enjoy a leisurely lunch or a late afternoon cocktail, the trip to New Jersey is well worth it.

Although the Binghamton now moves only when it is nudged by tides and currents, much of the ship's original detail remains intact. On the upper deck you can lunch in the galley, an airy space surrounded by windows and decorated with well-polished brass, mahogany and stained glass. Wander downstairs to the engine room to view one of the original steam engines, as well as two 1,000-gallon fish tanks. When the weather is fine, you can sit on the portside deck for a view of the New York skyline. A casual afternoon lunch or drink can easily be transformed into a shipboard romance.

◆ *Romantic Warning:* The food is not the Binghamton's strong suit. The chowder and sandwiches are fine, but unless you relish fried foods and seafood awash in sauces, stay away from the so called fancier entrees. During the week this is as subdued a spot as you could ask for, but on the weekends the scene changes markedly; you might even call the weekend crowd a bit wild, and they dance to all hours. Unless that fits your notions of romance, we recommend that you stay away on Friday and Saturday nights.

DELAWARE WATER GAP
NATIONAL RECREATION AREA
Information: (908) 496-4458

From the George Washington Bridge take Route 80 west to the Delaware Water Gap. The park is located where New Jersey and Pennsylvania meet.

As soon as the magnificent Kittatinny Ridge of the Appalachian Mountains rises up before you, you know without a question that you're coming into direct contact with the vast grandeur of nature. There are 70,000 acres of it in this dynamic park and exciting activity to go along with it in every season. Hiking and sightseeing are possible all year round, and there are so many trails and paths that you can pick and choose to suit your energy levels. In the summer, bring your swimsuit for an aquatic dip in Sunfish Pond, or trek up a hill, find a generously shady tree, unpack your picnic basket, sit back and watch the hawks glide soundlessly below. If you prefer, rent a canoe, hop in, relax, and commune with the blue vaults above.

If it snows here, pack the cross-country skis. Be prepared for brisk strides that take you across the crunching snow-packed ground and past trees dressed in white. Regardless of what you choose to do, you'll find the park a perpetual nature study: You might see anything, including deer, fox, birds, and yes, even the elusive mink, coyote, and black bear. Most important of all, you and your partner will never have a problem with a private kiss in this park because of its size and secluded vistas.

Note: For comprehensive and expert advice on what to do and where in the park to do it, consult the rangers at the **Kittatinny Point Information Center, (908) 496-4458**, which is on Route 80 near the toll bridge that crosses the Delaware River into Pennsylvania. They're friendly, courteous, and eager to help, not to mention full of excellent suggestions.

◆ *Romantic Warning:* After once spending a few hours driving all around the park with my husband in desperate search for a cup of coffee, I learned my lesson and brought my own provisions on subsequent trips. There is also an absence of inns or bed & breakfasts, although the park's historic buildings are slated for conversion into such in the near future.

HIGHLAWN PAVILION
Eagle Rock Reservation, West Orange
(201) 731-DINE
Expensive to Very Expensive
Jackets Required

From the Lincoln Tunnel, take Route 3 west to the Garden State Parkway and get off at Exit 145. Take Route 280 west and get off at Exit 8B. Follow Prospect Avenue for one-half mile and turn right onto Eagle Rock Avenue; 600 feet down and on the left-hand side of the road is the entrance to the Reservation.

This renovated early 19th-century casino at the very top of a mountain offers one of the most spectacular panoramic views of Manhattan — and parts of the Bronx, Brooklyn, and Staten Island, if you care to look. In its present incarnation as a posh, Mediterranean villa-style restaurant replete with tile floors, antiques, Spanish grillwork and tapestries, the central attraction is the floor-to-ceiling picture window which makes for ethereal city-gazing any time of day or night. The quiet and airy lounge features an extensive oyster bar. The bartenders are friendly and talkative only when you want them to be, and the servers are attentive and easygoing. For as long as you're here, you'll have the giddy feeling of being above it all.

◆ *Romantic Suggestion:* You won't have to go far for a moment (or much more) of privacy as soon as you step out of the restaurant, because you'll be standing in 408 acres of county park. Walk over to the scenic overlook and take in the view without the window.

LAMBERTVILLE

Take the Holland Tunnel to the New Jersey Turnpike south. Pick up Route 78 west to Route 287 south. Head south again on Route 202. Take Route 29 south along the Delaware River. Turn right at the traffic light at Bridge Street into the center of town.

This artists' colony, snugly ensconced on the bank of the Delaware River, is a unique combination of a colonial town and a European hamlet with a dash of Greenwich Village, the dash that's provocative and romantic. It's a cozy town to simply walk in because of its picturesque beauty, and every inch of street has something interesting to look at or step into: antiques stores, art galleries, historic landmarks, restaurants, and specialty shops. The shopkeepers are noticeably friendly. The other pairs of lovers taking in the town won't notice if you stop and kiss, because chances are they're doing the same, especially where a particularly exquisite stretch of the wide river comes into view.

◆ *Romantic Suggestions:* For all of the place's quaint attractiveness, there is a somewhat hidden gem here which should absolutely not be missed no matter what the season, and that is **the bicycle path** that lies between the river and the Delaware & Raritan Canal and can be reached by heading just past the Inn at Lambertville Station. In spring, summer, and fall, pack a picnic and hike or bicycle to your thighs' and hearts' content (the best area is to the south between Lambertville and the park at Washington Crossing). On either side of you is a crystalline body of water and, when you see the impressionistic reflections of the variegated fall leaves or bright spring flowers on the canal surface, you may have the idea that you're in the French countryside. You can cuddle on the grassy bank because the area is never crowded. In winter, cross-country skiing is the preferred activity.

◆ *Romantic Options:* Your palates and sentiments will be appropriately tended to at the **Golden Pheasant Inn, River Road, Erwinna, Pennsylvania (215) 294-9595,** (Expensive to Very Expensive), a stone farmhouse that has been refurbished with special attention to romance and dining comfort. Dine in a glass-enclosed atrium on marvelous French food.

Among the many less expensive places to dine, our favorite is the **Full Moon Restaurant, 23 Bridge Street, (609) 397-1096,** (Inexpensive), where the cuisine is always excellent and the service perfectly paced. Be advised, however, that it's closed on Tuesdays and only serves dinner on Fridays and Saturdays. For an aperitif, try the secluded **Boathouse, 8½ Coryell, (609) 397-2244,** (Moderate), just off Coryell Street. The reception desk at the Inn at Lambertville Station provides maps of the town and surrounding area.

Chimney Hill Farm Bed & Breakfast
Goat Hill Road, Box 150, Lambertville
(609) 397-1516
Moderate to Expensive

Call for directions.

The person who recommended Chimney Hill described it in glowing adjectives: a country manor with designer rooms, gourmet breakfasts, a beautiful landscape, and on and on. As we approached this attractive stone residence, with plenty of windows, framed by a well-tended garden and lawn, it appeared, at least from the outside, that this could be one of the more affectionate spots around. Thank goodness we were not dissappointed. The interior was wonderful. From the quaint dining room arranged with tables for two, to the sunroom with floor-to-ceiling windows, and the bedrooms with canopy beds and floral fabrics (some with fireplaces), it all adds up to a remarkable bed & breakfast experience. Mornings began with a full breakfast and cordial service.

◆ *Romantic Alternatives:* Lambertville has several other inns worth investigating. The most romantic is the **Coryell House Bed & Breakfast, 44 Coryell Street, (609) 397-2750**, (Reasonable), which features charming antiques-furnished rooms and a country-style breakfast served in bed. Reserve well in advance. Other places, such as the **Bridgestreet House, 67 Bridge Street, (609) 397-2503**, (Inexpensive), and the **Inn at Lambertville Station, (800) 524-1091**, (Moderate to Expensive), offer more units but aren't quite as private.

PALISADES INTERSTATE PARK, Alpine
(201) 768-1360

Drive across the upper level of the George Washington Bridge to Palisades Parkway North. Exit 2, Alpine Closter, is seven miles north. Once off the exit, follow signs to the Alpine Boat Basin.

The park that lines the New Jersey side of the Hudson River along the cliffs of the Palisades is a bastion of country relief astonishingly close to Manhattan. Isolated, varied, and rich in history, the Palisades are a gorgeous example of the enclaves of nature that thrive in the city air, giving testimony to the ability of urban and country life to coexist in harmony. You enter at one end and leave the city world totally behind. What you will find inside is green wilderness strewn with surging creeks and hiking trails.

Drive into the boat basin parking lot and pick up a map of the trails that run through the Palisades. Ask for a schedule of activities, too — you might want to return when there's a concert or a crafts fair in the park. At Alpine you can view the yachts, then choose from either the Shore Trail, which hugs the Hudson for more than ten miles, or the Long Path, which is cut into the cliffs that rise hundreds of feet above the water. Six sets of stairs connect the two so that you hike only as far as you wish, then loop back without retracing your steps. With every twist and turn, the trails offer new wonders for your eyes. Notice the hillsides, thick with vines, and stand next to your beloved to watch some waterfalls cascade over moss-covered rocks. Be sure to climb to a lookout point where you can see the whole length of the Bronx across the river. When you're ready for a rest, follow the spurs off the main trails to remote spots of sandy beach, where you can cuddle undisturbed to your hearts' content.

◆ *Romantic Suggestion:* The drive across the George Washington Bridge can be an exhilarating experience, but unless you're "lucky" enough to be trapped in a standstill, the traffic will move too quickly for the driver to witness the spectacular view or for the two of you to sneak a kiss. If you want to enjoy this romantic vista together, park your car in Manhattan's Washington Heights or in Fort Lee, New Jersey, or take the the A train to 179th Street (if you're not averse to subways), and walk along the protected pedestrian path as far across as you would like. From the south side of the bridge, you will have a kaleidoscope view of the Midtown skyscrapers against the Hudson River. The center of the bridge provides an open vista of everything due north and south. Below you'll see the famous Little Red Lighthouse, where it stands still in time like a page from the storybook. Here you'll come face to face with the more serene, magical side of this megalopolis and, for a total change of pace, there will be almost no one up here but you.

PALISADEUM, Cliffside Park
(201) 224-2211
Moderate to Expensive

Take the upper level of the George Washington Bridge to the Fort Lee exit. Make three left turns at the next series of intersections until you are LeMoine Avenue going south. This will become Palisades Avenue. At the fork in the road stay left and soon thereafter, turn left, when you see the sign for the restaurant.

You won't catch my husband and me near one of those heart-shaped, champagne-filled bathtubs in the Poconos (we claim to be too "sophisticated" to be persuaded by such tacky, commercial gimmicks). So please don't tell anyone that once in a while we sneak over the GW Bridge for this restaurant, which probably evokes the exact same feeling. When we were seventeen, this is the kind of place we would have described as elegance personified. Now that we're older and wiser we realize that the Palisadeum is hardly elegant, but we have also learned that elegance and romance are not necessarily synonymous. What this restaurant lacks in finesse, it makes up for in excessiveness. In no way subtle, everything at the restaurant is LARGE: from the giant water goblets to the grandiose (faux) fireplace to the golden wine buckets, from the sweeping views of New York City to the flaming Baked Alaska, from the mirrored ceilings to the very high-backed circular booths. To say the least, this place is obvious in its attempt to impress.

It's important to go to the Palisadeum on an off-night when it is not crowded or catering to singles and when you will be seated in a private booth near the window. Many of the items on the menu are made for two and are prepared tableside. The portions are huge and the food is good. The desserts, on the other hand, are superb. Consider sampling the Chocolate Grand Marnier souffle which needs to be ordered at the same time as the main meal. If it is late in the evening or not crowded, you can take your sweets and cappuccino out to the porch and enjoy them along with the astounding view.

◆ *Romantic Note:* There is ballroom dancing in the lounge after 8 p.m. if you're so inclined. (There is only valet parking.)

SPRING LAKE

From the Holland Tunnel, take the New Jersey Turnpike south to Route 78 south to the Garden State Parkway. Take the Parkway south to Exit 98. Pick up Route 34 east to Route 524 (Allaire Road); follow it east to Spring Lake.

Spring Lake is an ideal destination for a long, lazy summer weekend. Don't try to see it all in a day. This elegant, turn-of-the century, Victorian seaside resort is a romantic charmer in all respects. It's a marvelously picturesque town for walking or bicycling because nearly every wide avenue is lined with magnificent hotels, cottages, mansions, and estates, many of which are historically notable. But that's not all. This place is a favorite of ours because at every other turn is a choice spot for tender interludes. Most dreamlike are the long wooden bridges which span the lake for which the town is named and the gazebos on the peaceful (non-commercial) two-mile boardwalk overlooking the wide ocean beach on the other side of town. You'll never feel crowded, especially in the long off-season, and once you've shared a blissful sunrise over the Atlantic here, you'll surely remember it always.

◆ *Romantic Suggestions:* In season Spring Lake has no shortage of restaurants; for a casual bite, try the moderately priced **Beach House, 901 Ocean Avenue, (908) 449-9646**, for its excellent fare and view of the ocean and sun-filled sky. For a romantic setting, we recommend you dip into your wallets at **Anne's, 200 Monmouth Avenue, (908) 449-3330**, nestled right beside Spring Lake. Or turn up Old Mill Road to **Old Mill Inn, (908) 449-1800**, for a moderately priced delicious brunch or seafood lunch or dinner. The large restaurant is perched above a pond with swans and ducks. **Note:** Many Spring Lake restaurants are closed in the winter, and so if you're planning a trip here in off-season, call ahead.

◆ *Another Romantic Suggestion:* On your way to Spring Lake or on the way home, take a drive along the ocean (when the road takes you away from the Ocean, drive back to it) passing through, among others, the fascinating and quaint towns of Ocean Grove, Belmar, Asbury Park, Avon, and Deal.

The Grand Victorian
1505 Ocean Avenue, Spring Lake
(908) 449-5327
Inexpensive to Moderate

If you are looking for breathtaking views of the ocean, a sandy beach only a few feet away from your front door, and the inviting, cozy interior of a Victorian bed & breakfast, then surely you will want to spend at least one night at The Grand Victorian. This lovely hotel dates back to 1883 and the past sweeps through the rooms like a gentle friend reminding you to slow down and enjoy the ocean breezes. The yellow canopied porch is an amiable place to relax and listen to the sound of the surf in the distance. Each of the rooms is designed in bright floral prints, and some are smaller than others, so be sure to specify your preference. In spite of the size variation, all the rooms have a warm inviting appearance that will be hard to ignore and difficult to leave. The quaint dining room on the main floor features a full breakfast that is thoroughly enjoyable.

◆ *Romantic Alternatives:* Besides The Grand Victorian, there are two other establishments here that can effortlessly provide all of the interior, heartwarming amenities you desire. **Sea Crest by the Sea, 19 Tuttle Avenue, (908) 449-9031**, (Moderate), is a large Victorian home that has been carefully renovated into a remarkable bed & breakfast. Here we found some of the prettiest rooms the town has to offer. Nine of the twelve rooms have ocean views and private baths, and several even have working fireplaces. Breakfast in the dining room is an attractive buffet of freshly baked muffins and scones and fresh granola. From all points of view, this is indeed a very romantic place to stay.

The Hollycroft Bed & Breakfast, (908) 681-2254, (Moderate to Expensive), is the second alternative. Even in the heat of summer this unique rambling stone and wood home closely resembles a mountain hideaway. Sheltered beneath sprawling shade trees, Hollycroft overlooks Spring Lake about four blocks from the ocean. The interior is an intriguing mix of rustic sophistication. Upon entering you will be immediately impressed by the log-beam ceiling, enormous stone fireplaces, brick floors, and ivy-covered windows. There are six rooms here, some with private balconies, a glass-covered private entryway, and canopy beds. Each room has its own unique flavor and all have private baths. A generous Continental breakfast is served by the fireplace, or on the flagstone terrace during the summer.

◆ *More Romantic Alternatives:* There are many other Spring Lake hotels that we recommend. You might try, for example, the hundred year-old **Normandy Inn, 21 Tuttle Avenue, (908) 449-7172,** (Reasonable to Moderate), an Italianate villa with colonial revival and neo-classical interiors. All of the rooms have charming private baths.

Request the Tower Room for a view of the ocean or rooms 101 or 102 for their unique headboards and canopied beds. The inn is open all year and is renowned for its hearty full Irish breakfasts. As in many of Spring Lake's better hotels, from March through November there is a two-night minimum on weekends, and there is a four night minimum during July and August.

Or seek out **Ashling Cottage, 106th Sussex Avenue, (908) 449-3553,** (In-season: Inexpensive, Off-season: Inexpensive to Reasonable). This peaceful Victorian has ten, large airy rooms (eight with private baths, which are always more romantic) and features breakfast with delectable home-baked items. Ask for the room with the sunken bathroom or, for complete privacy, the one with its own entrance and porch.

◆ *One More Alternative:* **The Bluffs Hotel, 537 East Avenue, Bay Head, (908) 892-1114,** (Expensive) is one of the only hotels we found along the Jersey Shore that is located directly on the beach. The view is one of a kind and the ocean is its backyard. Although The Bluffs does not offer the romantic ambience several of the other bed & breakfasts in the area do, if you request a beachfront room with a deck, it can be a wonderfully intimate way to enjoy the beach and feel like it's part of your room.

THE PARK in the town of WEEHAWKEN

Go through the Lincoln Tunnel right into the Hoboken Tunnel. At the first light turn left and at the next light turn left again onto Boulevard East. Stay on Boulevard East through Weehawken; you'll see the park on the right. There's also a ferry from the pier near the Javits Center that will take you right there. The ferries run between two points in Weehawken (Lincoln Park and Port Imperial) and 38th Street in New York, Monday through Friday, 6:45 a.m. to 10:30 p.m. Call (201) 902-8850 for ferry information.

One night I announced to my husband that we were going off in search of yet another romantic nightspot. We commiserated with each other over the fact that there is very little to do at night if one (or two) doesn't want to eat or drink. That's what we were discussing as we passed through the Lincoln Tunnel straight into Wonderland. If you think New York ends at the Hudson River, you've never been to Weehawken. When we arrived, we wondered how we could have lived so long in New York and never thought to see what it looked like from the most unjustly maligned state in the country? After sunset, we gazed out from the park overlooking the sparkling clear view of Manhattan that spread from the GW Bridge to the Statue of Liberty. We agreed that we would come here many more times and that we would reluctantly share our secret. You want more of a description? It's a long rolling park along the Hudson; there are benches, green lawn . . . Oh, forget the description, just go there.

◆ *Romantic Suggestion:* Don't let the evening end so soon. The park is very close to **Shanghai Red's** (see next listing). Go there for drinks or a meal.

SHANGHAI RED'S
Pier D-T, Weehawken
(201) 348-6628
Expensive

From the Lincoln Tunnel, turn right into the Hoboken Tunnel. Once through the tunnel, make the first left. Make another left at the first light. At the second light, turn right onto Baldwin Avenue. Follow to Shanghai Red's in Lincoln Harbor. Commuter ferries run between two points in Weehawken (Lincoln Harbor and Port Imperial) and 38th Street in New York, Monday through Friday, 6:45 a.m. to 10:30 p.m. Call (201) 902-8850 for ferry information.

What a remarkable place! The first vision of it, a huge mansion of weathered wood designed to resemble a shack, against the mighty backdrop of New York City seems an impossible dichotomy — and it is. Built on a pier right in the middle of the Hudson, Shanghai Red's is the kind of magic "shack" you'd find at Disneyland. With its ten dining rooms filled with antiques, hammocks, and farm tools hanging from the rafters, warm lounges, and blazing fireplaces, it can appear — if you don't look too closely — to be charmingly rustic. On closer inspection, however — like Disneyland — it really is a high-tech, opulent pastiche. Regardless of its inauthenticity, the restaurant is indeed impressive; the breathtaking views that abound from every room and the delicious Continental cuisine are anything but illusions.

◆ *Romantic Option:* The restaurant houses a cabaret that changes its atmosphere each night, catering sometimes to rock 'n' rollers and other times to those who love to dance to a Latin beat. There is a separate admission to the cabaret which can be peeked at through a window in the cocktail lounge.

◆ *Romantic Warning:* Shanghai Red's is a popular place, and for Friday and Saturday nights, reservations are sometimes required a month in advance.

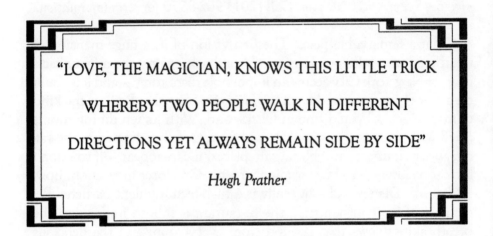

"LOVE, THE MAGICIAN, KNOWS THIS LITTLE TRICK

WHEREBY TWO PEOPLE WALK IN DIFFERENT

DIRECTIONS YET ALWAYS REMAIN SIDE BY SIDE"

Hugh Prather

◆ Pennsylvania ◆

BARLEY SHEAF FARM BED & BREAKFAST
Route 202, Holicong
(215) 794-5104
Expensive

Call for directions.

There couldn't be a more suitable place for a romantic getaway than this 18th-century country home surrounded by trees and thirty acres of prime Pennsylvania farm country. It turns out we are not the only ones who think so. As we arrived at the Barley Sheaf, a couple soon to be married also arrived, planning to profess their vows in the lovely backyard, beyond the swimming pool, in the afternoon shade of majestic old trees. (Wedding parties must rent the entire place; so don't worry about the house being inundated with someone else's relatives and best friends.)

The Barley Sheaf has an eclectic assortment of rooms, each one more unique than the next. Some are located in the main house, others in an adjacent cottage, the latter appointed with sitting rooms and stone fireplaces. All the rooms are tastefully furnished with bright fabrics, interesting antiques, and private baths, some of which have been beautifully renovated. Be sure to ask for one of the brighter rooms that takes full advantage of the sparkling sunshine. The staff offers a hearty full breakfast and will dazzle you with home-baked breads, fresh jams, and even honey from the farm's own hives. The peace that awaits you at the Barley Sheaf is unsurpassable anywhere else in this region.

◆ *Romantic Alternative:* **Aberdare Bed & Breakfast, 201 Pineville Road, Wrightstown, (215) 598-3896,** (Inexpensive to Moderate), has everything you would need for a romantic excursion out to the country. This 1850 stone farmhouse has been perfectly renovated. The attractive rooms are spacious, each with private baths and ample windows that let in plenty of sunshine. Breakfast is served around one large dining table, which, unfortunately, is great for family gatherings but not private conversations. However, the fresh baked breads, pastries, and egg dishes make it all worthwhile. There is even a large swimming pool with a wrap-around deck overlooking the pond and forest.

BEACH LAKE HOTEL
P.O. Box 144, Beach Lake
(717) 729-8239
Inexpensive

Take Route 84 east to Route 6 north to Beach Lake. In the town of Beach Lake, turn left just before the Fire Station. The inn is one-half mile down on your left.

We weren't going to go to Beach Lake. It seemed to be on the outside of what we considered an appropriate drive for a quick Manhattan getaway. A friend insisted it was worth the trip and a place we should include in this collection. It sounded promising, and we were up for an adventure, so we decided to find out for ourselves. The drive through the countryside was spectacular. The scenery in and of itself was worth the trip, but then came Beach Lake Hotel, which was nothing like a hotel at all. This building is a three-story, turn-of-the century boarding house that has been renovated to become a romantic bed & breakfast. The dining room is simply enchanting, and dinner, served Thursday through Monday, is fabulous. Each of the six rooms is extremely appealing and filled with charm, and all have private baths (but only double beds). There are antiques everywhere, and, surprisingly, price tags as well; almost everything in the hotel is for sale, including all of the furnishings in the rooms. Once a piece is sold, the owners replace it with another.

Breakfast here is superb. A full meal, complete with fresh baked coffee cake, a huge cheese omelette or a specialty egg dish, with fruit, juice and toast is included in the price. There is one thing we should mention, however: Management was not great about telling us what to expect. At night the only way to leave the building is with your key (the door is locked both from the inside as well as the outside), and the owners don't live on the premises, so there is no one available to answer questions after 10 p.m., and there also seemed to be some confusion about the dining hours. But none of that should diminish your considering this step into the romantic past.

BRIDGETON HOUSE

Upper Black Eddy
(215) 982-5856
Moderate to Expensive
No Smoking Anywhere

Take the Holland Tunnel to the New Jersey Turnpike south to Exit 14 (Newark Airport). Follow signs to Route 78 west. Take Route 78 west to Exit 15 (Clinton/Pittstown). Exit and go to the light and turn left. The road becomes Route 513 south. Go four miles. After Hoff Mill Inn (on the right) turn right for Frenchtown. In Frenchtown, cross the bridge to Pennsylvania. At the end of the bridge, turn right onto Route 32 north. Go three-and-a-half miles. Bridgeton House is on the right. It's a terra-cotta building with green shutters. If you pass the Texaco Station, you've gone too far.

When we just want to loll about on two rocking chairs, explore country roads, go tubing, and discover new farmhouse restaurants, we go to Bucks County, and this is one of our favorite little inns in Bucks County. Our special hideaway, 150-year-old Bridgeton House, situated right on the tranquil bank of the Delaware River, is the epitome of old country charm. Sit on the the porch and watch the canoes and tubers float by in quiet bliss — or better yet, join them! The rooms are decorated, of course, with pretty antiques, and several have four-poster canopy beds. Our favorite room is the downstairs suite on the southern end of the house with a porch overlooking the river. The suites overlooking the river all have baths and showers; the rest have showers. Breakfast is a treat, and afternoon tea and sherry are served in the main room.

◆ *Romantic Suggestion:* Venture over to **Point Pleasant Canoe & Tube** (River Road; first call 215-297-TUBE) and find out if tubing is for you. We enjoyed it thoroughly. Although kissing is not recommended while floating down river on inflated inner tubes, holding hands is sometimes possible. Afterwards, take a stroll on the nearby section of the 60 mile **towpath**, and stop in the general store for an ice cream cone. Walk over the bridge into New Jersey and visit the little shops and delectable bread bakery.

DELAWARE WATER GAP – (See Worth the Trip, New Jersey)

ISAAC STOVER HOUSE
PO Box 68, Erwinna
(215) 294-8044
Moderate to Very Expensive

Take the New Jersey Turnpike south and exit onto Route 78 heading west. Then take the Clinton-Pittstown exit and turn left at the end of the ramp onto Route 513 south. Stay on Route 513 south for eleven miles to Frenchtown. You'll cross over a bridge where you turn left onto Route 32 south. Two miles down on Route 32 you will see the house on the right hand side of the road.

The talk show host Sally Jessy Raphael owns this spectacular Victorian Federal country bed & breakfast located out here in the rolling hills and fields of Pennsylvania. Situated across from the banks of the Delaware River, this superbly renovated home is filled with every imaginable whimsical flourish. There are fabric-draped ceilings in some of the rooms, crystal chandeliers, thick plush Oriental rugs, scads of stuffed animals, overstuffed down quilts and handsome antique furnishings every place you look. Each room is more wonderful than the last. A full breakfast is served in the dining area that can be described as nothing less than charming. We noticed that there aren't any televisions at the Isaac Stover House; apparently Sally realizes that television and romantic getaways don't go well together. And here everything goes well together.

◆ *Romantic Suggestion:* Next door to the Isaac Stover House is an extraordinary restaurant of the first order. Out here, in what seems to be the middle of nowhere, is **Evermay, River Road, (215) 294-9100**, (Expensive). Located on the ground floor of an 18th-century country estate, the interior is unpretentious, though decidely quaint, and, if there were a few less tables, it would be perfect. Nevertheless, dinner is a six-course, prix fixe procession of delicacies that may include champagne laced with cognac, an endless array of hors d'oeuvres, chippino with saffron croutons, a salad of seasonal blossoms and local greens, and roast loin of veal with wild mushroom sauce, and desserts that are too seductive to describe. You may be too full to kiss after this event, but try, it's the only thing you'll have room for. Evermay is also a bed & breakfast, but this isn't our first choice for romantic accommodations. We found most of the rooms to be large and stark, but parents are discouraged from bringing children. And so it's up to you: The price is reasonable, the inn is peacefully lovely, and the breakfast is wonderful.

THE STERLING INN
Route 191
South Sterling
(717) 676-3311
Moderate

One-hundred-ten miles from New York. Take Interstate 80 through the scenic Delaware Water Gap (bypassing Stroudsburg) and bear right on to Interstate 380 to Route 423 (Tobyhanna exit). Go north on Route 423 seven miles and bear left on Route 191 a half-mile to the inn.

A perfect retreat all year long, but a colorful dream in autumn. Well named, The Sterling Inn is a precious find. The facilities are numerous and they're spread out over the property like a sleeping cat. Just a few of the amenities are tennis courts, hiking trails, a riding stable, a creek, a pond, a lake, an indoor pool, a heated whirlpool, and a sauna. What's most lovely and surprising at such a sprawling resort of 40 rooms and 16 suites is the sense of non-institutional privacy and trust you'll feel. There isn't someone always there watching your every step. There aren't signs pointing everywhere and people telling you what to do and what not to do. You don't need to ask for towels at the pool; they're there. It's easy to imagine this is your own private estate for the week or weekend. Still, people are discreetly present and always available when you do need them, and every detail is carefully attended to. When we arrived, they were hand trimming the fuschias that line the front porch where people rock on swinging chairs. The rooms are individually decorated with country antiques. On the property away from the main inn are very private wayside cottages with wood-burning fireplaces and porches. The food is well prepared and the menu, featuring home-baked goods such as pineapple almond bread, changes every day.

◆ *Romantic Option:* If the Sterling Inn is booked, **The Golden Goose Country Inn,** also on **Route 191 in Cresco, (717) 595-3788,** has some adequately cozy accommodations and a lazy porch for rocking and listening to soothing piano music. Note, however that although they're less expensive, these rooms do not compare with those of the Sterling Inn. The best room has a tub but no shower, and the shower in the hall isn't great.

◆ *Romantic Suggestion:* Whether you choose to spend an inexpensive night at the Golden Goose or not, be sure to enjoy a meal in the comfortable old farmhouse inn-restaurant serving huge and satisfying meals. The dining room feels a lot like grandma's 1920 parlor. As in Rick's Cafe, the fans throw muted lights around the rooms, creating a wonderful mood. From the soft muted faded florals, to the bordello lamp in the corner, from the flickering gas lights to the old crank-up Victrola, this inn will have you walking out arm in arm, slow, calm, and relaxed. For evening fun, there's a real saloon out back. People in the area like it, and so it gets crowded on weekends.

◆ *Another Romantic Suggestion:* Explore the country roads, and while you're at it, stop and be kids for a while at **Callie's Pretzel Factory, Route 390 & 191, Cresco (717) 595-3257.** After you sample one of the many pretzel varieties like Cheddar Cheese and Chocolate, you'll lick your lips (then you can kiss some more).

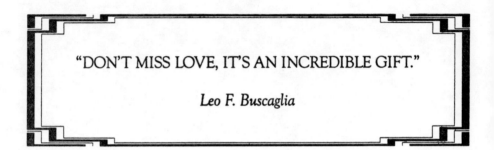

"DON'T MISS LOVE, IT'S AN INCREDIBLE GIFT."

Leo F. Buscaglia

Dutchess County

From Hyde Park to Rhinebeck to Amenia to Millerton, Dutchess County provides a wide variety of possibilities for romantic interludes.

BEEKMAN ARMS
Route 9, Rhinebeck
(914) 876-7077
Inexpensive to Moderate

Take the Taconic Parkway north to the Red Hook Pines exit. Turn left off the exit onto Route 199. Go a few miles to the first light and bear left onto Route 308. Four miles later at the very next light is Route 9. You're there.

The Beekman Arms Main Inn is at the crossroads of the charming upscale town of Rhinebeck. Dating from 1700, the inn itself is one of the oldest in America. The main inn has a quietly elegant dining room, a tap room with high-backed private seating, a vine-filled greenhouse for breakfast and Sunday brunch, and some well-appointed rooms furnished with antiques, but the reason to stay at the Beekman Arms lies one-quarter mile away at its satellite inns. Most notable is the **Delameter House** (an authentic and beautiful Colonial house), but especially in the winter we prefer the new rooms in the building that have working fireplaces — even though they're less authenticly antique.

If you don't insist on authenticity, request room 82 or an equivalent room in the **Delameter Courtyard**. Room 82 is actually a tremendous suite with a four-poster canopy bed, working fireplace, comfy couch, kitchen with microwave, and TV with remote. You could be happy to stock up the kitchen and not leave for days. The modern room, done up in a classical country style with many trompe l'oeil touches is exceptionally clean and well cared for. Clean, comfortable, pretty, and pampering: what more could a couple want from an inn? Real antiques, you say? In that case, spend the night at the Delameter House.

◆ *Romantic Suggestions:* Late summer of every year Rhinebeck plays host to an outstanding Crafts fair. But what do you do in Rhinebeck when there's no crafts fair? Go skiing, antiquing, berry picking, explore the countryside and visit the shops. When you have nothing in mind but a quick escape from the city together, this is a good destination.

BRASS ANCHOR
River Point Road, Hyde Park
(914) 453-3232
Moderate to Expensive Seafood
Dinner only

Going North on Route 9 in Hyde Park, look for the Brass Anchor Restaurant sign, which will direct you to turn left toward the water.

This restaurant is sandwiched between a small marina and the majestic Hudson. We highly recommend coming here in summer for appetizers, light entrees, and exotic drinks on the higher outside deck. Dinner outside on the lower deck is also recommended. Inside is not romantic, but as the omnipresent crowds indicate, the food delivers joy.

BYKENHULLE HOUSE
21 Bykenhulle Road, Hopewell Junction
(914) 226-3039
Moderate

Call for directions.

This Georgian country home is set on several acres of green lawn bordered by dense forest. With its large sunny windows and bright colors, the entire house has an expansive feeling. Each of the six rooms in this delightfully elegant bed & breakfast is an oasis of privacy and comfort. The bedrooms are lovingly fashioned with floral fabrics and linens, canopy beds, and antique furnishings. The room on the top floor has a large whirlpool bath that would fit two nicely and windows that look out over the tree tops. The common rooms are wonderful, each with its own fireplace and plush furnishings. The owners have recently added a glass-enclosed sunroom with floor-to-ceiling glass doors that open out to the lawn and the nearby built-in swimming pool. Every corner in Bykenhulle House is a delightful place to spend time catching up on quiet, tender moments. Breakfast is an array of fresh baked pastries, walnut and cream cheese spread, fresh preserves, fresh fruit, and cereals. It would be better if there were separate tables for each couple, but the presentation is so wonderful, you can forgive almost anything.

◆ *Romantic Warning:* The owners of Bykenhulle House are new to running a bed & breakfast and they are still working out the nuances of managing their potentially successful business. From what we can tell, once they get it all ironed out, this will no doubt be one of the premier properties in the area.

INNISFREE GARDENS
Tyrell Road, Millbrook
(914) 677-8000

From the Taconic Parkway, exit onto Route 44 heading toward the town of Millbrook. Just past the small town turn right on Tyrell Road and follow the very small signs to the gardens. Open May through October.

In all our years of seeking peace and solace in nature, never have we found such a magical corner of the world as Innisfree. Wondrous moments are waiting here for those who appreciate the subtle enchantment these unusual grounds can provide.

Innisfree is renowned for its use of the cup garden design – an ancient Chinese concept wherein separate garden groupings are individually showcased in a way that does not interfere with the larger landscape. The visitor happens upon these distinct groupings one by one, providing one lovely surprise after another. When something interesting in the distance catches your eye, only on closer inspection are you aware that the waterfall cascading down an intriguing array of rocks, the vines intertwined around a rock sculpture, or the flowered arbors draped atop a stone wall are all creations of gifted artisans and not nature. Everything here, from the terraces, sprawling lawn, and foot bridge, to the forest and rock arrangements will spark your creative longings, pique your imagination, and encourage you to explore further.

The entire garden wraps around a lake where wooden chairs are placed randomly, so you can stop to rest and bask in the harmony of the setting. Innisfree is a perfect place for an afternoon walk together; time to let yourselves roam and dream.

◆ *Romantic Option:* Whether or not you are a botany buff, you will want to visit the perennial gardens of the nearby **Mary Flagler Carey Arboretum, (914) 677-5359**, (Free). Over 1,000 taxa of various plants are displayed for those looking to soothe the senses while wandering through nature's remarkable offerings. There are over 1,900 acres of gardens, streams, fields, and forests here, with bicycle paths and hiking trails that will take you deep into the heart of the arboretum.

MAXIME'S RESTAURANT FRANCAISE
Old Tomahawk Street, Granite Springs
(914) 248-7200
Expensive French Cuisine

Heading north on Route 684 take the Katonah exit. Follow Route 35 west until you reach the intersection of 118 and 202 where you will see the sign for the restaurant.

Who would expect to find hidden in the trees of Granite Springs a sumptuous gourmet experience like the one you will find waiting for you at Maxime's? You can relish perfectly seasoned appetizers and entrees from a talented kitchen staff that knows the true meaning of the word delectable. You dine on the outdoor terrace overlooking the forest beyond during the warm months, while the rhapsody of the cicadas accompanies your conversation. Or inside you can be enveloped by soft music, enticing aromas, and beautifully appointed furnishings. Regardless of the season, you will savor every bite, wanting to linger on and on as long as you can. On our way home, we knew that not only would we remember our experience here, we knew we would come again soon, because we found ourselves missing the ambience (and the soup).

MILLBROOK WINERY
Wing Road, Millbrook
(800) 662-WINE

Take the Major Deegan Highway north to the Saw Mill River Parkway north. Follow it to the Taconic State Parkway north and then exit onto Route 44 east. Turn right onto Route 82 heading north. Three-and-one-half miles down the road, turn right onto Shunpike Road and then go another three miles to Wing Road. Turn left into the vineyard.

We stumbled upon this 130-acre vineyard while we were lost along one of the many backroads through the Hudson Valley. (We don't get lost often, but when we have, we've discovered some of our favorite kissing places.) The winery itself is an unusual sight to behold because it doesn't look anything like a winery. Once an expansive dairy barn, the building has been fastidiously refurbished into a wine making facility and tasting room. Perched atop a breathtaking vista of rolling hills, flourishing vines, and picturesque forest, this is a special place for a picnic and a sampling of the fine wine the valley is capable of producing.

MARGARET LEWIS NORRIE STATE PARK
Mills-Norrie State Park, Staatsburg
Route 9 and Old Post Road
(914) 889-4100

On Route 9, a few minutes north of Hyde and Vanderbilt Mansions, enter the park and follow the signs to the Environmental Center and Marina. When you see the Marina on one side of a long parking lot, turn left and continue to the other side of the parking lot. Walk past the Environmental Center out to the end of the pier and watch the sun set the way it was meant to be watched.

The park offers camping, picnicking, and hiking, but we usually arrive here much to tired to hike. This is a special choice spot for one thing: the sunset. Take turns using each other's knees for pillows and get lost in the mystique of the whirls, swirls, and laps of the Hudson. River fish jump, the boats hum by, and the birds fly effortlessly. A perfect moment.

◆ *Romantic Option:* All of the Hyde Park mansions offer exceptional views of the Hudson and thrilling spots for taking in the sunset. The special appeal of Norrie Park is that it is less traveled, and you can drive right up to the water without a hike. You can stay there until dusk, when the park officially closes, and you don't have to hike back to your car in the dark.

OLD DROVER'S INN
Old Route 22, Dover Plains
(914) 832-9311
Expensive

Take the FDR Drive to the Triboro Bridge to the Major Deegan Expressway (87) north to the New York State Thruway. Exit Cross County Parkway (exit 4 east) to Hutchinson River Parkway to Interstate 684. In Brewster pick up Route 22 north, and in Dover Plains follow the signs right to the inn. A more picturesque route would be to take the Henry Hudson to the Saw Mill to Interstate 684 (then follow directions above). Or take the Metro North train for an hour-and-forty-five minute trip from Grand Central Station. Transportation to and from the inn is available at the Dover Plains Station.

Every moment here at this year round retreat is a second honeymoon. Snuggled in front of the crackling fire in our cozy room, wrapped in terry robes; it doesn't get more romantic than this. Having dined like royalty in the elegant Tap Room and bathed in luxurious style, here we are — thinking, of course, of tomorrow's sumptuous breakfast in the muraled mahogany Federal Room. The 250-year-old inn creaks and groans. The floors slope. The muted colors and floral prints beckon and seduce. The many fires pop; their woody sweet aroma relaxes and comforts. The food and soups entice and nourish. Every room speaks of days long past. The food and atmosphere of the Drover's Inn Tap Room restaurant alone is worth the trip: The candle-

and fire-lit, low-beamed mahogany room is a trip back in time, say to 1750 when the old inn first opened. But once you see the bedrooms, you won't want to leave, and after you eat the meal you may not be able to walk to the car, much less drive 75 miles home.

The inn has only four rooms, and they're all charming. The only thing uninspired about The Meeting Room — the only room with shower and bath — is its name. This is the largest and most expensive of the four, but with its remarkable barreled ceiling, it's our favorite, and once you've stayed in it, nothing else will do — unless, of course, it's booked. The Cherry Room with its cherry wood outfittings is our second favorite.

◆ *Romantic Note:* Although it is expensive to stay here, the inn offers deals from January through April. When you stay Saturday plus another night, the rate includes a three-course dinner and Continental breakfast for two.

◆ *Romantic Suggestion:* Relaxing and rejuvenating in every season, the inn is accessible to every country pleasure. Bicycles are provided for your riding and exploring pleasure.

◆ *Romantic Option:* Thirteen miles north in a remote elevated area is the **Cascade Mountain Vineyards and Restaurant, Flint Hill Road, Amenia, (914) 373-9021.** Go for an inexpensive lunch. It's a beautiful drive to a lovely setting. Take Route 22 north and turn left on to Haight Road. Follow it to the end and then go left on Flint Hill Road. **Warning:** No matter what the Drover's innkeeper tells you, the back roads are very difficult to drive after rain. Go to the winery only in beautiful dry weather.

ROOSEVELT-VANDERBILT NATIONAL HISTORIC SITES ◆◆◆◆
Albany Post Road, Hyde Park
(914) 229-9115
FDR Library: (914) 229-8114

On Route 9 about six miles north of Poughkeepsie. (80 miles north of NYC).

This is a particularly good area to explore if you're staying in Ulster or Dutchess County. The Hyde Park mansions are possible to enjoy in a day — that is, a long tiring day. Here as at other similar sights in the area, the museum is open until 5:00, but the grounds are open until dusk, which as we all know can be deliciously late in the summer. Go after the museum closes, and you'll have the grounds virtually to yourselves.

◆ *Romantic Option:* From the FDR Mansion, they'll give you directions to **Val-Kill** (Eleanor Roosevelt National Historic Site, her home after FDR's death). It's about two miles east of the FDR Mansion on Route 9G. Not on the Hudson like the other mansions, but instead on quiet Val-Kill pond, the property offers lovely gardens and trails through the woods — all of the ingredients necessary for a pleasant afternoon (well, good weather helps, too). It's more private, too, because it is not on everyone's Hyde Park itinerary.

◆ *Romantic Suggestion:* Leave in time to see the sunset from **Norrie Point at Margaret Lewis Norrie State Park** (see earlier entry in this section).

RUTH LIVINGSTON MILLS MEMORIAL STATE PARK ◆◆◆◆
Mills-Norrie State Park
Old Post Road, Staatsburg
(914) 889-4100

Connected to Norrie State Park on the north side, the grounds of the Mills' Mansion is — distinct from the mansion itself — its own state park. The sloping grounds provide picture-perfect locations for picnics. While everyone else is busy touring the mansions, especially the FDR and Vanderbilt mansions, this can be your secret treasure. Picnic on a blanket, toss a Frisbee, and walk and talk on this magnificent sprawling property. The tour of the mansion is enjoyable if you like to gawk at life as it was for a wealthy financier. For the romantically inclined, the reason to come here has everything to do with Mother Nature. Scenic hiking trails around the mansion and down to and along the Hudson are spectacular. The trail along the river has a marble seat for gazing out over the Hudson between kisses.

SIMMON'S WAY VILLAGE INN
Main Street, Route 44, Millerton
(518) 789-6235
Moderate to Expensive

Ninety miles from NYC; follow directions to the Drover's Inn. Continue on Route 22 north to Route 44 east (Main Street). The inn is in the center of town on the right.

The grandfather clock will seem to wink knowingly as you enter this full-service country inn. Don't trip over Baden, the lazy Bernese Mountain Dog, who will probably be snoozing in his usual place on the rug. As you wander about the eclectically furnished commons rooms, Richard Carter, the proprietor, might entertain you with tales of his travels all over the world where here he picked up the exotic Chinese fan, and there he found the handsome chess set, and so on. We enjoyed touring the inn very much, with its warm international decor, feasting our eyes on such items as a Moulin Rouge Service Bar, many museum-quality knickknacks, an art deco Chinese carpet, stained glass doors and walls, and magnificent dried flower arrangements everywhere.

Each of the ten rooms is different, but all are equipped with bath and shower (not necessarily a tub, though), and all are decorated impeccably with a fine selection of antiques and linens. The very white bridal suite with its queen size half-canopy bed and its private covered porch has, understandably, been witness to many a wedding night, but it's not for brides and grooms only. The sunny bay window room (number five) is rather lacy and flowery and comes equipped with an uncharacteristically giant European-style shower/tub and its own porch. Room number three has a canopy bed and a little sitting area to recommend it. Really, they're all nice. If it were possible, we'd be happy to stay in a different room every time until we've stayed in them all.

High tea and cocktails are served every day in the front room cafe, where sits an elaborate cappuccino machine and many sunny little tables for two. The adjacent room with its unusual inlaid wood table from Harrods is the setting for the day's breakfast, and dinner in the back dining room is an elaborate affair. Tables are set with sterling silver plates, unusual blown glass candles, and little bowls of flower petals. The chef is a Culinary Institute graduate, and so the food here is a special treat. Although the menu changes each week, a typical meal might include caviar and chilled vodka, beef aged for flavor, and cherries jubilee followed by a round of Stilton cheese and fine port.

Note: A service charge includes breakfast, tea, and all gratuities. Dinner is a la carte, except in winter when it's MAP. There is a two-night minimum.

◆ *Romantic Warning:* This 184-year-old house has seen many a wedding. Here as everywhere, avoid booking your stay when nuptials are in progress — unless, of course, those nuptials are your own.

TROUTBECK INN
Box 26, Leedsville Road, Amenia
(914) 373-9681
Expensive to Very Expensive

Take Route 684 North to Brewster where the road will narrow and become Route 22. In the town of Amenia turn right onto Route 343. The sign for the inn will be about two-and-one-half miles down the road.

The roads that wind through the Berkshire Mountains take you through some of the most serene countryside anywhere. In the midst of all this beauty, hidden from civilization in a pristine corner of Amenia, is the Troutbeck Inn. There are over 400 acres of privacy waiting for you here, replete with landscaped gardens, the rushing waters of the Webatuck River, indoor and outdoor swimming pools, tennis courts, outstanding accommodations and a truly splendid four-lip restaurant. Sprawling sycamores shade the slate-roof of the country mansion where several of the rooms and restaurant are to be found. The rooms in the main house have a somewhat simple, though charming appearance, while the others in the 18th- and 20th-century farmhouses next door are a bit more modern. All the rooms are handsomely refurbished with floral prints and antiques. The common rooms are lush places to snuggle close, next to a crackling fireplace, or to lounge through precious moments together. Once you arrive at Troutbeck Inn, this is where you stay. The weekend packages offered here ($575 to $790 depending on the type of room) include three meals for two, all beverages (including wine and cocktails), your room, and all facilities available at the inn. This Garden of Eden, however, is a weekend getaway only. During the week management books only business conferences, so kissing would definitely be out of the question.

Rockland County

THE OLD '76 HOUSE
110 Main Street, Tappan
(914) 359-5476
Moderate American Fare

Take the upper level of the George Washington Bridge to the Palisades north. Exit 5S (Route 303) Tappan. Continue to second traffic light and turn right onto Oak Tree Road. At the Stop sign turn right on Main Street. It's right there.

Exceptionally close to NYC, this rustic Colonial built in 1755 is a very large old stone house with wood-beamed ceilings and several fireplaces. The restaurant is divided into a number of rooms — each with a slightly different atmosphere but all evoking an earlier time with authentic colonial furniture, old prints, flags, lanterns, swords, and wine bottles. The best tables for two are near the fireplaces in the front room. At night the rustic decor is slightly transformed by candlelight and quiet piano music. When the pianist isn't there, classical music is piped in.

◆ *Romantic Warning:* We enjoy the brunch buffet here, but we must warn you that, especially at brunch, many large family groups enjoy the atmosphere here as much as do couples. Seeing how the atmosphere is like an old farmhouse, we don't find that terribly distracting — particularly when we score one of those corner tables for two. But for a truly intimate or quiet tête-à-tête, this popular place is not your best choice.

◆ *Romantic Alternative:* Down the road, you may find **Giulio's, 154 Washington Street, (914) 359-3657**, a stately and ornate gabled 1880 Victorian house more to your liking. On Friday nights for the past fifteen years, guitarist Ricardo has serenaded diners here with love songs.

PIERMONT

Take the upper level of the George Washington Bridge. Stay right for the Palisades Parkway north to exit 4. Turn left to 9W north. Continue two-and-a-half miles. Bear left onto Route 340. As you go down a hill, turn right onto Ferndon Avenue. This will lead you one mile into Piermont Avenue, the town center.

Say you wake up on a beautiful Saturday or Sunday morning and you feel like going for a drive — but not too far — and you wouldn't mind doing some lazy exploring together. This quaint town on the water has just what the doctor ordered. The sleepy town of Piermont, just a stone's throw from Manhattan, is a shopping, strolling, sipping sort of place with many fabulous views of the Hudson.

Piermont on the Hudson
701 Piermont Avenue, Piermont
(914) 365-1360
Moderate Italian

This is a pleasant enough restaurant with a terraced interior accented by pink walls and brass rails, but we give it high lip ratings purely for its deck, one of the most scenic we've every kissed on. Go on temperate summer days and enjoy the sea breezes on your faces. Just below, geese and ducks strut and dip in the quietly lapping waves of the tiny cove. Boats go this way and that, some sailing under the majestic Tappan Zee, which spans the whole horizon. The bucolic hills beyond finish the scene like a perfect watercolor. Although full dinners are served inside or on the deck, we prefer to do the town: Have drinks here and then dine at the heavenly Xaviars down the road.
    ◆ ***Romantic Alternative:*** When it's too nippy to sit outside, do your sipping in the small art deco **Freelance Cafe and Wine Bar, 506 Piermont Avenue, (914) 365-3250**.

Xaviars at Piermont
506 Piermont Avenue
(914) 359-7007
Expensive prix fixe
Contemporary French Cuisine with Oriental Embellishments

It's amazing that jackets are not required here because this intimate restaurant is the ultimate in posh and tasteful elegance. The perfect setting for a romantic date, there are just a few tables here, and they're set comfortably apart like jewels in the tiny candlelit room. Each table, set up slightly differently – showing a personal touch – is provided with two large bouquets of fresh roses in Waterford crystal vases, Cartier salt and pepper shakers, and its own crystal figurine. Classical pianoscapes fill the air and encourage quiet talk. As far as the food is concerned, let it be said that eating here is sensual serious business.

Putnam County

COLD SPRING

Take the Palisades Parkway north to Bear Mountain Bridge and turn left on Route 9D. Travel 9 miles on 9D farther north to Cold Spring (not to be confused with Cold Spring Harbor on Long Island). Once in Cold Spring turn left on Main Street to the end. Looking past the train tracks you'll see the Hudson River in front of you, but the car can't cross the tracks here, so follow the signs which will take you around the block to the water. Park your car there at the public boat-launching ramp.

Start your day in Cold Spring right there in the company of giant graceful white swans, ducks, and seagulls. To them you'll look just like everyone else they see every day locked in a sweet embrace, looking out over the water and breathing in the clean air. Perhaps take a walk along the water one block to the **Dockside Harbor Restaurant, (914) 265-**

3503, (Moderate). Wipe the lipstick from your sweetheart's cheek and have lunch or make your way back to Main Street (pedestrians can go through a tunnel under the tracks). The quaint little town is an antique and craft admirer's paradise.

◆ *Romantic Suggestions:* Although Cold Spring is close to New York and can be enjoyed comfortably as a day trip, there are so many things to see and do here that you couldn't go wrong making a weekend of it. Besides shopping, two special outdoor sites are the **Boscobel Mansion Restoration and Gardens in Garrison, (914) 265-3638**, and **Constitution Marsh Sanctuary, (914) 265-3119**. Two of our favorite bed & breakfasts are the **Plumbush Inn, Route 9D, Cold Spring, (914) 265-3904**, (Moderate) which also serves superb European-style food and has wonderfully appointed rooms, one with private bath; and the **Pig Hill Bed & Breakfast, 73 Main Street, (914) 265-9247**, (Moderate). Also, **The Olde Post Inn, 43 Main Street, Cold Spring, (914) 265-2510**, (Inexpensive), an 1820 landmark building which is a delightful bed & breakfast with a very unromantic name, has a basement tavern open from 8 p.m. until 1 or 2 a.m. where jazz musicians play on Friday and Saturday nights. (The inn only has shared baths, which explains its inexpensive rating; not a romantic preference, but an economic one.) **Xaviars, Highland Country Club on Route 9D in Garrison, (914) 424-4228**, (Expensive), is quite highly recommended for very special personal occasions. The Continental menu includes fresh venison and rabbit creatively prepared and served in a truly romantic setting. On the weekends a violinist and harpist will serenade you with the music of the angels. For a very out-of-the-way interlude the **Bird and Bottle, Route 9, Garrison, (914) 424-3000**, (Moderate to Expensive), is a fine place to dine and toast the evening away.

◆ *Romantic Option:* Don't go home without making a stop at **Garrison's Landing**. In fact, this is best enjoyed as a detour on your way to Cold Spring rather than on your way home. When you get on 9D (coming from New York) turn left at the blinking light, (Route 403) to the artists' colony that is Garrison. Walk behind the houses, and be sure to take in the view of West Point from the Gazebo. You'll probably see an artist or two entranced in the process of creation. Everywhere you'll see evidence of their work. Stop in at the **Art Center**, too, before you leave.

Rockland County

ROCKLAND LAKE STATE PARK
(914) 268-7598

Take the George Washington Bridge to Palisades Parkway. At Exit 4 turn onto Route 9W north. Stay on Route 9W until you see a sign for Rockland Lake South entrance.

A fumy turnpike or a dark, thronged tunnel can threaten romance right at the start of your excursion out of New York City, but the 40-minute drive to Rockland Lake will be scenic and serene. The tree-lined Palisades is fast and Route 9 affords enchanting glimpses of the Hudson River and Tappan Zee Bridge as you pass through the well named town of Grandview.

The 2.8-mile path that winds around the lake is paved and flat, posing no obstacles to the exchange of soulful thoughts. As the vista changes subtly with each curve, you'll marvel at the tranquillity and freshness so close to a bursting metropolis. Scattered among the lakeside trees are grassy nooks, some with benches and tables.

Although the seclusion is far from complete, a cuddly, discreet picnic would not be out of place or easily observed. You can rent a rowboat at the ducks' gathering place and float through your surroundings.

◆ *Romantic Warning:* At least one of the park's two swimming pools is open on weekends from Memorial Day to Labor Day. A June dip will enliven the senses, but once school is out, stay away! Those romantic urges will wither with the first chlorine-bound tot's cries of delight.

◆ *Romantic Suggestion:* Wear outfits that can be dressed up so that you can take advantage of the lovely **Bully Boy Chop House, 117 Rte. 303, Congers, (914) 268-6555**, (Moderate to Expensive). It is a Rockland gastronomic gem just minutes away. Be sure to reserve a table overlooking their pond for a perfect backdrop to a British-inspired feast. Scones with honey, succulent curried beef, and savory rack of lamb are among the pleasures of the cordially served bounty.

Ulster County

The choices of romantic excursions in and around Ulster County are limitless. Tool around and discover this emerald yourself. You almost can't go wrong. Here you'll find the best antiquing, picnicking, strawberry picking, and hiking anywhere. In the summer, you can just lose yourself in the fresh vegetable stands (sweet sugar corn is the area's best specialty). Some of the many places to visit nearby include Lakes Minnewaska, Mohonk, and Awosting, and the towns of Stone Ridge, Woodstock, Kingston, and New Paltz. Try the other direction, and it's a fairly quick and pretty drive over the Hudson to Hyde Park or Staatsburg in Dutchess County.

AUDREY'S FARMHOUSE B&B
Route 7, Walkill
(914) 895-3440
Moderate

The best route: Take the George Washington Bridge upper level to the Palisades Parkway north to Exit 17 Newburg. Pay the toll and then take the first right down the ramp and around to Union Avenue. Go straight on Union Avenue for one-and-a-quarter miles to Route 5. Turn left onto Route 52. When you enter the town of Pine Bush, count to the second light and turn right onto County Route 7. Drive six miles, bearing right at one point to stay on Route 7. When you see Corey's Greenhouse on the right, you'll know Audrey's is right across the street on the left. Turn in.

Two of the rooms here present a special treat. We've stayed in both and can't decide which we prefer. One is upstairs. It's a very large room with bath, angled ceilings, uneven floors, comfortable bed, woodburning stove and a pretty view of the meadow. The most unusual, perhaps, is the suite on the first level. Thinking romance? You better be. This room is all bed — and what a bed: done in snowy white, large, covered with a fluffy feather mattress, down comforter, lots of cushy pillows, and topped off with two little lacy potpourris to take home. By the headboard is a decanter filled with brandy for two. The suite has its own private entrance from the outside, a small vestibule and separate bath. In the bath you'll find a big old bathtub on legs and a separate shower stall. We would've been tempted to stay in our suite if other delights didn't beckon outside. At Audrey's you can watch deer and birds play in the adjoining meadow as you stretch out on twin rafts or lounge chairs at the small pretty built-in pool. Or in the house itself, enjoy the country comfort of the beautifully decorated restored old 1740 farmhouse. Read in the library, snuggle by the fire, or play Frisbee on the lawn; you may even be able to arrange a barbecue on the patio. Audrey will make you feel right at home.

◆ *Romantic Suggestion:* Located nearby in the town of High Falls is the four-star **De Puy Canal House Restaurant, (914) 687-7700,** (Moderate to Expensive). Like Audrey's, it is an old stone house with many rooms filled with antiques and blazing fireplaces. We have dined there many times, and more than once we have been seated in our own such room (although this is very unlikely on a weekend when reservations are strongly recommended). The food is exceptional and the multi-course meals have been known to take four hours, but guests are encouraged to roam about the beautiful mansion while awaiting courses, and there are several interesting spots for embracing and kissing. One such spot is a catwalk which overlooks the sparkling clean kitchen; you'll discover the others.

◆ *Romantic Option:* Right next door to Audrey's, dine on delicious seafood at the **Bruynswyck Inn Seafood Restaurant, (914) 895-3877,** and drink wine with impunity because you can walk back. Or ask Audrey to direct you to **Soudani's, 73-77 Main Street, Walden, (914) 778-2149.** There you'll find an eclectic Continental menu that ranges from hamburgers to lobster tails. Somewhat large and resembling a disco, it's surprisingly easy to settle in at a candlelit table. There's usually someone taking requests at the piano. Play it for me, Sam.

JINGLE BELL FARMS B&B
1 Forest Glen Road, New Paltz
(914) 255-6588
Moderate

Take the New York State Thruway (87) to exit 18. Turn left on 299 through New Paltz to the last light. At David's Cookies, turn left onto 208. After 3.3 miles turn right onto Forest Glen Road. Then turn into the first driveway on the right.

A splendid place to call home for the weekend, this is year-round country heaven. Jingle Bell Farms is a place to be pampered in low-key comfort. On a hot summer day, the secluded pool is a welcoming sight (midnight swims permitted). The old stone house itself stays remarkably cool indoors without air-conditioning. On a cold winter day, snuggle up together by one of the three fireplaces or play backgammon in the game nook. You're free to roam the whole house, which includes a brick-floored porch. The common rooms are comfortably decorated beyond compare with country antiques. Most notable are the collections of spinning wheels and colorful glass bottles. Request the master room with library, piano, and half bath.

Wake up to the sounds of roosters crowing, songbirds singing, and sheep baaing. Take a stroll around the pretty property as you wait for your deliciously late individually prepared candlelit country breakfast served at tables for two! This special touch is very unusual for a B&B where you're usually forced to make small talk at big tables before you've downed your morning java. Before you leave, take some deep breaths of air home with you.

◆ *Romantic Warning:* None of the rooms has a private bath. One room has its own half bath, but four rooms share two showers. This didn't diminish our enjoyment. Don't let it keep you away.

◆ *Romantic Note:* April is birthing season for the 15 sheep, all of whom are named for flowers. There are also 13 chickens, 7 peacocks, 2 horses, and a partridge in a pear tree. (There is a Christmas room, but we're only kidding about the partridge.)

MARCEL'S
Route 9W at Floyd Ackert Road, West Park
(914) 384-6800
Moderate French Cuisine; Dinner only

Follow the directions to West Park Wineries. Marcel's is one mile north of West Park Wineries on 9W.

Marcel's has its own bottled water, and on every bottle is etched "Where Fond Memories Are Made." Unless you're thinking about proposing here, that may be going a little far, but one can certainly expect a tasty French meal in one of the two cozy dining rooms. One room even has a fireplace with white sparkly lights above. The same room — our favorite of course — has a poster of a couple kissing. It says "l'amour." And they didn't even know we were coming!

◆ *Romantic Warning:* No reservations are taken for Saturday, and so expect a wait.

◆ *Romantic Option:* Before going to Marcel's, work up an appetite at **John Burrough's Sanctuary** a short drive behind Marcel's. To get there, turn left on Floyd Ackert Road. Bear left over the railroad tracks and continue a mile or so to John Burroughs Drive. Park your car and walk or, if permitted, turn left and park outside of **Slabsides**, the hand built home of John Burroughs, naturalist, preserved along with the surrounding land as a sanctuary in memory of this man. What else is there? Blissfully fragrant, peaceful, and private short trails through the woods.

MARINER'S HARBOR
46 River Road, Highland
(914) 691-6011
Moderate Seafood

From New Paltz, take 299 east to Route 9W. Make a right on 9W south. Go one mile to Grand Street and turn left. Follow Grand (it turns into River Road) all the way to the end at the river.

Go on a summer day to this busy restaurant on the water. Either dine outside or, better, just have drinks on the deck. It's a large and noisy place, and the food is not exceptional, but if you're lucky enough to score an outdoor table, the exceptional view of the Mid-Hudson Bridge looming large right beside you will probably make you think of other things beside food. If you only have an appetite for love, this is a choice spot for cocktails or soft drinks and appetizers.

◆ *Romantic Note:* Many people come here by boat. Free docking is available.

LAKE MINNEWASKA STATE PARK
Route 44-55, New Paltz
(914) 255-0752

Take the New York Thruway (87) north to Exit 18. Turn left on Route 299
and go through the town of New Paltz. Continue to the end and turn right on
Route 44-55. Follow the road up the mountain, about four miles past the hair-
pin turn. Turn left into the park. Pick up a map at the gate; then continue slowly
up the windy road to the parking lot near the lake.

The lake is only ninety miles from New York City, but it might as
well be ninety-million. Your first view of the water will be through the
trees. The water at first appears emerald green, but as you draw nearer
it becomes turquoise. Both colors are astounding from any perspective.
But even more than the color, the clean, clear water has a magical
quality; swimming in it is like swimming in silk. There are no fish, just
an occasional scuba diver exploring the 100-foot deep bottom of this
glacial lake. The lake is said to have a high copper content, which accounts both for its color and lack of fish.

Don't miss taking a walk around the lake trail which winds up and
around the white cliffs that preside over half the lake, and don't hesitate
to try a few side trails, where it's not unusual to see a deer or two. You
may also want to take out a rowboat or a paddleboat on the lake. The
park closes at 5 p.m. but be sure to leave at least one hour to take the
easy one-mile walk to Beacon Hill, very probably the most restful spot
there is with a spectacular mountain view so close to New York City.

◆ *Romantic Note:* There's a cascading waterfall called **Awosting**
Falls which you can dip your feet into from above or swim in beneath. It is
just inside and near the entrance to Minnewaska State Park, but wait until
you're leaving the park to see it, or you may never get to Lake Minnewaska.

◆ *Romantic Warning:* Until recently the park was owned by a
private family. Now the state owns it. Although they are maintaining
the beautiful grounds, they have restricted swimming to a very small
area, making it somewhat less pleasurable than in the old days when
swimmers could go where they pleased.

◆ *Romantic Suggestion:* If you're spending more than one day
in the area, here's an excursion idea, but it's for serious hikers only.

Lake Awosting (not to be confused with the falls mentioned above) can only be reached by taking a 4.5 mile (each way) hilly path. One of two such paths begins from Minnewaska and is on your map. Along the way there are some little waterfalls and running brooks on the left just off the path. The water at Awosting is not as blue as Minnewaska's, but early in the swimming season it is remarkably clean and clear. Like Minnewaska, Awosting is surrounded by white cliffs and plateaus, one of which juts out into the water and serves as a beach where there is usually a lifeguard on hot summer days (otherwise there's a ranger enforcing no-swimming rules). Along with the lifeguard and a few other hearty souls like yourselves, you're sure to bask in the beauty, peace, and privacy that will have made the rigorous trip worthwhile.

MOHONK MOUNTAIN HOUSE   
Lake Mohonk, New Paltz
(914) 255-1000
Very to Very, Very Expensive

Take exit 18 off the New York State Thruway and turn left onto Route 299. Follow Route 299 through New Paltz and over the Wallkill River bridge. Take the first right turn after the bridge (the sign says "Mohonk"). After approximately one-quarter mile, bear left at the fork onto Mountain Rest Road and continue up the mountain for about four miles to the Mohonk gate.

There are two ways to love Mohonk: one is the cheap way and one is the expensive way. The first way means you check into a lovely B&B in Ulster county, pick up a picnic in New Paltz, tie on your walking shoes, take the winding roads to one of the most scenic private estates in the world allowing public access, and proceed to inhale the delicious scenery as you meander up and down trails, along breathtaking cliffs displaying venerable vistas, up a mountain to the well-named Sky Top Tower, and shimmy through caves with such names as Lemon Squeeze. The expensive way? Stay at the European-style country elegant Mountain House, of course.

◆ ***Romantic Warning:*** Day guests, who pay as much as $7.00 for a day pass, may not swim in the emerald green gem of a lake, and there are other amenities available to hotel guests only. If you couldn't bear to look at the lake without swimming in it and you can't afford the steep rates, you may want to do your hiking and swimming at the very beautiful Lake Minnewaska State Park where you'll feel more welcome.

◆ *Romantic Note:* If you do stay at Mohonk, where there is often a two or three night minimum, don't expect to party all night in a disco. A typical night's entertainment may include a nature talk with bird slides or an outdoor viewing of *The Yearling* on the porch.

◆ *Romantic Exception:* Mohonk specializes in Theme Weekends. You may do nothing but dance if you choose to come on "Ballroom Dancing Weekend" or "Vintage Dance Weekend." Call ahead for information.

UJJALA'S B&B
2 Forest Glen at Route 208, New Paltz
(914) 255-6360
Inexpensive

Follow directions to Jingle Bell Farms, except turn left into driveway.

Spiritual-health-oriented country travelers really feel at home across the street from Jingle Bells Farms here at Ujjala's. This is an excellent "alternative" in more ways than one. With California flair, Ujjala presides over a downhome B&B that specializes in healthy gourmet breakfasts, and exercise. Ujjala, a dedicated rock climber, teacher, and practitioner of stress management techniques and holistic health, has her own indoor wall for practicing rock climbing. On the grounds, there are many unique sites, such as a teepee where authentic Native American purification ceremonies are conducted. There is an exercise, yoga, and meditation room for use by guests. The rooms of this Victorian frame cottage are all comfortable, but none of the others competes with the skylight room. Be sure to request it. It is the only one with a private bath. It also has a fireplace, a murphy bed, air-conditioning, and a skylight, of course.

◆ *Romantic Option:* In a less traveled area of the valley, when all the other B&B's are full, you may be able to get an excellent room at the 1866 Queen Anne Victorian called **Orchard House, Route 44/55 at Eckert Place, Clintondale, NY, (914) 883-6136.** Accommodations are inexpensive, and there is one exceptional room, with a balcony and private bath. A door from the room leads onto the balcony. Suddenly you'll find yourselves in an enclosed solarium loft overlooking the first floor inside and the garden outside. You'll also find peace and inspiration on a moonlit night, and, in the morning, country breezes. This B&B has a more homelike European sophistication as opposed to Ujjala's funky flavor.

WEST PARK WINERIES
Route 9W and Burroughs Drive, West Park-on-Hudson
(914) 384-6709
Inexpensive
Lunch only

Take the New York State Thruway (87) to New Paltz (exit 18); turn right and go east on Route 299 for approximately five miles to Route 92; turn left approximately 2.8 miles to the winery on the left.

An easy drive from our favorite places in Ulster or Dutchess County, we love to stop here for lunch in temperate weather. This is the procedure: We march past the self-guided tours and the 50 cent wine tasting area. We browse in the gift shop and usually buy things. Then we purchase a luscious picnic consisting of something like curried chicken salad in two tomatoes (fresh, fresh, fresh) and a bottle of oaky, buttery Chardonnay. We carry our feast up the hill to a magnificent meadow where we lay out a red checkered blanket, pop open the wine, and take in the view of the pretty winery below and the sprawling Hudson below that. Pure bliss. Try it yourselves.

Westchester County

ALEXANDER HAMILTON HOUSE Bridal Suite
49 Van Wyck Street
Croton-on-Hudson
(914) 271-6737
Expensive

We love this route out of the city: Take the Westside Highway to the Saw Mill. Take exit 25 and turn left onto 9A. Drive seven to eight miles on 9A until it becomes Route 9. From Route 9, exit at Route 129. Turn right going east to the light at Riverside Avenue. Turn left onto Riverside for one block. Turn right on Grand Street. Go one block. Turn left onto Hamilton which intersects Van Wyck right in front of #49. Go down the drive into the parking lot. Climb the porch steps and ring the bell.

For a local honeymoon, anniversary, or quick weekend getaway, you can't do better. A mere 32 miles from NYC, The Alexander Hamilton House is situated in a neighborhood that can't seem to decide if it's the country or the suburbs. Luxurious without being ornate, everything here is comfortable, clean, and new, and every touch was carefully planned with a careful eye toward the puckering of the lips.

Of the six available accommodations, the bridal suite on the third level is the only one that's expensive, but is it ever worth it!

Picture this: an enormous suite with five skylights, a king-size bed with the firmest of mattresses, real lace curtains, a pink marble fireplace, a remote control TV, VCR, and sound system, a refrigerator and microwave, and last but far from least, the most tastefully opulent crimson-tiled brass-fauceted fantasy bathroom we've ever seen. Get waterlogged together in a giant porcelain double Parisian whirlpool under the exotic influence of candles and moonlight. In the morning, a full home-cooked breakfast will be delivered to your door.

This startlingly well-kept 102-year-old house is yours when you're there: sun porch, living room with piano, TV and VCR. There are many amenities not typically offered in a bed & breakfast such as a bathroom basket and terry robes. We haven't even mentioned the 35-

foot swimming pool set in a manicured yard that presents glimpses of the Hudson far below.

◆ *Romantic Alternative:* On the second level, there are four lovely moderate rooms that share two baths. (Note with caution that one of these has twin beds.)

◆ *Romantic Suggestions:* There are many things to do in the area. Be sure to take a picnic to the intimately small but magnificently grand, serene, and picturesque **Croton Gorge Park (on Route 129) in Cortlandt.** It's an idyllic spot for a picnic. Before you drive away from the park, drive a little farther on 129 and turn right onto Croton Dam Road to gaze down at the view below.

Another nearby treat is the **Van Cortlandt Manor on the Croton River, (914) 631-8200**, where you'll be whisked back in time to the early 19th century. When we arrived, the first thing we saw were two blue herons involved in a loud mating ritual up ahead. And what is it about white swans gliding gracefully around a pond? Depending on the your inclinations, take a guided tour of the manor house or explore the grounds yourselves.

Dine at **Guida's, 199 Main Street, Ossining, (914) 941-2662**, an expensive Italian restaurant with moderate prices. If they don't have it on the menu, they'll make it for you. A less obviously romantic dining spot, is the boisterous and fun **Amawalk Inn, Route 35 (Chambers Boulevard), Amawalk, (914) 245-4388**. The atmosphere here at this inexpensive to moderate seafood establishment is noisy and crowded, but we enjoyed it, and in fairness I must mention that we did see not fewer than three couples KISSING!

While you're in the area, consider visiting the wonderfully romantic **Bear Mountain, (914) 786-2701**. Though this scenic area draws a crowd, a stroll around **Hessian Lake** is always renewing and there are more than 5,000 emerald acres in which you can easily find an area all to yourselves. Perhaps on a different trip, make it a point to tour the **Storm King Art Center, Old Pleasant Hill Road, Mountainville, (914) 534-9115**, an immense and beautiful sculpture park where you can picnic on rolling hills beside great works or art or take in an evening concert in summer. Storm King is open from April 1 to November 30, daily from noon to 5:30 p.m., and there is an admission fee.

BRONX RIVER PARKWAY PATH

The path extends from Bronxville north to the Kensico Dam in Valhalla, Westchester. Take FDR Drive in Manhattan north, cross the East River on Willis Avenue Bridge to Major Deegan Highway (Route 87), north to Cross Country Parkway, east to Bronx River Parkway, north to Bronxville or other towns. One half-hour mid-Manhattan to Bronxville.

What a wonderful piece of wilderness remains in Westchester. Conservationists and romanticists alike are proud and delighted by the foresight of the creators of this ten-mile park. Those in need of refuge from the city will find it to be a desirable place to enjoy peace and togetherness.

A wide stretch on each side of the Bronx River Parkway has been maintained in its original pristine, sylvan state, safeguarded for those who relish nature and woods undisturbed by civilization. In recent years, a paved path winding through this park has been handsomely constructed between Bronxville and Valhalla. It is ideal for arm in arm touring or bicycling about the countryside together. The terrain is varied along the path, except for the bubbling Bronx River, which will accompany you most of the way. Many parts are secluded, and the two of you could well imagine yourselves in a remote section of the Adirondacks. In direct contrast, other sections are wide open including a spacious grassy area in Bronxville with an aqua blue pond filled with seasonal birds and occasional swans. There are a few benches along the way, where you can sit and talk, or just rest.

Note: The Kensico Dam area at the northern end of the path has some dramatic points of interest. The dam and surrounding grounds were artistically designed, although their maintenance has been less than perfect. A brick road winds through the woods up to the top of the dam, which provides an all-encompassing view of Westchester to the south and the beautiful Kensico Reservoir to the north. Cars as well as hikers can easily traverse the top of the dam. Also, the parkway is closed to autos some Sundays from May through October from 10 a.m. to 2 p.m. Call the Westchester County Parks Department at (914) 285-2646 to inquire.

♦ *Romantic Warning:* The parkway goes through several suburban towns, the paved path continues all the way except through Scarsdale, which can be walked through on side roads. At the White Plains

Station, the path becomes a quiet road for about one-quarter mile. The path also stops at the North White Plains Station, where one must walk through a parking lot to reach the resumption of the path.

◆ **Romantic Option:** If you're near White Plains and hungry for good Continental cuisine, head for **Gregory's Restaurant, 324 Central Avenue, White Plains, (914) 428-2455** (Moderate to Expensive). Just north of White Plains Station, you will see a large building, the Westchester County Center, and its parking lot. Gregory's is one-third mile south from there on Route 100 (Central Avenue). The walk is not in the least bit romantic, but the restaurant is. The interior of the renovated old house with weathered wood walls and beamed ceilings invoke a nautical feeling. With soft lights, a quiet atmosphere, and flowers on each table, it is a comfortable place to enjoy the pleasures of food and time with your companion.

THE CHART HOUSE
Foot of High Street, Dobbs Ferry
(914) 693-4130
Moderate Brunch, Lunch and Dinner. Specialty: Seafood

Take the Henry Hudson Parkway to the Saw Mill Parkway north. Exit at Ashford Avenue. Turn left at the end of the exit ramp towards Dobbs Ferry. Go through Dobbs Ferry, 3 blocks past the stoplight at the intersection of Route 9. Turn right onto Walnut Street. At the intersection of Main Street, veer left down the hill, over a small bridge. You're there. Or take the Hudson Line from Grand Central Station to Dobbs Ferry. Then, weather and shoes permitting, walk or take a cab.

Specializing in good basic seafood, steaks, and drinks, this is a national chain, but you wouldn't know it. By city standards, it's special. So close yet so far, the Chart House offers as panoramic a view of the Hudson as can be found anywhere in the tri-state area. Stand on the deck and from one spot you have a life-size postcard of the George Washington Bridge ushering in the Manhattan skyline on your left, and the Tappan Zee on your right. Unfortunately, the outside tables which are blissfully tranquil compared with the bustling interior, are reserved for appetizers and drinks. If you want a full dinner, you'll have to dine inside in a modern nautical setting where, yes, it's noisy when crowded, but you may not notice. With a view from every table, chances are you'll both be mesmerized by the sunset and the passing boats and, we hope, each other's company. Nevertheless, try to come during the week if possible. Or better, satisfy your appetite with appetizers on the deck.

◆ *Romantic Suggestion:* Depending on the time of day and year, take a drive a few miles south on Route 9 and visit **Untermeyers Park and Gardens in Yonkers**. This is a large park, but only a small part of the sprawling acreage is maintained for strolling, concerts, and picnics. For that reason, we don't recommend making a special trip here, but do stop when you're nearby. The sloping green lawn just begs to be picnicked on. Pass under the arch of the goddess Artemis into a formal Roman garden. The first thing you'll see is a shade tree over a bench that we can personally testify has been witness to many a kiss. The park, built on several levels with lush green trees and Romanesque marble "ruins," overlooks the Hudson and provides a grand assortment of idyllic spots for osculating.

◆ *Romantic Warning:* Groups of teenagers are said to convene down by the river and we were advised by a neighborhood regular to stick to the maintained park areas well above the water.

◆ *Romantic Note:* The park is most gorgeous in the early hours of the morning when it isn't unusual to spot a deer or two romping into the woods.

THE DONALD M. KENDALL SCULPTURE GARDENS
Anderson Hill Road, Purchase

From Manhattan, take the Hutchinson River Parkway north to the exit for Route 120 North (Purchase Street). Go one mile and turn right onto Anderson Hill Road. The Gardens are located at the Pepsico building on your right a mile down Anderson Hill Road.

A nude couple dances wildly in a clearing in the woods. A marble bear guards a graceful pond that's home to cranes and geese. An absurdly giant trowel stands at the edge of an expansive lawn. What a kissing place! And it is also a corporate headquarters. In the Westches-

ter town of Purchase, the Pepsico Company has created a most romantic setting for a weekend stroll or picnic. This is a special place in which
to share a combination of nature, art, and each other's company. Paths
wind through 112 landscaped acres, past forty works by noted 20th-
century artists like Calder, Miro, and Dubuffet. There's a piece for
every mood and taste — from the dramatic Eve by Rodin to sensuous
abstracts and fanciful etchings. The plantings here are exceptionally
beautiful as well. There are groves of birch trees, water-lily ponds, exotic
trees and plants, and seasonal blooms. The gardens are rarely crowded.
For extra privacy, try the woodchip paths through the surrounding
woods to the right of the main entrance.

Three small courtyard gardens in the center of the building complex
offer moments alone, too.

◆ *Romantic Note:* The grounds are open every day during day-
light hours. There are a handful of picnic tables beside the pond.

LA PANETIERE RESTAURANT   ◆ ◆ ◆
530 Milton Road, Rye
(914) 967-8140
Expensive French Cuisine

Call for directions.

La Panetiere captures the aura of southern France with its authentic
Provencal antiques, atmosphere, and cuisine. The stucco walls and natural wood beamed ceilings enclose a snug interior and promote intimate dining. The lace-covered windows, copper kettles arranged
throughout the dining room, santons (regional French dolls), and
terra-cotta floor all evoke a soothing, richly southern French feeling.
The farmhouse exterior with ivy covered windows and forested backdrop helps enhance the out-of-country experience. The culmination of
all this is the menu with its outstanding cuisine. This restaurant would
be worth the trip for the romance alone, but you get the added bonus
of fabulous food.

Le Chateau Restaurant
Route 35 at Junction 123, South Salem
(914) 533-6631
Expensive French Cuisine

Call for directions and reservations.

Le Chateau sits atop a dogwood-lined driveway that winds through acres of hillside and woodland. The restaurant is housed in a stately, almost gothic, mansion with a rich chestnut interior accented by dark, dense colors. J.P. Morgan built this little chateau for his minister, Dr. William S. Rainsford, in 1907. The mansion itself has more than twenty rooms and is a mass of brick and stone outside, while inside grand wood staircases, stunning stone fireplaces, and hand-crafted wood paneling throughout create a unique place to dine. Le Chateau offers a vast selection of classic French cuisine from onion soup to Muscovy Duck. Here you can savor the taste of exemplary cooking and enjoy the expansive, glorious view of the New York countryside. In fact, besides the impressive menu, the most spectacular part of dining at Le Chateau is that amazing view of the countryside, brimming with rolling hills covered in trees, and fields that extend as far as the eye can see. During the summer you might share an embrace in the flowered courtyard, while you enjoy the view and fresh summer breeze before you slip in for dinner.

TARRYTOWN

Take the Henry Hudson Parkway to Route 9 north into Tarrytown.

Ever since the early explorers sang the praises of the Hudson River Valley centuries ago, travelers have been drawn to Tarrytown. It offers everything you can think of: cultural attractions, rich history, and beautiful scenery, with ubiquitous views of the surging river. And yes, romance. Of course some Tarrytown locations are more amorous than others, and they are well worth seeking out. At the very top of my list is **Lyndhurst, 635 South Broadway, (914) 631-004**, the luxurious 67-acre estate that once belonged to railroad magnate Jay Gould.

The centerpiece of this manor is the breathtaking Gothic Revival mansion (which can be toured with a guide, although it's preferable to go it alone), but what surrounds it will steal your breath away: rolling hills and sweeping lawns, groves of stately trees, abundant foliage, rocks, and rose gardens. As you look over these august grounds, you're the reigning royalty of your own kingdom. Spread a picnic and breathe deeply the fragrant air. Enjoy a delicious moment in the gazebo off the rose garden or simply watch the river flow.

If you prefer literary opulence, take Route 9 south from the center of Tarrytown and follow the signs to **Sunnyside**, at the Tarrytown-Irvington townline, (914) 631-8200, the somewhat smaller estate of author Washington Irving. The house itself can be toured in the company of costumed guides. Take yourself on a tour of the gently undulating grounds that feature ponds, gazebo, picnic benches, exquisite greenery and, winding pathways with views of the Hudson. Irving preferred the view here to any he's seen in all his wide travels. As you tour the grounds, the murmurs from the river will drift into your ears and woo you with thoughts of country living.

◆ *Romantic Note:* Lyndhurst is open to the public May 1 through October 31, and in December, Tuesday through Sunday, 10 a.m. to 5 p.m.; January through April and in November, weekends 10 a.m. to 5 p.m. Closed on holidays.

◆ *Romantic Option:* If you are in the mood for more solitude, explore the 750-acre **Rockefeller State Park Preserve in Pocantico Hills** just above North Tarrytown (take Route 9 north to Route 117 east to the park entrance). Here you'll find a network of shady river lanes, intimate wooded paths, and panoramic vistas. Permits are available for horseback riding and carriage driving. If it snows, pack your cross-country skis.

◆ *Romantic Suggestion:* The perfect conclusion to the perfect day can be found at **Isabel's, 61 Main Street, Tarrytown, (914) 631-9819**, (Inexpensive to Moderate). The atmosphere is extremely cozy and the ambience endearing. The specialty here is dinner and snacks. The wine and cheese menu is extensive.

Tappan Hill Restaurant
81 Highland Avenue, Tarrytown
(914) 631-3030
Expensive
Restaurant Open Weekdays; Catering on Weekends

Major Deegan Expressway (87 North) to Exit 9. Turn right onto Route 119.
At first traffic light turn left onto Benedict Avenue. At the fourth traffic light
turn right onto Highland Avenue. Make a left at the stop sign.

Mark Twain once owned this estate perched in the heights of posh Tarrytown. Now it is a mecca for lovers of food, beauty, and each other. Arrive in winter and you'll be welcomed by fireplaces blazing in the mansion's regal vestibule and adjoining cocktail lounges. The profusion of lights conspire to replace those chills with a toasty glow of expectation. In the summer months the area is full of enchantment. Walk the verdant promenade that leads from the restaurant to a semicircular second tier and watch the sun descend over the powerful waterway below.

It's worth the wait for a window table in the spacious dining room; the unobstructed view of the Hudson River and the Palisades is stupendous. You'll savor the panoramic splendor over good and often delicious contemporary American food served with hospitality and elegance. Steak, fresh fish, and rack of lamb are all impressively prepared, and the award-winning espresso fudge cake is itself worth a trip.

♦ *Romantic Note:* The restaurant is open on weekdays for lunch and dinner. On weekends it is always closed for weddings and private parties. Incidentally, if you're planning a wedding in the area, consider Tappan Hill.

♦ *Romantic Suggestion:* It's summer and the Westchester air is cool and fragrant. Why return to the stifling city? Or it's winter and the ground out here is blanketed by pure white drifts of snow, so why return to a slushy frozen city? A few minutes away the **Tarrytown Hilton, 455 South Broadway, (914) 631-5700,** (Moderate to Very Expensive), offers excellent accommodations at low weekend rates. Not the height of romantic sleeping arrangements, but it can be better than returning to the city. This Hilton also has a nice restaurant and a delectable brunch on Sundays.

◆ *Romantic Alternative:* An activity-packed alternative retreat can be found at **The Tarrytown House Executive Conference Center, East Sunnyside Lane, (914) 591-8200**, (Moderate). It offers clean and comfortable standard hotel rooms, sprawling acres, several dining rooms in different settings, a complete and fabulous health spa and recreation center, including indoor and outdoor pool, a heated whirlpool, tennis, and racquetball — and all the equipment you need. Only a half hour out of the city, this is a real find for couples who like fun and games.

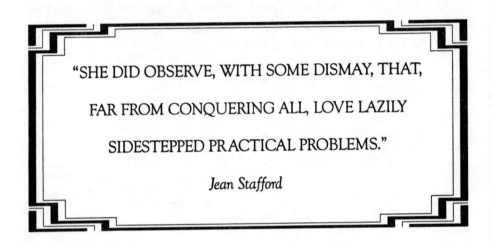

"SHE DID OBSERVE, WITH SOME DISMAY, THAT,

FAR FROM CONQUERING ALL, LOVE LAZILY

SIDESTEPPED PRACTICAL PROBLEMS."

Jean Stafford

Your Own Personal Diary

This is the section just for the two of you, so you can keep your own record of the romantic, fulfilling moments you've shared together — where you went, what you discovered, the occasion celebrated, and whatever else you want to remember long after the weekend, evening, or morning has passed. Keeping a record of special times together to read to each other when the moment is right can be an adoring gift, at a quiet moment, sometime in the future, when another magic-filled romantic outing is at hand.

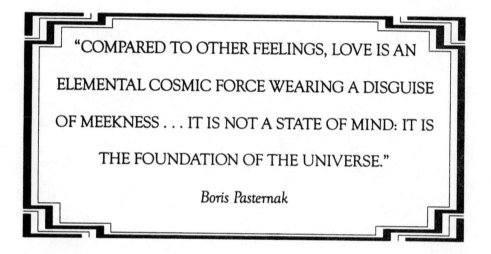

"COMPARED TO OTHER FEELINGS, LOVE IS AN ELEMENTAL COSMIC FORCE WEARING A DISGUISE OF MEEKNESS . . . IT IS NOT A STATE OF MIND: IT IS THE FOUNDATION OF THE UNIVERSE."

Boris Pasternak

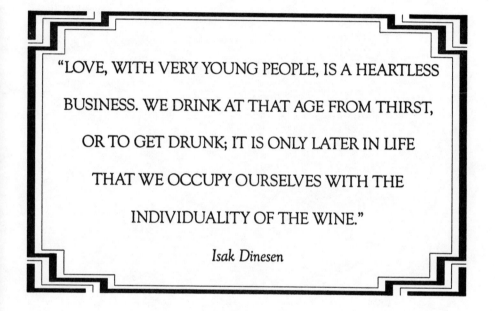

"LOVE, WITH VERY YOUNG PEOPLE, IS A HEARTLESS

BUSINESS. WE DRINK AT THAT AGE FROM THIRST,

OR TO GET DRUNK; IT IS ONLY LATER IN LIFE

THAT WE OCCUPY OURSELVES WITH THE

INDIVIDUALITY OF THE WINE."

Isak Dinesen

Index

D

P

S

Z